PALANTE

Young Lords Party

Photographs by Michael Abramson
Text by the Young Lords Party
With a new foreword by Iris Morales

Haymarket Books
Chicago, Illinois

Art Direction: Harris Lewine
Design: Herb Lubalin
Cover Design: Eric Ruder

This edition published in 2011 by Haymarket Books, PO Box 180165, Chicago, IL 60618
info@haymarketbooks.org, www.haymarketbooks.org

ISBN: 978-1-60846-129-5

Printed in Canada by union labor on FSC-certified paper.

Published with the generous support of Lannan Foundation and the Wallace Global Fund.
Discounts are available for bulk orders to organizations.

Library of Congress CIP data is available.

10 9 8 7 6 5 4 3

Proceeds from the sale of this book will be donated in the name of the Young Lords Party to nonprofit organizations working with Puerto Rican Youth in the United States.

To my partner, Erika Jakubassa, for providing a lifetime of inspiration and wisdom —Michael Abramson

Dedication

The Young Lords Party wishes to dedicate this book to—

Don Pedro Albizu Campos, the President of the Nationalist Party, who from the 1920s to his death in 1965, carried the message of freedom throughout the nation

and to Puerto Rican prisoners of war—

Oscar Collazo, imprisoned since November 1, 1950, for the attempted assassination of President Truman at Blair House

Lolita Lebron, Rafael Cancel Miranda, Irving Flores Rodrigues, Andres Figueroa Cordero imprisoned since March 1, 1954, for shooting at politicians in the House of Representatives, Washington, D.C.

Martin Gonzales Sostre, imprisoned since July 14, 1967, in Buffalo, New York, on alleged drug charges, but really for raising Third World consciousness in that city

Carlos Feliciano, imprisoned since May 16, 1970, on alleged bomb charges; the government claims Carlos is a member of MIRA, an underground Puerto Rican revolutionary organization

POWER TO THE PEOPLE

In 1971 when *Palante: The Young Lords Party* was first published, we were young people in the throes of organizing for revolution. The *Palante* book captured the ideas and dreams that moved us to deep and passionate commitments and to bold and dramatic actions. We believed in a world of economic and social equality, and of human possibility. So many decades later, young activists continue to be inspired by the Young Lords, attracted by our freedom dream, the idea described by Robin D. G. Kelly in *Freedom Dreams: The Black Radical Imagination*, which poses the question, "How do we produce a vision that enables us to see beyond our immediate ordeals?" The Young Lords' vision, expressed in a 13-point program written in 1969, began, "We want self-determination for Puerto Ricans: liberation on the Island and inside the United States. We want self-determination for all Latinos and liberation of all Third World people." It ended with, "We want a socialist society. We want a society where the needs of the people come first and where we give solidarity and aid to the people of the world."

The Young Lords Organization emerged from two historical currents: the social justice movement in the United States, specifically the African American liberation struggle—from the slave rebellions to the Black Panther Party of the 1960s—and the struggle against colonialism in Puerto Rico—from the early resistance of the Taino Indians and enslaved Africans to the Nationalist Party led by Don Pedro Albizu Campos. Our oppression tapped deep into our collective understanding and into our hearts about creating social change, removing the oppressor class from power, and improving poor peoples' lives in the United States and around the world. We saw ourselves as part of a larger movement that sought to change power relations and connected with millions of people in opposition to the war in Vietnam. Moved by the Cuban and Chinese revolutions and by liberation struggles in Africa and Latin America, we believed that we could change the economic, political, and social system, and that in the process, we could also transform ourselves.

The Young Lords began in Chicago, a street gang turned revolutionary under the leadership of Jose "Cha Cha" Jimenez, the organization's Chairman. On September 23, 1968, they began a militant challenge to powerful forces including real estate developers who were evicting Puerto Rican families from the Lincoln Park neighborhood. Like the Black Panther Party, the Young Lords set up "serve the people" programs, organized protests, and took action against unresponsive institutions located in neighborhoods where we lived. The Young Lords Organization inspired young Puerto Ricans across the United States to take a stand.

It was not by accident that the New York chapter began in East Harlem—El Barrio, a first home and cultural hub for generations of working-class Puerto Ricans. The disdain and systemic neglect was visible on the streets overflowing with trash and sent the message, "Puerto Ricans are garbage." The Young Lords entered the political stage armed with brooms in the summer of 1969 and, for several Sundays, swept the streets and burned the garbage on the main avenues. The resulting traffic jams and media attention forced the sanitation department to clean the streets, and the city administration to take notice. With this action, known as the "Garbage Offensive," the Young Lords announced, "We want respect, and we want justice!"

The members of the Young Lords shared a deep sense of urgency and were determined to change the status quo. Puerto Ricans lived in the poorest slums and were unemployed or in dead-end jobs. Our communities lacked health care and quality schools, and suffered under institutional indifference, racism, and marginalization. By imagining what society should and could be, we were inspired to action. We set up storefront offices in Puerto Rican neighborhoods in New York, Newark, Philadelphia, Bridgeport, Boston, and other areas. We were, first and foremost, community organizers—"25 hours a day, 8 days a week." We were young people, mainly 16 to 26 years old, from working-class families raised in Spanish-speaking homes—primarily Puerto Ricans, first-generation born or raised in the U.S., but also Cubans, Dominicans, and Mexicans. African Americans made up about 20 percent of the membership. Women joined from the beginning and constituted one-third of the members at the highest point and helped shape a unique politics that took into account racial, class, and gender oppressions. We fashioned a broad reproductive rights agenda that included demands for legal and safe abortions, voluntary birth control, end to sterilization abuse, affordable child care, and a quality public health care system. We understood the power of mobilization and believed it necessary for our collective survival.

The *Palante* book beautifully details the intensity of the time with photographs and essays; it shows the Young Lords in action, in the streets, organizing. The men and women of the Young Lords conducted weekly political education classes in storefronts, housing projects, church basements, and schools to study Puerto Rican history, labor movements, political economy, feminist ideas, and contemporary events. Through these sessions, we developed a common language and strategies, became better organizers, and built community relationships. The Information Ministry skillfully communicated our message through the *PALANTE* newspaper and pamphlets; a weekly radio show on WBAI, the New York Pacifica radio station; and press conferences. We joined many artists, poets, and musicians to create revolutionary political culture. We collaborated with other Puerto Rican activists in the Movement Pro Independence, El Comite, and the Puerto Rican Student Union among others, and with other people of color organizations, most closely with the Black Panther Party, I Wor Kuen, the Third World Women's Alliance, as well as white progressives. Bold collective actions, civil disobedience, and confrontation brought attention to the systemic neglect, exploitation, and suffering of our people. Even those who disagreed with our tactics agreed that the injustices we pointed to were clearly present. We woke up each day to serve the people and went to sleep analyzing what we had accomplished, and at night we dreamt about the new society that we would create, convinced that the richest country on the globe had the resources needed to sustain a better world for everyone.

The *Palante* book reveals the dreams that motivated the Young Lords and was dedicated to Don Pedro Albizu Campos (1891–1965) who spent more than twenty-five years in prison for his beliefs. It was also dedicated to other Puerto Rican Nationalists then in U.S. prisons: Oscar Collazo (1914–1994), Lolita Lebron (1919–2010), Rafael Cancel Miranda (1930–), Irving Flores Rodrigues (1931–1994), and Andres Figueroa Cordero (1931–1978), who won clemency in 1979. The book was also dedicated to Martin Gonzalez Sostre (1923–), pardoned in 1975 after the main witness recanted, and to Carlos Feliciano (1929–), who was acquitted of attempted bombing charges in 1972, but later spent two years in prison.

The *Palante* book survived even after the publisher stopped printing it. Latino/a students, educators, and artists determined to keep the history alive circulated photocopies for many years. The book and "El Pueblo Se Levanta," the cinema veritè documentary also produced in 1971 and distributed by Third World Newsreel, persist as unique firsthand accounts, about the Young Lords' ideas and organizing strategies. More than two decades later, another generation supported the production of *¡Palante, Siempre Palante! The Young Lords*, which was broadcast on national public television in 1996 and continues to be screened in schools and community venues connecting with new generations of young people and activists to dialogue about the relationship of past social justice movements to the present and to the future, as a way to learn from one another about how to strengthen the ongoing struggle for human liberation.

So what happened to the Young Lords? Not long after the publication of the *Palante* book, the Young Lords Party (YLP) opened two branches in Puerto Rico. The move called Ofensiva Rompe Cadenas (Break the Chains Offensive) can only be understood within the context of centuries of colonialism and geopolitics. In 1898, the United States took Puerto Rico as a prize of the Spanish American War. In 1917, Congress declared Puerto Ricans to be U.S. citizens and drafted islanders to fight in U.S. wars as absentee American corporations appropriated Puerto Rico's wealth causing extreme poverty, and then promoted the mass exodus of the working poor as a solution. Almost half a million Puerto Ricans migrated to the United States after World War II in search of work settling primarily in northern cities. The Young Lords were the sons and daughters of this migration and grappled to understand the relationship between the Puerto Rican struggles for equality in the U.S. and the independence movement in Puerto Rico. Relating the migration to the island's colonial status, we identified with the Nationalists who, since the 1920s, had battled the U.S. government to free the island.

Early in 1971, the YLP leaders in New York announced that they would set up branches on the island. The move was a disaster as the shifting of people and resources from the States to Puerto Rico began the dismantling of the organization. Even the members sent to organize in Puerto Rico concluded that it was a mistake and that the YLP's role should be in the United States. Yet the leaders refused to listen, insisting on the failed strategy, and more and more members left the organization. A year and a half passed before the leadership admitted the mistake and took another direction, sending members to organize in factories, hospitals, and other workplaces in the U.S. and changing the name from Young Lords Party to the Puerto Rican Revolutionary Workers' Organization (PRRWO). It also failed in these efforts, and, by the mid-1970s, PRRWO had faded into history.

A complex set of factors account for the demise of the Young Lords and other revolutionary organizations of the time. By the early 1970s, the socioeconomic-political landscape was changing rapidly as U.S. capital shifted to a global export economy, moving manufacturing out of the country in search of cheaper labor and even higher profits. In tandem with this globalization process, the elimination of manufacturing and service jobs devastated and restructured American cities. For Puerto Ricans concentrated in the lowest level jobs, the shift resulted in great unemployment, instability, and poverty that triggered large migration back to the island. Of course, Puerto Rico was in no better situation and the result was a circular, back and forth, migration in search of work. The Young Lords and similar organizations were not positioned or equipped to address the economics and politics of globalization.

Simultaneously, the U.S. government invested heavily in COINTELPRO, the FBI's secret counterintelligence program to repress and eliminate the protest movements. COINTELPRO undertook activities intended to "discredit, disrupt and otherwise neutralize" all progressive organizations, targeting the African American movement, particularly the Black Panther Party, because of its militancy and role in galvanizing domestic and international support for peoples' movements. While the full story of COINTELPRO with respect to the Young Lords remains to be written, documents acquired through the Freedom of Information Act reveal that the FBI sent informants to recruit members who carried out treachery and betrayal within the organization. Across the country, COINTELPRO operatives spied on, manipulated, beat, tortured, framed, imprisoned, and even murdered revolutionaries and activists.

Another factor—lack of democracy—weakened the Young Lords Party from within. A hierarchical structure concentrated power and decision making in a few leaders, stifling creativity and initiative. Centralism prevailed even as members attempted to have their voices heard, and, by extension, the community's views reflected. Without mechanisms to engage differing viewpoints, like the challenges to the decision to move to Puerto Rico, the organization degenerated into dogmatism. In the end, a few remaining leaders resorted to violence against members who disagreed with them. Accounts of physical threats and beatings circulated by word of mouth. Like a plague, sadness and cynicism spread, and the mythology that social change is impossible descended like a thick and heavy fog.

Years passed before we collectively assessed the Young Lords experience. A few never recovered from disillusionment and resumed their lives as if untouched by the freedom dream. But others continued to pursue the politics we had learned and believed. Former Young Lords organized workers, fought police brutality, protested racist media, built women's collectives, and created community and arts organizations. Former Young Lords joined other activists to free the Nationalists in prison since the 1950s and took over the Statue of Liberty in 1977, placing the Puerto Rican flag on its crown to bring attention to their incarceration. Two years later, President Carter commuted their sentences to time served. After twenty-five years in prison, they returned home to Puerto Rico to a jubilant welcome. The fight for political prisoners continued. In 1999, eleven members of another generation of Puerto Rican political prisoners were given clemency and released. As of early 2011, Oscar Lopez-Rivera and Avelino Gonzalez Claudio remained behind bars.

The story of the Puerto Rican community in the United States reflects an intense and persistent struggle for justice seeking to end job, housing, and racial discrimination, to gain access to quality education and health services, for Puerto Rican studies programs and cultural institutions, for voting and language rights, for fair media representation, and in every other arena. Puerto Ricans have had to fight for everything!

As of this writing in 2011, Sonia Sotomayor, a Puerto Rican from the Bronx, sits on the U.S. Supreme Court, and Barack Hussein Obama, an African American, is president—achievements only possible in our imagination decades ago. While the *Palante* book presents a seemingly long-ago history, the disparity between the "haves" and "have-nots" is even greater now than in the 1960s. Wealth concentrated in just a few hands contrasts with the intense poverty lived by the majority of the world's people. When U.S. bank and corporate heads created a global economic crisis in 2007, they shamelessly lined up for taxpayer bailouts and paid themselves bonuses as they pushed millions of Americans into an avalanche of home foreclosures and job losses. The contradictions would have been clear except that the corporate media, among others, stepped in to distract and deflect the public's attention away from the issues at hand, obfuscating the inherent defects of the capitalist system.

Since the social movements of the sixties and seventies, the Latino/a population in the United States has grown to 48.4 million or about 16 percent. Census data shows ancestries from every Latin American and Caribbean country, the majority from Mexico, with Puerto Ricans being the second largest group. Yet despite the tremendous cultural, political, and economic contributions made by Latino/as, xenophobia and anti-immigrant politics are at an all-time high with passage of laws that blame Latino/as for the country's problems—everything from the lack of jobs to the drug epidemic.

The Puerto Rican population has also undergone tremendous change. The twenty-first century began with more Puerto Ricans living in the United States than in Puerto Rico. Now New York is no longer the first stop as Puerto Ricans migrate directly to smaller U.S. cities and towns, reflecting both the upward mobility of the middle class and the dispersal of poor and low-wage workers from large urban areas. Even with greater numbers of Puerto Rican politicians, professionals, journalists, and business owners than in 1970, large numbers of Puerto Ricans continue to live poverty, and Puerto Ricans, 16 to 24 years old, in New York City face a bleak future according to a Community Service Society of New York report in 2010.

Puerto Rico remains a U.S. colony, poorer than the state of Mississippi. In 2009, the island's governor announced mass civil service layoffs, prompting thousands of workers to take to the streets in protest. In 2010, students opposed tuition increases and other changes by occupying the University of Puerto Rico campuses for two months. The people of the Puerto Rican island of Vieques continue to clean up poisoned land, attempting to alleviate the ecological devastation and high cancer rates caused by uranium, aluminum, lead, arsenic, and mercury left behind by U.S. Navy military maneuvers conducted over the course of sixty years. The United Nation's Decolonization Committee continues to call on the United States to allow Puerto Ricans their right to self-determination and independence as Congress, with President Obama's support, recommended yet another plebiscite to determine whether Puerto Rico should remain a U.S. territory, but offered no plan to withdraw the U.S. military from the island.

The relentless and ever-expanding exploitation of social and natural resources has created an imminent threat that affects every human being on the planet. Centuries of domination of the Earth and its people in the quest for profit have brought us to this point. We face an energy crisis, a food crisis, a water crisis.... All symptoms of the same sickness—a global system based on greed and monetary gain. The massive environmental destruction evidences the need for a human rights approach and screams out for radical change—a transformation that entails more than simply switching the current set of politicians and rulers. We need a change that puts working people and human values at the center, equitably distributes wealth, and advances structural changes that envision different ways of living and organizing our societies beyond the engines of capitalism and its unyielding pursuit of profit.

The *Palante* book reminds us of the revolutionary vision that young Puerto Ricans, Latino/as, and African Americans in the United States fought for in the 1960s and '70s: "We want a society where the needs of the people come first, and where we give solidarity and aid to the people of the world." Today, the struggle for social, racial, and economic justice in the United States and for the independence of Puerto Rico continue, and across the world people are building networks, grassroots alliances, and coalitions from a wide range of sectors bridging local and global struggles toward the end of capitalism and other systems of oppression. Our hope for the planet and for human liberation lies in these movements. As the Zapatistas of Mexico say, "Another world is both possible and necessary."

IRIS MORALES, 2011

INTRODUCTION

HISTORY OF THE YOUNG LORDS PARTY

**Our cry
is a very simple
and logical one.
Puerto Ricans came
to this country
hoping to get
a decent job
and to provide
for their families;
but it didn't take
long to find out
that the American
dream that was
publicized so nicely
on our island
turned out to be
the amerikkkan
nightmare.**

DAVID PEREZ

"Wherever a Puerto Rican is, the duty of a Puerto Rican is to make the revolution."

GLORIA GONZALEZ, FIELD MARSHAL

Many people ask us, "How did you begin?" A few people have the idea that "some foreign power" organized us, or that we are a gang. This is our story:

In New York City, in January of 1969, some Puerto Rican college students got together because they felt something had to be done to connect them with the people they had left behind in the ghetto. The intentions these people had were good, but vague. They didn't quite understand which was the best way to proceed. As the months wore on, the group met many times in *El Barrio*. People came and went, the group kept changing, and those who stuck around felt things were going nowhere.

Yorúba came into the group in late May (by this time it was called the *Sociedad de Albizu Campos* [SAC]). He was a student at the State University of New York at Old Westbury, and had just returned to the States from a stay in Mexico, which was part of his schooling. He was eighteen at the time. Most of his life before going to Mexico was related more closely to the struggle of Black People in Amerikkka than to that of Puerto Ricans. This was because his dark skin and Afro hair made it difficult for Puerto Ricans to relate to him, especially light-skinned ones.

However, Yorúba's stay in Mexico had made him aware of his Latin roots, so when he returned to Amerikkka he was looking for something to get into. A friend of the brother's who also went to Old Westbury was one of the people who stuck it through with the SAC from the beginning. He introduced Yorúba into the group.

Two weeks after the first meeting he attended sometime in May, Yorúba met David Perez. Old Westbury needed more ghetto spics to maintain its image of a "with it" institution, and it sent people out all over the country looking for these strange animals. They had found David in Chicago, where he was hustling an anti-poverty group. Whereas Yorúba was born and raised in New York, David was born in Lares, Puerto Rico. At ten, he came to Chicago, because his family, like hundreds of thousands of other Puerto Rican families, nearly starved due to the effects of "Operation Bookstrap."

When David arrived in New York, he was nineteen years old. He and Yorúba quickly got along, and they went to stay at Yorúba's mother's house on David's first night in the city. They stayed up all night rapping about the SAC in particular, and politics in general. Their points of view on a lot of things were similar, and one thing was especially agreed on: the SAC had to stop meeting and get into the street.

On June 7th, the Black Panther newspaper had a story about an alliance in Chicago called the Rainbow Coalition which the Panthers had formed with two other organizations and a story about one of the groups in the Coalition—the Young Lords Organization (YLO). The Young Lords were Puerto Rican revolutionaries!

The Lords had entered into an alliance with the Young Patriots Organization, a street gang of white youths that had also turned political, and the Black Panther Party. This was called the Rainbow Coalition.

The Rainbow Coalition sent representatives to the annual Students for a Democratic Society (SDS) convention in Chicago, held in May of 1969. An SDSer from Florida, José Martinez, who was looking to get back to his Latin people, met Cha Cha, one of the founders of the YLO, at the convention. Martinez told Cha Cha he was going to New York, and wanted permission to start a Lords chapter there.

When Martinez got to New York's Lower East Side, he soon managed to start a group that met regularly. This group heard that there was another group doing what they were doing—except in East Harlem. These young street bloods would clean up the streets of *El Barrio* at night and leave the garbage in the middle of the street the next morning. In this way, the Garbage (Sanitation) Department was forced to clean it up so traffic could get by. José met with this group's leader, Pickle, and the two groups became one, with the intention of getting recognition from Chicago. It was decided that the new group would work out of *El Barrio*.

At its June 7 meeting, the one where we discussed the Lords, the SAC talked about both New York groups. We felt that it was important for all the little groups that kept popping up to form one national party, and we felt the Young Lords Organization was that party. The SAC met with the group that had just merged, and a new merger was made. This merger represented the uniting of the street people with the students of working-class background.

Together, this new group, already calling itself the Young Lords, cleaned up the streets of *El Barrio*, rapping to people as they went. On July 26, the group was recognized by Chicago as the New York State Chapter of the Young Lords Organization.

On Sunday, July 27, the Lords of New York blocked the avenues of *El Barrio*. This action grew in size through the summer, as the frustrated, forgotten mass of Puerto Ricans joined in barricading the avenues and streets. Soon the garbage action turned into a confrontation with police, and the YLO became experienced in street fighting, in basic urban guerrilla tactics, the hit and run. For the first time in years, the pigs came into the ghetto with respect and fear in their eyes. This period of the summer of 1969 is referred to by us as the Garbage Offensive.

By September, we felt that our people had accepted us, and that we were now a part of people's lives. We opened an office in a storefront at 1678 Madison Avenue, between 111th and 112th Streets. The leadership of the organization at that time consisted of David Perez, Deputy Minister of Defense; Felipe Luciano, Deputy Chairman; Pablo "Yorúba" Guzmán, Deputy Minister of Information; Juan Gonzalez, Deputy Minister of Education; and Juan "Fi" Ortiz, Deputy Minister of Finance. This was the Central Staff.

Juan Gonzalez joined the *Sociedad de Albizu Campos* just before we merged with Pickle's and José's group. He had just come out of jail, having done thirty days for contempt of court arising from the 1968 student uprisings at Columbia University. Born in Ponce in 1947, Juan came to the States at an early age. His parents felt that they should always "do better," and Juan's family kept moving from place to place, one step before the Puerto Ricans, two steps before the Blacks, and three steps after the whites.

Juan entered Columbia on a scholarship. To support himself, he took a poverty program job on the West Side of Manhattan. Here, as a community organizer, Juan would go from house to house, getting to know people, and seeing all that his parents kept moving away from. This led him to junk the books his professors would give him for books on how to change the people's conditions, books on revolution. He joined SDS and became a leader of the 1968 uprising.

Fi was a member of Pickle's group, stayed with the merger of José's group, and wound up a Young Lord. He was fifteen at the time of the merger. His father is a preacher who managed to save enough to buy a house in Queens. Most of Fi's time was still spent in *El Barrio*, and he rarely visited the house in Queens.

The brother refused to accept the

nonsense taught in school, and he had been tossed out of practically every high school in Queens, until, in 1969, he wound up at Benjamin Franklin in *El Barrio*. Fi is a brilliant photographer whose work of the street scenes has been exhibited in museums. Many of the people in the photo workshop in 117th Street that he belonged to were also with him in Pickle's group. Although he was not a part of the central leadership in the beginning, the Central Staff soon saw the level he was on, and in September he was promoted to Deputy Minister of Finance.

The Central Staff decided that we would shift the Organization's tactics from street fighting to programs which served our people and which would also build the Organization's theoretical level. We began Free Breakfast and Lead Poisoning Detection programs, supported the struggle of the welfare mothers that year, began organizing hospital workers, and studied revolutions in other countries.

In October of 1969, we wrote the Thirteen Point Program and Platform (revised May, 1970) and Thirty Rules of Discipline (revised December, 1970).

That same month, we went to a Methodist church on the corner of 111th Street and Lexington Avenue, and asked if we could use some space to run a Breakfast Program. We couldn't even get in the front door. We wrote letters, began attending services, and talked with the congregation, but the church's Board voted no. December 7 was the church's testimonial Sunday, when people from the congregation spoke. Felipe rose to speak, and twenty-five uniformed pigs, in addition to the plainclothes pigs that had been going to church with us for six weeks, ran in, attacking the Lords and our supporters. The ambush netted thirteen Lords and supporters. They and others who got away were treated for broken arms and heads.

For the two following Sundays, we went back to the church and interrupted services again. The fact that blood was spilled in the church showed us the level the pigs wanted to go to. On December 28, we took the church, renamed it People's Church, and for the next eleven days, we ran free clothing drives, breakfast programs, a liberation school, political education classes, a day care center, free health programs, and nightly entertainment (movies, bands, or poetry). Three thousand people came to the church. This was our Second Offensive, the People's Church Offensive, and the action spread our name around the world.

Two things happened: our membership increased rapidly, and we were now seen as a legitimate threat to the enemy's balance of power.

It was obvious that we were no street gang; as Socialists and revolutionary nationalists, we had become a political force to be dealt with. Those in power knew, perhaps better than we, what could happen if Socialist, revolutionary nationalist Puerto Ricans in Amerikkka hooked up with the other two-thirds of our people living on the island. The explosion would be tremendous.

Our intention after People's Church was to build our organization, to get back in regular touch with our people through our daily organizing programs, which had been suspended for the eleven days of the church. From January through March we did this; during this period there was a series of street battles with the police around drugs. We attacked the police for allowing the drug traffic to come into the neighborhood, and then busting junkies instead of the big pushers. The YLO became involved in getting junkies to kick and in having them serve our people.

In October of 1969 we opened our second office, in Newark, New Jersey; the fact that we managed to run an office there, plus the success of People's Church, prompted National in Chicago to recognize us as the leadership for the East Coast Region, with the responsibility for organizing that area. The Central Staff moved up in rank and became the Regional Central Committee with the titles of Regional Ministers.

The Bronx Branch was opened in April of 1970. This was also the location of our Information Center. The leadership for the East Coast now noticed that Chicago was not providing guidance or example; a few things that bothered us were that the newspaper, *YLO*, was not coming out regularly; that there was no political line to follow (which meant that we developed on our own—the Thirteen Point Program and Platform is an example), and that the only branches of the Organization were in Chicago, *El Barrio*, the Bronx, and Newark, while our people were calling for us everywhere. There was also a branch in Heywood, California, but they were in less contact with Chicago than we were. They are now disbanded.

To offset the problem of not having a newspaper which regularly gave our position to the people, in October, 1969, we began publishing a mimeographed packet called *Palante*, the voice of the YLO-East Coast. On May 8th it came out for the first time as a full-size newspaper. The paper has grown in content and circulation. We also have a weekly New York radio program called "Palante" that went on the air on WBAI–FM in March.

In May of 1970, the East Coast Regional Central Committee went into a retreat. We discussed where we had been, and where we hoped to go. We knew that we could not continue to run an effective organization on our own personal dynamism, that definite political principles would have to be laid down for others to follow. As a group, we started studying more, and formulated methods of work that would develop other leaders. One of the main areas that we attacked was *machismo* and male chauvinism. If we wanted to have power in the hands of the people, it would be necessary to have *all* the people fighting *now*. The attitudes of superiority that brothers had toward sisters would have to change, as would the passivity of sisters toward brothers (allowing brothers to come out of a *macho* or chauvinist, superior bag).

It was felt that the vague relationship with Chicago would have to be cleared up. We went deeply into what we felt were the responsibilities of a National Headquarters, responsibilities that Chicago was not fulfilling. After the retreat, we went out to Chicago. After a series of meetings, we felt that we had to split from the YLO and move ahead with the work that was urgently needed. We had now become the Young Lords Party.

Since October of 1969 we had been active in the field of health, both from the patient's point of view and the hospital worker's. Our work in lead poisoning detection led to deep investigations in New York City that uncovered epidemics; we did the same for tuberculosis.

Ninety per cent of the hospital workers in New York City are Black and Puerto Rican. To meet their demands for better conditions, and to serve the needs of patients, the Health Revolutionary Unity Movement (HRUM) was created, made up of these hospital workers, in the early fall of '69. HRUM has the ideology of the Young Lords Party. It became involved in several health struggles, like Gouverneur Hospital on the Lower East Side.

The Young Lords Party and HRUM, along with the Think Lincoln Committee, a patient-worker group, took Lincoln Hospital in the South Bronx in July of 1970. This was our Third Offensive; we ran programs, like TB and lead poison detection services, and a day care center, in a building the hospital was not even using. This highlighted the oppressive conditions in Lincoln (the building was condemned by the city), which could have been found in any ghetto hospital. Just before Lincoln was taken, a city-run TB x-ray truck was liberated in *El Barrio*. This was a good education for our people as they saw the difference between what the government did and what we did: whereas the city was lucky if it tested 300 people in a week, we examined 300 people in one day.

On July 26, 1970, the Party celebrated its first anniversary. Soon afterward, in August, a branch was opened on the Lower East Side.

In August of 1970, Felipe Luciano was demoted from the Central Committee to the position of cadre in the Party. He left the Party in October. This was one dramatic example of a series of internal problems, and the Central Committee met in early September to get the Party moving again. One of the results of this was the establishment of a definite system of work and responsibility within the Party. This is called democratic centralism; briefly, it means that there is a top-down, centralist chain of command in the Party, and that at each level (central committee, branch staff, etc.) democracy is practiced.

For this series of meetings there was a new minister, Denise Oliver; afterward, there were some changes on Central Committee, and also, another minister was added, Gloria Gonzalez. Juan was now the Minister of Defense; Fi was Chief of Staff; Denise was Minister of Finance (now Economic Development); and David and Gloria were Field Marshals.

Denise had joined the Party in October of 1969, when she was twenty-three. Before, she had attended the State University at Old Westbury, the last of several universities she had attended, all filled with empty promises. Denise had been raised in a "Black Bourgeois" (really middle-class) family, but she knew that reality was in the ghetto, with the people of the streets, and the workers who came home late for little pay. This is where Denise made her home.

Once, Denise worked in an *El Barrio* anti-poverty program. In the Lords, she rose to her natural level, and went through the ranks to become a minister. Besides contributing to the struggle against male chauvinism and female passivity, she has helped in eliminating the racism that exists both within the Party and among our people.

(In March of 1971, Denise Oliver left the Young Lords Party to join the Eldridge Cleaver faction of the Black Panther Party. This was not part of a collective decision by the Central Committee, but rather was an individual decision on Denise's part. We in the Lords still relate to Denise as a sister, in the same manner as we would relate to any Panther. As a result, the position of Minister of Economic Development is now vacant.)

Gloria became a Lord in February of 1970. Born in Puerto Rico, she was a strong supporter of the Nationalist Party. To make a living in New York, she became a health worker in Gouverneur Hospital. There she saw conditions which led her to join community struggles for better health care. For this, the sister was fired, but not until she had helped found HRUM and its newspaper, *For the People's Health*, two people's tools that still fight on. That ain't bad for a junior high school drop-out.

Through HRUM, she came in contact with the Party; Gloria went through the People's Church Offensive, and joined the Party afterward. She rose through the ranks, aided by her organizing of our Health Offensive that reached a peak in Lincoln Hospital in July. In August she and Juan celebrated a revolutionary wedding. She joined the Central Committee in September, at age twenty-six.

On September 22 and 23, the Young Lords Party and the Puerto Rican Students Union sponsored a conference for Puerto Rican students at Columbia University. The theme was the liberation of Puerto Rico. Over 1,000 high school and college students attended. September 23, El Grito de Lares, the conference marched for a celebration to Plaza Borinqueña in the South Bronx.

In August, our branch in Philadelphia was recognized. This has been one of our most effective branches, having dealt with the drug problem (pushers) in the colony, taking over a church to support the demands of rebelling prisoners, and now organizing a conference for church people on the problems of brothers and sisters in the prisons. For this, they have undergone practically the heaviest attacks of any branch; there have been numerous beatings, false arrests, and several firebombs which have wrecked their offices.

We first got involved in the prisons struggle when the prisons in New York City first got taken by the inmates. Many of the sisters and brothers in jail had come from the streets we had worked in, and had read *Palante*, or were reading smuggled copies. In October of 1970, an organization that arose from the prison rebellions came from the concentration camps to become a section of the Young Lords Party. This was the Inmates Liberation Front (ILF).

Our attention had turned from the prisons toward organizing a national demonstration when we were brought sharply back to the brutal oppression of the inmates. For years, there had been reports, many published in the press, of Puerto Ricans and Blacks committing suicide by hanging in precincts and jails. Such a large number of these deaths were reported that the circumstances were highly suspicious. On October 15, 1970, a Young Lord joined the statistics. Julio Roldan, arrested on the whim of a pig in *El Barrio*, was said to be found hung in his cell in the Tombs, the Manhattan Men's Prison. We were told it was a "suicide."

We knew we were being taken for a ride. Julio was a Young Lord, and we are not about useless, wasteful suicide. There had to be some action taken to provide an example for our people; a demonstration just wasn't going to make it.

On October 18, at the end of a funeral procession of 2,000 people for Julio Roldan through the streets of El Barrio, we took the People's Church once again. Only this time we took it armed, with guns. Our message was clear: When attacked, defend yourselves. This was the Party's Fourth Offensive.

Where does the Young Lords Party go from here? At this point, we are going ahead with plans to step up the forward progress of the Puerto Rican national liberation struggle. On October 30, 1970, the anniversary of the day in 1950 that the Nationalist Party started a rebellion in Puerto Rico, we organized a march to the U.N. of 10,000 people. On March 21, 1971, we held a demonstration in Ponce, Puerto Rico, in remembrance of the massacre of innocent people in 1937 by Amerikkkan orders. We announced that day that a YLP branch had opened in Ponce. This has been done to unite our people on the island and the mainland with a common goal: liberation. Wherever a Puerto Rican is, the duty of a a Puerto Rican is to make the revolution.

Our new branch in Bridgeport is carrying the Party line to Connecticut. This line carries our belief that national liberation will be won by uniting the most exploited parts of our society, the street people and the workers, in a common effort. We also believe that our fight here on the mainland is fought at the side of many peoples, particularly the people of the Third World, people of color. We are eliminating the racism that divides us.

Our past examples, our present work, and our future successes make victory certain, because we are backed by our people. The enemy, the United States Government, respects us because of our people; we are always humble before our people, and will always be vicious before the enemy.

Liberate Puerto Rico now!
Venceremos!
Central Committee

ROOTS

"You're either a victim or a rebel."

RICHARD WRIGHT

"I want people to wonder at what forces created him, terrible, vindictive cold, calm man-child, courage in one hand, the machine gun in the other, scourge of the unrighteous—'an ox for the people to ride.'"

GEORGE JACKSON, ON THE DEATH OF HIS BROTHER JONATHAN, FROM *SOLEDAD BROTHER*

"I become the one that translated ...the go-between."

IRIS MORALES

My family can not be called typical, because it excludes a lot of things that other people experience. But there are a lot of threads in the family structure which are typical of all Puerto Rican families. My family just happens to be a very straight type of Puerto Rican working-class family. We weren't affected by drugs. We weren't affected by daughters going out and getting pregnant. Instead, we were affected by daughters going out and doing organizing, becoming political.

Both my mother and father came to New York in 1947. They met here at a dance, got married, and in 1948 I was born. In Puerto Rico my father was a cane cutter. He was the oldest son of about nine children, so when things got rough, he came over here to make some money to be able to send back to the family. My mother was the oldest of nine children also (an older sister had been killed by a lover). After her parents died she became the one who took care of all the other children, so she never knew any kind of childhood. My father worked in a hotel when he first came here, as a dishwasher. Then I guess he graduated to elevator operator—and he's been there ever since. My mother at first didn't work, she just devoted herself to having a family and taking care of the house—the traditional role of women. But, financial things got kind of tight and she was forced to go out and get a job, and that's when problems between them started, because my father, in very strong Latin tradition, felt that was threatening—that a woman should go out and work and have her own money and gain her own independence.

My mother didn't speak any English—she still doesn't—so I became the one that translated. It meant that she was ashamed to go to school because she couldn't speak English and talk to the teachers, and she didn't look as good as the other Americans, the other mothers. It meant that she always had to play a behind-the-scenes role, and she could never assert herself in dealing with any kind of institution.

I was the one that was the go-between. This happens to a lot of older children in Puerto Rican families—they become the link between the Puerto Rican culture and the American culture and the Puerto Rican way of life and the American institutions. They become, in a sense, the ones that come up against oppression the most. For example, when the landlord comes to the house to pick up the rent, it's the oldest one who speaks English who has to translate for the mother. When they go down to the unemployment office, it's the oldest one who goes as a translator, or when they go to the hospital.... So that the oldest child usually comes in contact with all these institutions, and feels, you know, the way that Puerto Rican people are treated.

We first lived on 124th Street, but it was torn down to build a project. So after that we lived on 106th Street, and they're still living there. The apartment has about five little rooms, and I always had to share a room with my younger sister because we always had to have boarders to help pay the rent. although at that time the rent wasn't very high.

My mother worked in the factories and my father worked two jobs in the hotel. He would leave the house about five-thirty in the morning, and he wouldn't come home till four or five. I don't really know what wages he was making because that's one thing that was kept from us. You know, this is something that happens in Puerto Rican families, where the parents have all the authority and the children don't question. There's even a saying in Spanish to the effect that children should speak only when spoken to.

The mother's just one step above the children—she doesn't question anything that the father does—and that's the way it was in my family. If I ever wanted any money, my mother would tell me to go to my father and ask for it. If I ever wanted to go anywhere, I would have to go ask my father. If I ever wanted to have anyone over to the house, I would have to ask my father. And my father was not very close to us—he was very distant. He was maintaining his role as an authority figure, and an authority figure doesn't get involved with children or with the wife.

And then, of course, you also have the thing, *machismo*, which is very strong, so that the man feels he has to go out with other women. My father always did that—there was always another woman—and all I remember is my mother sitting and crying. So I developed very negative attitudes toward Puerto Rican men.

My mother's not that old, she's in her middle forties, but she looks like she's in her fifties or sixties—completely destroyed, constantly sick. They say she has a nervous condition. Actually, it's just a reaction to oppression. She's worked in a factory for twenty-three years.

There was one thing that was always very big in the family, that there were no brothers, that my father didn't have any sons. He himself was the oldest son of the oldest son of the oldest son. I was supposed to be a son but I wasn't, and then there were no other sons to carry on the family name. That really got to my pops, so I guess that's one of the reasons he started running around, trying to develop a son somewhere else.

My father can be sick or whatever, but he's never missed a day of work—not even a day—because you've got to support, you've gotta do it. It's a strong thing, you know: "In Puerto Rico I worked and got my money, and here I'm working and getting my money. But I can't make ends meet. I can't pay the rent, my wife went out to work. . . ." He's completely crushed. His whole conception of manhood, which is fucked up anyway, is destroyed.

One time he was dealing in running numbers so that he could supplement, but he got caught, so he stopped that. What happened was that he just kind of gave up trying to deal with things and tried to pretend that everything was okay by developing something else on the outside. He would have nice clothes that he would buy for himself and for his other woman, and in that way pretend that things were okay. Or he goes to Puerto Rico and gives out money to relatives, like he's rich.

In the beginning I remember they used to talk a lot about going back to Puerto Rico. When I was four we went, and then after six years we went again. My mother would always tell me how, although it was hard for her there, it was much nicer—she didn't have to deal with the cold and people who spoke English and people who were in the factories. That at least she would be among her own. My father was coming from a more mercenary kind of thing where he wanted to go back and show that he had made good here, and buy a house and maybe some land and stuff like that. But as we got a little older we started seeing that it was kind of a fantasy, so that now my mother just talks about going back to visit, because she knows she doesn't have any hope of going back there to live. She doesn't have any hope of ever leaving that apartment—and she's been wanting to move for the last ten years. She filed an application with the projects because, you know, when you live in a tenement, the projects are always better. They're cleaner, they don't have rats and roaches, or it doesn't appear that they do. So that's what she aspires to now.

When I went to school I was placed in a class where I was the only Puerto Rican. That helped me a lot in one sense, and it fucked me up in another. The way that it helped me was that I began to see contradictions. Like, we lived on the West Side, a liberal white community, and all the white kids would go home one way, and I would go home another. All the white kids dressed a certain way, too. Like, the girls' skirts didn't get wrinkled, and mine did. They talked about going away to camp, and I would talk about going to *El Barrio* for the summer. I got to see these contradictions very young, but as a result I became timid and felt inferior. I became very ashamed of my family, because they weren't what it was to be American.

You know, we lived in a typical kind of ghetto apartment—no hot water. Sometimes we would go for days without taking a bath, and I would see myself next to the other kids and feel that I was dirty, because I was not white. Or, you know, there'd be rats, and I'd stay up sometimes hoping that the rats wouldn't get into the baby's crib. I'd keep the light on all night and take turns watching with my other sister. My sister and I slept in one room that was divided by a curtain into two. The baby slept on the other side of the curtain, and my sister and I slept in the same bed. It'd get so ridiculous, you'd fight over blankets, you'd fight over... I mean, everything is always very antagonistic in that kind of setting. You don't have any privacy, so that if you feel upset or you want to cry, you can't slam the door to your room and go upstairs—you just lock yourself in the bathroom. You could even hear the neighbors next door, there were always people out on the street.... I remember when I got into a really big school thing, the guys in the summertime would be playing the congas and it'd get really noisy out on the block, and I'd get pissed at them because I couldn't do my schoolwork, you know.

I started blaming my parents for not giving me anything better. I started hating them—feeling that it was their fault and that they were stupid and that if they'd really worked hard they could have gotten something better, rather than realizing that they were just being victimized and that there was no place for them to go, there was nothing for them to do.

In our family it has always been us two older sisters who have played the pioneer roles. You go to school, coming from a very strict, patriarchal type of family, and you have a conception of things that you can do and things that you can't, and these conceptions start to be broken down. For example, you find that other kids stay over at each other's houses, which is something that you would never be allowed to do as a female. And I wasn't allowed to go to the library until I was in junior high school, when the teachers forced me to go, 'cause my mother and father, coming from a rural thing, didn't know what that was all about.

I was supposed to always come home right from school. I could never visit anyone and no one could visit me—you didn't have strangers in the house because of the fear of strangers, the feelings of inferiority. And I developed these feelings too. I wouldn't have people over to my house—especially the kids that I went to school with, the white kids—because I felt that my house didn't live up to their standards. So I was in a kind of limbo situation. I hung out with the kids on the block, but I went to school with other kids who didn't really consider me part of them because they considered me part of the Puerto Ricans, whom they didn't exactly like.

When I was in seventh grade, I was very friendly with this girl named Susie whom I'd known since kindergarten. She knew that her parents didn't like Puerto Ricans, but she was gonna show them that I was okay—so she took me to her house for lunch. I went and I was very uncomfortable, because I didn't know all this table etiquette and shit. At home we usually ate on the bed or on the floor or in front of the TV or wherever we could eat, 'cause the kitchen wasn't big enough to hold the whole family. I had tried to dress right and speak correctly and not let my accent show, and I thought everything went okay. But that afternoon at school, her father came in and told me that he had a pair of gloves lying on the kitchen table when I was there and when I left they weren't there anymore, and did I know where they were. So I got very indignant and said, "Yeah, that's all we Puerto Ricans do is steal." I just told him off. I refused, I refused to degrade myself and deny that I had taken them—I just said, "Fuck it." You know, you wanna think that, I can't change your ways. Eventually the gloves were found and he wrote me a letter apologizing for this, but I just couldn't accept it.

When I was in eighth grade I got involved in a thing with the kids from the neighborhood where we stole a hundred dollars. I got caught. The truant officer—his name was Big John—caught me counting the money out on the street, 'cause I was *stupid*. They took me to my father's job, and he was humiliated because I had put him through such shame, and they took me to my mother's job and she cried. We came home and my father gave the hundred dollars to the truant officer, plus fifty dollars so that he wouldn't take me in and give me a JD card. And after that I wasn't in with that group of kids. When I went back to them, they said, "Where's the money?" And I said, "Well, you know, I don't have it 'cause my father gave it as a bribe." And they said, "Oh, man, you fucked up, and you're full of shit!" I said, "Fuck it, man. You know, it was either me getting a record or giving the money." But they didn't understand.

My sister—the one two years younger than me—would go to school, but she wasn't part of it either, and she never got into being with people on the block. She was quieter and more timid.

Since the two of us older kids had not turned out so hot because we had gone to public school—which my mother thought accounted for it—she put my other sister into a Catholic school so she could turn out better. The Catholic school had a lot of Irish kids, and the nuns were coming from a thing very oriented toward *them* and not at all toward Puerto Ricans—so that my sister wouldn't even admit that she was Puerto Rican. Finally she turned into a whole street thing. She just decided that she was gonna deal with the people on the block and fuck everything else. She didn't deal with school at all, although she's very bright. She became very rebellious.

And the youngest one—well, you know, all of us got scared because the public school didn't work, my mother said, and the Catholic school didn't work, so we found a way of putting her in private school. *She*'s fucked up because she knows she doesn't belong there. She gets into fights with the kids all the time. They organize gangs and they fight each other, and there's a lot of racism going on.

All of us, you see, went through different kinds of things, and yet there's that common thing where we didn't fit for some reason or another, because we were labeled from the beginning, we were made tokens. You know, when you're a kid and being oppressed, you don't understand that it's a whole system, capitalism. All you see is that your pops comes home, when he comes home, and that there ain't enough bread there for the family, or that your mother works at a factory and why can't she work someplace else, why doesn't she learn how to speak English. Like, I used to get on my mother about that all the time. As a matter of fact, the teachers in school used to tell me, "Make her speak English, so that you can speak better English."

The rest of the family—aunts, uncles, cousins, and everybody else—considered us kind of odd because we wanted to go on, get more education, and we were kind of rebellious. I started doing organizing when I was young, I started out with the people in my building, trying to organize them into a tenants' group. I was about fifteen, and they thought I was crazy, 'cause what kind of woman goes around knocking on doors and telling people all this kind of stuff? They just saw that I didn't have any respect, 'cause that's a big thing in Puerto Rican families to have respect—and especially in my age group, you have to have respect for your family, and you have to learn how to cook and take care of children, because that's what your role is going to be. When I or my other sister would go out, my mother would say, "Well, you think you're a man—you think you're a man." I got a beating one time for coming home at three-thirty, because I was always supposed to be home at three. I used to stand on the corner and talk to the guys and girls from school, and when I came home one time at three-thirty, for the third or fourth time in a row, I got a really bad beating. For weeks I couldn't walk well. And that's how you teach respect—very physically. You know, very authoritarian.

The Catholic Church was another thing too. What happens is you have to go through all the rituals—baptism, communion, confirmation—even if your family is not into a deeply religious bag. There's that whole thing about having to confess your sins—*everything* is a sin in the Catholic Church—you get that on top of the strictness and the patriarchy. And since the Catholic Church is kind of elitist, that whole cultural thing of inferiority is reinforced. The Catholic Church says you have to dress well to come into the House of God, that boys and girls can't mingle together. The Church also reinforces that authoritarian thing with the father and with the mother, and the kind of controls they have over you, 'cause, you know, God is looking out. It's just taken for granted that there is God and there is the Church, and that you have to respect it—and that goes hand in hand with the whole respect that you must have for elders, the whole respect you must have for your parents, the whole respect for your teachers, the whole respect for authority.

You know, sometimes I sit and I wonder how all my development came, politically. And I think it's happened in the last five years, when I decided to leave home. And that was, like, a big scandal in the family. But it was worth it. It was worth all the hassle and everything, because now I can see what is happening, and being in the Party, I can share this with more people.

You know, there used to be only four choices for the Puerto Rican woman—housewife, prostitute, or drug addict, and then, when the society needed more labor for its sweatshops, she would become a worker.

Now there's a new choice open to her that threatens the existence of the family and the state itself: The Revolution.

"America should never have taught us how to read, she should never have given us eyes to see."

FELIPE LUCIANO

The first ten years of my life were spent in the projects. Long, long, vertical buildings, shit-encrusted walls—there were no rats and roaches, but it was its own prison. It's always reminded me of a mental institution—people closed in, not allowed to expand at all. I grew up there like most of the other Puerto Rican Black brothers and sisters in *El Barrio.*

When I went to public school, I was a bright student, very bright, but I was always a behavior problem—that's what the teachers told me. I rebelled against everything. There was something that I was always looking for as a child. I always knew that I had to do something, as romantic and as weird as this may sound. What that thing was, I didn't really know. I had images and dreams of becoming a doctor, becoming a social worker. Of course before any of those very legitimate dreams, I wanted to be a cowboy on a horse, riding through the plains in my big sombrero. I read *Cowboy Sam* and *Curious George* and Dr. Seuss—very, very entranced. My world was expanded because I was able to read a lot at a very early age.

We were very, very poor. My mother was separated from my father when she was three months pregnant with my sister. They had been married for about three years, and had had one baby right after the other. We went through the welfare scene—the welfare syndrome as I call it—always waiting for that check, anticipating that check, heart beating, mouth dry, arguing with each other. My brother, sister and myself used to fight each other for scraps of food on the table. When that welfare check was supposed to come, we used to run downstairs, open that mailbox. You played a game with yourself—you turned the key very slowly and peeked in the box very slowly, and if that welfare check wasn't there, there were two reactions you used to have. Like when we wanted to be cruel, when we wanted to get back at my mother for a beating she'd given us, we used to go and tell her the check had come and then we'd tell her it hadn't. Otherwise we'd come up with morose-looking faces and say "The check didn't come." I remember those days, I remember almost begging for food.

You resign yourself to poverty—my mother did this. Your face is rubbed in shit so much that you begin to accept that shit as a reality. You've never seen anything else. Like the only thing we knew was that block. You never went out of that block. I didn't know there was a Museum of Modern Art. I didn't know that there were people who were living much, much better. I didn't know about racism. I mean we were just on that block—and that block was our home, it was all we knew.

The images of that poverty.... My stomach rumbling. My mother beating me when I knew it was because of my father—you know, they just had an argument where he almost hit her. The welfare investigator cursing out my mother because what she wants is spring clothing for her children and he's telling her how she just can't have it—when I read in the magazines that people—you know, other people—had spring clothes. Why couldn't we have clothes for Easter? And he's telling her, like, in a sense, "Fuck you." And I remember images of my saying, "When I grow up I'm gonna kill every welfare investigator I see, every one of them—you know, strangle them."

There's nothing extraordinary you know in my childhood—maybe just that I learned very early how to become accepted, how to rise above and beyond as they say. Even at that point we knew that to the extent that we became white—we would advance in school. To the extent that we spoke properly—we would get Satisfactory or Excellent on our report cards. To the extent that we conformed—we were accepted. And since I read well, and I spoke well, I rose in terms of classes. And I remember the teachers always saying, when I hit a teacher or would throw a chair through a window, or would lead a group of cats through a riot in the cafeteria—a near-riot in the fourth or fifth grade—the teachers grabbed me by the side, grabbed me by my ear, you know. Wrenching my ear and saying, "You know you have so much potential. Why do you act like that? I mean look at your marks—you have so much potential...." That thing went through all my school life—those words were uttered time and time again: "You have so much potential." Of course, what they considered potential was certainly not what I later became.

And my mother was very frustrated also. She couldn't get a job, she wanted to get off welfare. I never looked upon my mother as a woman; she was always my mother. I never looked upon her as a Black Puerto Rican woman who was oppressed—she was just Mommy. She's fat, she is a *bear*, you know, and I remember snuggling between her neck and... peace, you know it's peace, 'cause nobody can hurt you when you're with Mommy, 'cause Mommy's the big protector. Not Daddy, but

Mommy—Daddy wasn't ever there. And she too wanted to get out, but she didn't know how. You know, she always wanted me to do something, since I was the first born. I was getting into a lot of trouble. But she had these images of me becoming something.

Finally we moved to California to get away from New York and because my mother wanted to go back to my grandmother. California was such an enlightening experience because I saw all these people—Japanese, Chinese, white people—they lived together without the kind of separation that you see in New York. And it was sunny all the time, like there was no snow, you know—just eighty-five-degree weather all the motherfuckin' time. I got *black;* I got black as the sun, man, and I got fat and healthy. I entered the fourth grade and got good grades in school. We had fields—this was in Wilmington, California, before they industrialized—we had fields that we used to run through. After school that's all we'd be doing. I got into track because I always wanted to do that, but I didn't have the chance to do it in New York. I had a lot of happiness, a lot of fun there because the environment was completely different. There were trees, there were horses, which I had never seen. They had a corral, a stable just a block away from the house. Just to see a horse, just to touch him was like another kind of world for me.

But it wasn't to last long. We stayed there only four months. My father was supposed to send us money in a legal separation. But he didn't send it. He got very bitter when my mother took us away, it seems. And though he hadn't done a motherfucking thing for us—remember that when I say that, I'm just remembering the bitterness of my younger years, because I really don't hate him—at that point, he felt my mother had slighted him by taking the kids away. Without the money from him we couldn't survive because my grandmother couldn't take the burden. So we had to go back. And we had to ask the welfare in Wilmington for the money. I remember the very degrading experience of my mother having to go there and be insulted three, four times during that week.

We only had enough money to pay our train fare; we had no money for food. So my grandmother, in a little handkerchief, tied up all of the coins she had. Of course, it didn't last us beyond Union Station in L.A. But we left, and I'll never forget, man, we were starving, you know, literally starving on that train coming back. Big, plush train and no food. We would look at people—you learn how to look at a person to let him know that you're hungry—and they'd give us a little tidbit, but it wasn't much. And I was very concerned for my mother, because throughout the whole trip she held her head in her hands. And it was traumatic, it was horrible, having to see my mother go through shit like that. I felt so responsible for her that I felt like a little man, since I was the oldest. And I was always to my mother lover, confidant, trustee, everything rolled into one.

On that train, hungry as we were, the only thing that saved us were some Black brothers working in the kitchen, and they saw us and we would walk in, we sat down and had some water in front of us. My mother with those little pennies bought some pastries and some coffee and tea because she couldn't afford any more. And the cats knew we were starving, I don't know how they knew, but they just started bringing things to us—burnt blueberry pie, I'll never forget it was burnt, but it was all they could afford, and they gave it to us. And that's how we survived—by them giving us little things. I don't know where they are, man, but all power to them wherever they are. I mean they saved us, I don't know how we would have gotten through that trip without them, 'cause I would've started robbin' or something.

Anyway, we got to New York and we ended up living right back on 112th Street, but in a different project. And for three years we lived there. I went to another school, and again, the same shit. I was, as my mother says, fucking up. I was still into my thing.

At that stage I was living a double life. On the one hand I was going with my mother to church. I grew up in the Puerto Rican Pentecostal Church, which is a scene unto itself—I mean it's a different world. The Holy Spirit, speaking tongues, body contortions, jumping on the floor, vomiting out demons, people entering trances—*vahilias*, as we call them in Spanish—which are just seances almost, that are held overnight... all those things I was very involved in. Man, I was a *fervent* church-goer. Even with all the streetfighting I was getting into. That's not unusual. We find in our community—the Puerto Rican community—that things are compatible. For instance, people have Catholic saints and at the same time they'll have a Voodoo doll, you know, or a piece of bread above the door so that the evil spirits can eat that and leave in peace.

So I made the church and the fighting compatible, you know. I would always just shut up about the fighting. I would never tell her. After church or before church she would talk about people beating up each other and be condemning them for it. I might be coming in from a fight myself, but I'd be coming in goodie-goodie and go to church with her, right. And so I just led that kind of a double life.

In school, the same kind of thing happened. I happened to *love* to read. In fact I just raped books. I used to go to the library, get ten at a time, and just shut myself in my room, because that was my way of escape. Like getting into another world—with horses and trees and flowers, and fighting and adventures—going up on a mountain, and doing all those things that, you know, white folks do.

There were only a very few people that you could talk to about it. I mean, we still hadn't gotten to the point where we were that close to each other. But I had one or two friends—Big Ben, Richard as we called him, and June Bug, right, and we used to sit down and say, "Man, you know, Mount Everest is the highest mountain. I wish we could climb that one, man." We used to talk about riding horses, we used to talk about, oh, so many things.

But at the same time, I was of the street. I had to prove to my friends that I was just as bad as they were. I was always into fighting and scullies—Crack-top as we called it—using spinning tops to crack another guy's top.... That's really a ghetto game. Whoever couldn't spin his top had to put his in the middle, and all of us would take turns trying to crack his top—and yet each one cost fifteen cents, and for us that was a lot of money, right. Hot Peas and Butter, that's another game we played. Whoever is It takes a belt, and screams "Hot Peas and Butter," and goes around and whips the *hell* out of whoever he catches. Very violent games on *each other*.... We laugh about it now, but it was very rough, as you begin to think about it, how we murdered each other every day. I was vicious when it came to fighting, simply because I didn't want to be considered a schoolboy, you know.

When I was in eighth grade, I had a teacher—I'll never forget her—Mrs. Shapiro—she introduced us to Shakespeare. Here we were in eight-two, which is, of course, a step below eight-one, and they had told her she'd never be able to have us accept Shakespeare—but we loved it, you know. I was Puck in *A Midsummer Night's Dream*. We read *Twelfth Night*. We did *Romeo and Juliet*, which I thought was corn shit, and all kinds of things—but we began to enjoy Shakespeare.

And again I had to lead that double life. I enjoyed the fighting, you know. I enjoyed it—it was a release for all of us from whatever we were running from. We had our gang, we had our identity, we had our own community. We didn't realize it then—that the oppressor had taken away our community. What America has done is cause groups to fight each other to keep them from seeing the *real* cause of oppression. We didn't understand that then, man, we just understood that as far as we were concerned, you know, we wanted to be together. And we were very close to one another, and we used to goose each other—of course, had you called us homosexuals then, we would have just had a *fit*, but it was.... It mean, it's a natural stage for young cats to go through. And that was another factor involved in it....

Oppression binds you together, sometimes in a negative manner, because you have nothing else to look forward to, you have nothing else to look at. You bind yourselves in locales, and one locale will fight against another. All of the energy that we had against the oppressor was perpetrated on our own people.... If I just begin to add up the number of brothers and sisters who had lye thrown in their faces— 'cause we used to mix red lye in Pepsi-Cola and throw it in a cat's face—the number of brothers who are now crippled, the number of brothers who are *dead* because of those gang fights, it would number into the thousands.

There are very, very few survivors. Big Ben is a dope fiend, Charlie is a dope fiend.... June Bug is a very frustrated man—he was brilliant, brilliant as a child, brilliant mind, so was Big Ben, by the way. June Bug ended up as a hospital orderly, and that's what he's doing now. Peachhead is on drugs. Leon, his brother, was shot in the streets and died. The others have died in Viet Nam, or are out on drugs now. One, Angelo, is in Harvard—no, he went to MIT—but he's now working for anti-poverty and lost to the world.

And for me I saw no future. College was to me like a dream, I could never get there. I think that's one of the things—that fear—that led me into, you know, like, vicious, man, vicious fighting. Not knowing what to do with your life, even though you've been taught the American Dream. America has sown her own seeds of destruction, because she's made oppressed people eat that dream up hook, line and sinker and when they found it shattered, they decided that the only way to begin to build that dream for themselves—interpret it for all oppressed people—is to shatter it, shatter the reality that is ugly, and begin to build a new one. America should never have taught us how to read, she should never have given us eyes to see.

"All you had was your turf —there was nothing else."

BOBBY

When I was growing up, when I was a kid, the gangs were a very big thing. It was like hero worship. The heroes of the block were the Bad Motherfuckers and the Wizards. They were the thing we wanted to be, you know. I remember they used to kick each others' ass, fuck each other up real bad, man. They'd do all kinds of weird shit to each other. And I grew up in the middle of that. Like, cats would come up to us and say, "Someday you guys will be the protectors of the block." 'Cause it was a thing where you protected your turf. All you had was your turf—there was nothing else. All you had was this pride in being an *hombre*, in being bad and taking care of your people.

At that time, in the block you felt pretty safe. It isn't like now when the people close their doors and shit. You knew the gangs wouldn't fuck with you. People would just go in and out of each other's houses. And everybody loved each other—you'd go to the roof and hang out and drink beer at night, listen to music. Each turf was like a little country in itself. As long as you weren't a stranger, as long as you didn't come from somewhere else, you were safe in your block. But if somebody came in and was, like, the enemy, you fought him off, and you protected what was yours. 'Cause, like I said, that's all you had.

I became a Dragon when I was around fourteen. At that time the Dragons and the Viceroys were the two big gangs in *El Barrio*. We had a thing where we fought each other. But we honored each other too. We used to talk about how bad the Viceroys were. We used to tell stories about how bad Little Man was, and how bad this cat was, and how bad the other cat was. We'd try to, like, justify how strong we were when we went into battle. That pride was the thing. 'Cause you had a feeling when you walked down the street you were somethin'—fuck all the garbage and all the shit that was around you and how fucked-up your clothes were—you were somebody, man. If you were a bad motherfucker you had a rep, and you'd die for your rep if somebody fucked with it because that's all you had. It was like you were trying to say to the world, "This is *me*, man, I'm alive, you dig, and I got somethin', and I live in this community, and I'm somebody here. I'm a leader. . . ." Especially if you were a leader of a gang.

You know, going down was like a mixture of fear and excitement. It would be like a military move—one division would go to Fifth, another division would go to Madison, another division would go to Park, dig? You were afraid of what could happen. You were carrying a piece, and you didn't know if you were gonna get busted, dig. But the feeling of going down and proving yourself overcame all of that. It was actually a joy to go down.

You'd run into the block, burn, get chased out by the pigs or by the Viceroys, you'd do your thing and then you'd run out of there. And at the end of it, when you'd get together with your boys, you would say, "Yeah, I did this, and I did that," and your boys would say, "Yeah! Man, dig the shit this brother did! You see this motherfucker when he did that!" You know, back and forth, hugging each other and really being up in the air about the fucking thing. We felt like kings—like we were warriors. Man, we were channeling our warrior thing, you dig. We were a people, you know, we *are* a people—and it was coming out of that—that warriorness in us.

Now, the gang thing went through stages, dig. The first stage was what we call the rumbles, right. We used to go down in big numbers, like, ninety of us against the Viceroys and a whole lot of Viceroys against us, and we'd have these gigantic battles. Most of it was blades and sticks, and shit like that, and a little burning. It was very glorious at that time. Then it got a little more scary. It became like guerrilla warfare. Three cats would go down and burn one person. Now it was no longer a thing of the big gang but just a fighting thing. It became very vicious. We were just killing each other off, man, like fuckin' flies. And, many of us were goin' to jail, you dig—doin' like twenty to life.

You know, I shot this brother. It happened when I had stopped gang-fighting. But something happened with my younger brother, and we had to go down. The brother we shot was an ex-Viceroy. Me and my brother burned him, man—we put, like, seven bullets in him. It was a fucked-up thing, you dig, it was a fucked-up thing.

That brother is now a Lord. And we love each other, man. And the deep thing about it is, the brother's in a wheelchair—behind what me and my brother did, you know what I mean. And still, you know, he's political enough and I'm political enough that we understand, you dig, why the shit went down—it was the conditions we were living under. And that's why he and I now have dedicated our lives to fighting for the freedom of our people, so no more of our kids will fuck around like we did—'cause, like, we hurt him, and it's still there, you dig, and at the same time we hurt ourselves.

"We wasn't thinking about the other guys being Puerto Ricans ...if he was your enemy, you kill him."

GEORGIE

I think if I would have been raised up upstate, man, in a good community, I would've never become a gangbuster, I would've never shot nobody, I would never have stabbed nobody—but since I was raised up in this community, this is what it, oppression, teaches you—kill, stab, steal, and shoot dope—like, now the thing is dope, mainly. I got a lot of brothers out there, man, that are shooting dope—they used to jitterbug with me. They used to call me Little Man, 'cause I always was really small for my age. But smallness to me didn't mean nothin', because wherever there was a bat, it used to make me always the same size as the other person.

When I was a little kid, around seven years old, they used to have what they called the Lightnings. Later on, they became the Lightning Dragons. You know, little kids see those big guys and say, "Wow! Man, when I grow up I wanna be like them." Because that's all there is to do in your neighborhood—like if you don't learn how to be a pimp, you learn how to be a jitterbug. Those were the two big things then, because at that time there wasn't that much drugs around the neighborhood. I always wanted to be a pimp, because the pimps they were always clean, they had shoes, a lot of wing-tips, a lot of sharkskin, mohair suits, and they always had money in their pockets. I always used to say to myself, "Oh, man, when I grow up I want to be a pimp."

I started all my fighting when I was really young. My father used to have a very nasty attitude—anybody that looked at him, he would go up to them and say, "Have I got a monkey in my face or somethin'?" If it was a little kid, he would put me to fight against him. And I got into the habit of always fighting in the block—as a matter of fact, when the older guys wanted to play stickball in the block I used to tell 'em, "No, man, you people ain't gonna play in the block—me and my fellows are playing." And, my fellows were all guys six years old, seven years old, you know, against guys eighteen, And, since we wanted to be like them we used to, like, put on a show, and we thought we were *bad* 'cause we had stickball bats and shit.

My father and my mother used to give me everything I wanted. Except my father—he always told me, like, the only two things that he wouldn't give me in life was roller skates and bikes, because I might get killed by a car. And, that's where my trouble really started, because when I was around nine years old, like, I wanted a pair of roller skates *so bad*, and my father would never buy them for me. I remember, five of us went to Central Park and we dug these guys rollerskating. I was nine years old and I wanted some skates—and there was five of us, and we seen these guys skating down the thing, and like, we beat 'em up and we took off their skates. Anyway, the pigs came, and me and my brother got busted for the skates and shit, and I went to the Youth House for a few months.

The next year I got busted again—this time for robbing *La Marqueta* and I did five years in Children's Village.

When I came out I was tired. On 111th Street they had the Viceroys and the Dragons then. At first I really didn't want to join them. I said, "Oh man, if I join one of them, I'm just gonna go back upstate again."

But I used to live in Viceroy turf, right across from where their center was. I was raised up with a lot of those guys and I always wanted to hang out with them. A lot of the debs, the sisters, used to go for me, too. What happened was that the Dragons saw me hangin' out with the Viceroys, and thought I was in the Viceroys—you couldn't blame them, you know.

In P.S. 83, where I was going, they had around two Viceroys, and maybe fifty Dragons—so you know where that was at. One day I was playing dice and all these Dragons surrounded me and asked me, "Hey, man, are you a Viceroy?" I told 'em, "Look, man, I'm not no Viceroy," and I tried to explain to them that I had just come out of jail, but they thought I was bullshitting them.

I remember they hit me all the way from the schoolyard—for a whole block they were hitting me. And then they got me in this telephone booth and broke a telephone right over my hand. So now I was mad, but I still didn't want to join the Viceroys. Another time I was with this guy named Bimbo—he used to be an old Viceroy, he was from my neighborhood. Anyway, they caught me and Bimbo in the train station and they came over to us, and they told me, "Look, man, this is the second time we catch you—the last time we bust your ass, man, and you tell us you wasn't a Viceroy. And every time we see you, we see you with Viceroys."

What they did was, they waited around a minute before the train came and threw me on the train tracks. And I got up and I ran, you know. I said, "Damn, man, these guys are fuckin' me up every time they see me—so I'm gonna join the Viceroys, man. I might as well join them."

We used to jitterbug, right. Some times we used to go down to 103rd Street and, like, go up to the block and shoot up the candy store or shoot up the guys that were around. Sometimes we used to stab guys, sometimes we used to get stabbed. We wasn't thinkin' about the other guys being Puerto Ricans. Like, now we're political, but at that time Puerto Ricans were Puerto Ricans—if he was your enemy, you kill him.

When you used to go to school, like, the teacher used to tell you, "Oh, man, you dumb—like, you nothing but a little boy," and shit like that. So all the young brothers used to have that complex of the teacher calling them a boy, and they wanted to prove it to themselves they were a man. And they would go to any means to prove it.

When I first started jitterbugging, a brother named King Kong got shot at 117th Street. When he got killed I was hurt—that was my main man, you see, one of my brothers. A week after that, the Dragons came down to 112th Street in a car and they started shooting at us. We had a gun on us, so when they started shooting, one of the brothers was gonna run over to the car to, like, to shoot the Dragons. But the Dragons they shot him in the arm with a .38 and he fell. So this guy named Chico grabbed the gun. This other guy, Nate, opened up the door from the car and Chico shot the Dragon in the head, you know, shot him in the head. He fell against the horn dead, and the car went out of control and went into that store on the corner of 112th Street and Madison. Even though I knew Chico had killed this dude, I felt bad about it. You know, you say, "Ah, fuck it, yeah we killed a motherfucker, man." But inside, you really say, "Man, one of these days they probably come up to me and shoot me. . . ."

Some of us been lucky, that we stabbed a lot of guys, right, but never killed nobody, and we not doin' time. But some of the brothers, like, they're unfortunate—they're doin' life in jail. And right now I feel sorry for a lot of these brothers, even the Dragons, man. I know if they had another chance to live, they would never jitterbug no more or kill another brother. You know, they might turn political like I did and Bobby did, right—because, like, I cooled down.

I stopped jitterbugging because my enemy became my best friend. Like, they got this guy named Feather, from the Young Dragons—right now, man, he's like my brother—I love that cat, I love him. If anybody would try to hurt me, I know he'll kill for me—if anybody try to hurt him, I know I'd kill for him, man. Me and him were real together in jail. A lot of

Dragons that I met there, some of them are more friends of mine than my old, old friends the Viceroys, you know. And you go ask the Dragons, man—Dragons will tell you the same thing.

I guess it's because we got to know each other and that's what the Young Lords is really about, man—to show you you don't fight against brothers, because you might be angry against your brother today, and tomorrow he might be your best friend. Tomorrow, he might be the guy that saved your own life.

"It was just escape ...the easiest cop-out there is at this point is drugs."

CARMEN

We came from Puerto Rico—my family were all Puerto Ricans who come from Guayama. We had a good home at first when I was a little girl—everything was all right over there. Even money wasn't as big a thing because there was more. If you were middle-class you could go to the schools there. My father struggled a lot, and we went to school, we all went and we were well-dressed and well-fed. And my mother was well-known and my father was well-known, and I was a kid that everybody knew. And I would visit with the rich kids; I'd hang around with the rich kids—I even had myself a bicycle.

My father was right hand of one of the richest people but he heard that over here he could make more money, and that he could educate us better. We also have a very sick brother, and we felt that here he could have the right medical care. My brother had a fall in Puerto Rico when he was three and because over there medical care is very poor, he wasn't treated on time, and he became handicapped. He doesn't absorb anything—he will forever be a child. And that's why he had to be taken care of, and taken to hospitals—and treatment is done, but still no progress is being made on his condition.

So, my father came to this country a very proud man, but he went to a factory to work—that's the only job he could get—and he was getting forty dollars a week. And here he started drinking wine and became what is commonly called an alcoholic.

At that time I had to become the head of the family. Being the eldest, I had to handle all the situations going on in the house—and I was only ten, going on eleven, so I couldn't really do as good a job as I thought—but I was trying hard. I got part-time jobs in different small stores, I went to school, I took care of the family, I made sure they ate, I picked my father out of the hallways when he got drunk, took him out of the places where he used to hang out.

My mother was with the family, but my mother is a woman who has been a house woman all her life. She's never been to school and she was never educated whatsoever. But in Puerto Rico she did a lot of work. She's a very fine cook, and she could organize parties and things like that. But here, she doesn't speak English, and she's at home all the time—she doesn't know how to travel, she doesn't know how to do anything in the streets. I mean, here she couldn't learn anyway—because of my brother's handicap—she has to stay home and sort of babysit and be a nursemaid for my baby brother.

I was here six months before I really started to run away.... I was living on 121st Street, that was called in those days Korea, 'cause it was like a hassle, a struggle broke out every day—drug addicts stabbing each other, garbage being thrown out of the windows. Every weekend we had a movie—the neighbors would fight, and we'd watch through the windows, or we'd go to the street and watch the brothers kick each other's behinds out on the street. And drunken sisters and drunken brothers in the street, fighting and arguing and playing dominoes....

I was so tired of seeing my father work so hard. There was not ever enough food, and they were always struggling to keep me well-dressed—every day the same routine. I thought I could make it on my own and become wealthy. Like, I read in many places that kids run away from home and become owners of factories, and whatever. So I tried it. I ran the streets.

You start out—you live in the subways, you sneak in halls and sleep, you steal babyfood from the supermarket 'cause it's the easiest thing you could cop in your pockets, and that's what you eat. And then you hang around with the addicts, and these people see that you're so young and they feed you—if they had a piece of bread, they'd share it with you. And sometimes charitable people take you into their homes and feed you a couple of eggs, but then they have to throw you out because they're afraid of the cops.

I went to the Bronx, and I shined shoes—I shined a lot of shoes in my life. I slept in basements, and I fed myself, and did the best I could. I stole a bit, but you have to steal a lot to keep on living. It was escape—at least I didn't have to face reality. I could just sneak anywhere and be by myself and cry if I wanted to, without having a crowd on my back. In a three-room apartment—one room to sleep in and everybody hanging around—you didn't even have privacy to cry in.

I met a lot of addicts in the street.... I used to talk to them and they'd say, "Well, I feel good." And I said, "Well, maybe if I get high, I won't feel it, it won't bother me so much." And I started snorting with them—you know, they would give me the bag when they were finished, and I would snort it and it felt good—'cause I would cop out for a couple of hours, and I could sleep, and I didn't cry, 'cause I didn't feel like crying. So I started snorting, and then I watched them buy here and there—and I said, "Man, I could get involved in that." And I tried buying a little—two-dollar bags—and then I met some people who needed a kid to give them the look of decent people. They would buy me clothes and take me with them, and give me a lot of dope. And for me it was like a Christmas present. Then I learned how to shoot up in my arm, and I kept on. And because I never used dope before—I never knew what it was—I got a really big head out of it.

It was just escape. Everyone finds escape somewhere—the people in the factories find escape working to death; the mother in the house finds her escape beating, spanking the kids, or watching TV or hearing the serials on the radio. The man in the street drinks, gets drunk; the wino gets drunk and escapes. So, for people who cannot swallow and learn how to drink—the easiest cop-out there is at this point is drugs.

I got up quite a big habit. I bought over a hundred dollars' worth of heroin every day so I could keep myself set up. It doesn't mean I was high—just to keep myself from getting sick and having my fits.

At this point I was mugging and stealing galore—everything I found in sight. I had myself this partner—he's dead right now—and we went out, and we set people up. Like, people would say, "I need half a load"—that is, fifteen bags—and we'd say, "Yeah, we'll get it for you. We'll get the *best* there is in the market! Just give us the bread, wait right here, and don't worry. We'll get it for you." And we'd take away the money.

Otherwise, we'd wait for Fridays—in those days, everybody got paid on Friday. We'd wait by a train station and we'd follow people, and I would say, "Listen, I need a quarter for so-and-so," and then my partner would come in from behind, and I would stab them, or put a gun in their head. Or sometimes, when we had a gun, we would take their money away, knock people over the head, smash faces—anything to get the money we needed.

My partner was about thirty-eight. He was an old man, he'd been on drugs all his life. One time we was shooting up on the roof, and he said the stuff was kind of heavy. He shot up first. He didn't have no veins any more, he was too old. He was shooting up in the head, the vein in the temple. He was shooting up there, and he miscalculated; he passed out. When I checked him out he was halfway dead, so I looked in his pocket and I took all the bread he had, and the set of works. I let him die there, and I tipped. That's the last time I saw my partner.

Sometimes I'd be thinking of my family and my mother and that I wanted to come back, and I'd go back to the house. My mother, she could see that there was something wrong, but she would play blank, or she'd think I was just nervous and upset, and she let me get away with it. I guess most mothers are that way. Sometimes she even gave me money too.

I tried a couple of times, you know, to kick. I would stay in somebody's house, and just try to do something, but the chills were bad and heavy. I would stay clean two days—then somebody would come up and say, "Man, I got the best dope there *is*," and I would get tempted again and get high and start all over again. It was a vicious circle.

When you get high, you get really relaxed. You just want to sit down and nod, you wanna scratch yourself, and you wanna eat sweets, and you enjoy it, like, everything's passing you by. Sometimes you hear the radio, you hear the news and you say, "Oh my God, *really*—bad one, hunh..." but you don't really capture it—you're just dozin' off all day. But when you get down, when you need some dope I mean, you start sweating, your nose starts running, your eyes start running, you throw up a lot, you get diarrhea, and the pain in the bones is pitiful. You feel very uncomfortable, and very violent—like, very nasty about the whole situation, real, real, real upset about it. And if you stay too long that way, you get sick, completely sick. You start getting the shakes, and you are unable to get up. But nobody waits for that point, 'cause at that point you can't go out and hustle any more. So, when you start getting sick, then you *know* you have to go out there and start hustling for your next cure. You become... you're not really human any longer. You're like an animal, and your own cravings are the only thing you want to satisfy—you don't really give a damn about anyone. I mean, I wouldn't doubt it that if I knew my mother had money I would take it all if I needed it.

When I was sixteen they sent me up to Bellevue. I didn't want to stay there, but I started reading a lot. And I started doing a lot of thinking in there. I started reading about different people that started on dope.... I said, "If all this time I had to make money the way I make it... if I used that in a good purpose, I'd be rich pretty soon." And that was my first initiative to quit—my capitalist initiative. The same bread I was making for dope, I was gonna make it for my pocket. I wanted to become rich, and own a car, and really look good.

I kicked the habit then, and I went upstate to Hudson for eighteen months. I was always rebelling in that place. They would put me in confinement, do any kind of thing. They tried to impress me so bad. But then I found a kind woman, and she says to me, "Carmen, if you use your idea that you have here for the right purposes, I mean, you could really help your people." I said, "What people?" So she said, "Puerto Ricans." I said, "I ain't Puerto Rican! I'm in New York, I'm from New York. I'm an American citizen." I kept on telling her I was an American citizen. And she said, "That's very funny," and that what I was was Black. I said, "You're a New Yorker," and she said, "No, I'm African." And she started sort of giving me small training, small things to think about and make me proud of my people. And she started talking about certain people in my race, like one time she mentioned Pedro Albizu Campos, and she started telling me about how my people had struggled, and I didn't even know it 'cause I didn't know I had any history; I didn't know these things. And when I was in confinement, she would walk into my cell and talk to me and tell me how proud I should be of what I was. And when I came out of Hudson, I started checkin' things out, really checkin' 'em hard, and reading. And I was really getting to know my people, and many times I went down in the street, and "Hey, Carmen, I got something good—you want some?" And I said, "No, man, you don't wanna kill me anymore—I had enough."

When I came home, I saw that my brother—the one that is all right—was growing and trying to be like me, and I figured, you know, if he tried to be like me, we'd have another bum in the family. So I started giving a good example to him. And then, getting married helps a lot. I got married, and I started thinking of other persons' feelings. I really became sort of . . . at this point, I was halfway human. I started really seeing the problems of the people outside, and thinking about how they tried to escape. And I started talking, constantly—every time I would meet a junkie I would talk to him, and talk, and rap to him what happened to me. Out of ten junkies I would catch, one would quit. And that really done it to my pride, my ego. So I got to being proud of myself, and I have been clean since. Now I got three years, clean.

"Larceny in my heart..."

GEORGIE

The first time I went to prison, it was to the Youth House. I was ten years old and I was, you know, a real small guy. The big guys always tried to push on the small guys, so I had a real hard time there. Since I was so small and I couldn't fight with my hands, I'd hit 'em with a chair, hit 'em with a broom—anything that I could get a hold of to make me their size. I used to get into a lot of trouble with the counselors.

I think the Youth House instead of making me better, put larceny in my heart. The food was good, they had a swimming pool, they had every recreation—but still they used to make it hard for you. For any little thing you used to do, they used to come and smack you behind your head. Some of them used to punch you and hit you. I know guys who had their arms broken. Me, I got punched around a couple of times. Matter of fact, I also got kicked—they just kick you, like, up your ass and punch you around.

Later they sent me upstate to Children's Village. Now, Children's Village was the same thing. One time when my mother went up there to see me, they told her that she couldn't see me because I was under discipline. What happened was that they beat me up so bad that my mother, if she would have seen me, could have brought it back to court. This guard, he had me with a bat, and my arm was swollen, my two eyes were swollen and my lip was broken. So he told my mother I was disciplined, and my mother had to turn back, all the way back to New York, you know, from upstate all the way back to New York.

I did five years up there till I was fifteen years old because every time they used to hit me, that made me so mad and I'd do the opposite of what they wanted me to do. So what happened is that I ended up doing five years there.

In a way, I used to like the home, because I always did like sports. They had a baseball team, they had a football team, and a basketball team—they had track, they had high-jumping. As a matter of fact, I won medals for everything that happened. I didn't have a chance to do these things in New York City.

When I first went up there, I ran away three times because I was homesick. I wanted to be home with my mother, and I was trying to get back home. The first time I ran away I got as far as the highway, and they caught me. They beat me up, they gave me discipline, they put me in my room, they took away my privileges and everything.

The second time, it was a week later. As soon as they let me out from my discipline I ran away again. And the same thing happened. The second time they gave me two weeks locked up.

As soon as they let me out, I ran away again, because I wanted to be home. They caught me again, and they gave me discipline again. So, I saw for myself, I dug it, running away wasn't the thing, man, because I was just gonna get caught, so I said I might as well face it, so I stayed up there for the five years.

When I got out it was January. All winter I stood out of trouble because I was going to the center at 111th Street to play basketball. Then when the summer came, I was looking for a baseball team to join—you know, so I could keep out of trouble and stay out in the streets. But it was hard to find a baseball team. I used to, like, ask a lot of people—because I was lookin' and lookin' and lookin', and I couldn't find nothing—there was nothing there to find, there was no baseball team, there was nothing. So I got bored. I started to get into trouble—I started gang fighting. I assaulted this person, and they gave me four months on Rikers Island. First I went to the Tombs, since they didn't have an adolescent bureau at that time.

And the Tombs—they usually throw you in a cell with bums—bums that have crabs. Sometimes you can't use the same bathroom that they use, because you know that they're so infected, and when they throw up you can smell the vomit and everything like that. So I really got sick. I was in the Tombs until my hearing came up—that was a week. I pleaded guilty because I just wanted to get out of the Tombs because the Tombs is so fucked up. I was forced, in a way, to plead guilty, and I went to Rikers Island.

At Rikers Island I had the same problem that I had upstate. I was small, and when you're small and young a lot of people think they can have sex relations with you. They think of you as a girl when you go in there—they try to make you a girl if you don't have no heart. You become a homosexual if you don't fight for your rights. The first time I passed through the yard a lot of guys looked at me and started whistling. I told them to whistle to their mother, and we got into, you know, a big static, and we got into fights. The first time, like, I got into a fight, two or three pigs hit me. After that, they put me in the bing.

Now the bing is solitary—they put you in this little room, and in this room they give you bread and water. For instance, if they give you ten days, every two days they'll give you bread and water, and then the third day they give you a full meal. It's supposed to be a full meal, but what they really do is give you a quarter of a full regular meal. So you really don't get that much to eat. They throw you in there like you were a dog—just for a little fight or something. And if you give them a hard time, they open up your cell and they fuck you up. They punch you, they hit you with clubs.

One time this pig called me out, right, and he told me, "Clean up the recreation room." He told me to clean up the recreation room, and the recreation room was clean. So I went back and I told the pig, "Look man, the recreation room is clean." So he told me, "Okay, well, go back out there and close the windows." So I went back out there, and the windows were closed. I told him, "Look, the windows are closed." So, he told me anyway, "Wait for me out there." I went out there and waited for him. When he came in, he started rolling up his sleeves—so, I asked him, "Look here, man, whatcha gonna do?" He told me, "Look man, I don't like you, and to get it off my chest—I'm gonna deal with you." So, I told him, "Look here, man, you're not gonna hit me for nothing, because if you do—I'm gonna break your jaw!" I was honest with him, you know. I told him I was gonna break his jaw because I wasn't gonna let nobody hit me for nothing. So, he hesitated for a while and then he hit me, right—when he hit me we started fighting—his partner, instead of coming and breaking me off, he called the riot squad. Fifteen people come in and, like, all of them started hitting me with riot sticks. They hit me everywhere—they hit me in my legs, my arms, my back, my neck, and my head—they hit me so much that the next day I didn't get up, because when I tried to get up I fell on the floor. I tried to get up again, and I still fell, man—like, that's how much the pains were. As a matter of fact, two weeks later, I still had the pains, man—that's how bad they fucked me up.

Sometimes they would tell you to take a shower. In the shower, they got these clubs—I don't know how I can say it—it's a bad word.... We used to call them rubber dicks because they were made out of rubber, and they were hard, right. So they told me to take a shower, right. I thought I was just gonna take a shower, and they started hitting me with these rubber dicks. I don't know if anybody knows how painful it feels to get hit with a rubber thing under the shower, man—it opens up the meat of your skin, your pores, it really opens it up, and it stings like they're sticking a whole lot of knives into you. On one shot it feels like a million stings are hitting you—and they just kept on beating me with that, and I was trying to get out of the shower because I was hurting, and they kept on pushing me under the shower and hitting me with these things. After two weeks, like, I still had the pains. And every day they used to go in my cell and tell me to get up every time I heard that key. But I couldn't get up, so every day they used to hit me and hit me and hit me. This went on, for almost two weeks straight, man, they kept on hitting me and shit.

By the time I came out of Rikers Island—when I used to see a pig—and I don't care what kind of pig it was, man—I used to hate him—I used to just look at him and hate him.

At Rikers Island they had a school, a tailor shop. I used to work in the tailor shop in Rikers Island. It wasn't so bad, because it was a man from the streets that used to work the shop, so I did learn something—he showed you drafting, and sewing, he showed you how to work pressing machines. It really wasn't that bad—like, all that they showed you, in a way, was good to learn. But the larceny they used to put in your heart.... When you came out, you didn't want to work. You didn't want to work, because you figured why should you work, man, when you know how these people messed you around in jail, how they treated you. Now, you get to hate, you know, hate people. Really, you don't go out to work, man, 'cause true, you learned a trade and everything like that, but they say you're a menace to society—they used to tell me, "Georgie, you're a menace to society," as if I was a killer or something. Yet, they were more killers than me, because if I was a prison guard, I don't think I could hit a brother that's in there, hit 'em with a club, and mistreat them—I think I would be there to help 'em, not to fuck 'em up, man.

When the brothers took over the Tombs, I was happy. In a way I almost cried. When they were broadcasting it over the radio I knew how it was, man, how they felt—like when they said that roaches ran over their beds. It's true. In jail this is what happens—the rats, the roaches. When they give you coffee, the coffee tastes like rusty water, the oatmeal they give you in the morning tastes like glue, and the bread is so hard, man—like, they have a joke in jail that says the bread is so hard that if it falls on your toe it breaks your toe, and it's really something like that—it wouldn't break your toe, but it's hard. Then they give you this thing called Spanish rice, man, and it really ain't Spanish rice—what it is man, is gooey rice. We got a brother over here in the Lords that made some gooey rice upstairs in the mess hall. His rice was bad, and everybody talked about it. But you know, I was thinking, "All these people, they talking about Lefty's rice, but they don't know the rice they give you in jail."

What prison did was put more larceny in my heart, you know. After prison I couldn't dig living in society. When I came out in 'sixty-two, I stayed out almost five years working in a factory—but it really was against my will. Every time I used to work and I used to see that foreman, he'd remind me of the prison guard. It always bothered me. Sometimes I used to be sewing, right, and I really wasn't tired or nothing but all of a sudden I used to stop my machine and walk away. When I was working for my boss, like, it would remind me so much of a jail, it reminded me of working with people, man, that had tortured me, and this thing that was in me—it was put into me while I was in jail. I used to have hate for any boss I used to work for—I didn't trust no bosses, man. I used to think they were the same as prison guards. And my boss, sometimes he used to ask me, "Well Georgie, how come sometimes you come in so happy in the morning, and all of a sudden, like, you turn off your machine and just go home?" I used to tell him it was because I just felt sick or something. But I wouldn't tell him the exact point, you know, why I felt this way—that it was because I had a lot of larceny, like, real larceny in my heart. Really, like, you know, it was there—probably I would still be working if I hadn't heard about the Young Lords today. I probably would have still been working there, feeling that way. Feeling depressed, feeling like I was working under a ruler or somebody that... you know, if I didn't work, I was gonna get hit. Even though I knew I was free, I could have quit any time I wanted to and everything like that—but I still had that complex, man, I still had that thing. If I didn't work they would lock me up in the bing. If I didn't work, I would be outside and I was gonna go to jail, and everything like that. So, I was forced to work, working under pressure, you know, really under pressure. And I couldn't see that, man—and then I heard about the Young Lords, right.

Like, I joined the Young Lords Party, man. And I seen it, because I seen they were fighting against the system—the system that I always hated. Because when I was a kid, when I used to go to school, I used to pledge allegiance—I used to love the flag, man, you know. I guess I started hating the United States after I started going to jail. After I got arrested—the way they mistreated me, I used to draw, like, Nazi signs—everything against America, right, because, like, the system was so fucked up, man, to me. Okay, you go to jail when you do something wrong, and they're supposed to give you discipline—but not fuck you around so much that you get to hate everybody you see. It had got to a point that I didn't even trust my own mother, right—because I didn't trust nobody. I thought that everybody was the same, you know. And then I joined the Young Lords Party and it gave me a lot of trust in people again, man.

One day I heard over the radio that the Young Lords Party had taken over a church. It was the first time I'd heard about them. I really didn't understand what it was about. I didn't know it was a revolutionary group. I didn't know they were fighting against pigs—I just heard they took over a church, and I thought that they took it over just to help little kids, and it was, like, a group that used to help kids out and that was about it.

So, like, I dug it, you know, because I remembered when I was a kid I wanted help—and nobody wanted to give me help. But that still wasn't really my thing when I first heard about it, because I wanted to help kids out, but I also was against the system. So I didn't know what it really was about.

But that same night I went home after I heard that over the radio, and it was on television. I wanted to see how these guys took over the church, you know, what was happening, so I put the news on, and the first guy I see on television was my cousin. I didn't know that he was a Lord because I hadn't seen him for about six months. So, when I seen him on television, I said, "Oh man, you mean my cousin's a Lord, man," and I was curious to find out what he was doin' in the Young Lords takin' over a church for a free breakfast program. Because me and him, we had got into a lot of static with pigs when were younger, right, we had got a lot of foot up our ass when we were younger because we used to hang out together, you know.

So, I went down there and I asked him what's the Lords about, and he explained to me it was a revolutionary group, it was a group that was fighting against the system 'cause the system was fucked up—they were trying to get better housing for the people, and he told me about the health thing—in other words they were trying to help the Puerto Rican people, the Black people, all oppressed people. So, like, I dug it, I dug it because I knew I was oppressed, man, and this thing was something I was looking for a long, long time, right—something I knew, like, was in me. The only thing was, there'd been no group there to tell me, "Well, come on, be in it"—there was no group doing this, you know. So I told my cousin I wanted to join.

I went to the Young Lords' office. I wanted to join the first day 'cause I knew that this was my thing, but everybody was quiet. I just walked out 'cause I seen everybody not talking to me and everything like that. But the following week I went back because that's how bad I wanted to join. So I went back, and the people still kept quiet. One day, I wanted to join so bad that finally I opened my mouth—I told them, "Look, man, how do you join?" So, they talked to me, they told me how to go to Political Education class. I went to P.E. class, and then the following day, like, I became a Friend of the Lords. I was a Friend of the Lords for two weeks. I became a Lord-in-training.

Now I know I'm fighting for all oppressed people—people that I felt like meeting for many years, you know, and never had—people that had been suffering, man, people who had been getting mistreated not only in jail, but out on the street. And I'm fighting against people like the landlords, right, who have been fucking people around—we've started working on that now—and we're fighting in hospitals. You know, when they told me we were going to take over Lincoln Hospital—oh man, that was the happiest thing that happened to me in my whole life. In the meeting I told Fi, like, "Oh, man, that's beautiful, man." You know, he looked at me like I was crazy, because I was just a Friend of the Lords at that time, and he figured maybe I'd be shook up, I'd be a little nervous, you know—first offensive or something like that—but I wasn't, man. This was something I wanted to do. And, you know, when we took it over I was so happy, I wasn't even thinking of the pigs. I was really happy—even though I could have got killed in there, you know, or something like that—because I'd been to Lincoln so many times.

One time, I seen a brother there, he was shot three times—he was there on the table, you know, laying on the stretcher for two hours, *two hours, man*, with three bullets in him. I could see it if they would have took two x-rays and were waiting to see where the bullets were, I could see that, but they hadn't even brought him in for x-rays yet—and he was waiting there for two hours with three bullets in him. And I seen old ladies with pains, you know, sitting down.... I live around Lincoln, so I used to go to the emergency room a lot, and I used to see these old ladies and everything.

So, when they told me, like, we're gonna take it over to improve the thing there, I was happy, because I was thinking about those old ladies I seen there, I was thinking about the brother that was laying on the stretcher, and I knew that if we took it over, we might have got hurt, but yet, we was gonna improve the hospital one way or another.

I know there's gonna be a time we gonna have to pick up the gun, or they gonna kill us, man. I know, like, I might die, but yet I know, like, I'm gonna die for my people, so when my son grows up he's gonna live a better life, right. And I know when his kids grow up, they're gonna live a better life. You know, in time it's gonna be that way, man, because people are uptight, really fucked over.

For instance, they're over there in Viet Nam having all these people killed and spending all this money, but yet, they won't think about putting that money into a day care center, right. Mothers who have kids in day care centers, they could go to work, you know. They tell 'em, "Yeah, I'll give you welfare," but what good is welfare gonna do—welfare ain't gonna let them live like other people are living over here, right. Like they're not gonna give 'em luxuries, they're not gonna have cars, they're not gonna have nothing. So really, they're not doing nothing for the Puerto Rican people by giving them welfare and shit like that. The way they treat my people, man, my people—all oppressed people—the way they treat 'em is like dogs.

They'll send rockets up there to the moon, right? They're throwing these billions of dollars away to go some place where there's no life, there's no nothing, but they won't give them to our people. If they care for our people so much, how come they don't put that money to work, like, for them? And that's why I think I joined the Young Lords Party.

If a pig ever kills me and I'm fighting for my people, I'll die happy because I'll know I gained something by dying. Now, if I'm not in the revolution and I just die of a heart attack, I'll probably die sad because I'll know I didn't do shit for nobody.

REVOLUTION WITHIN THE REVOLUTION

"Let me say at the risk of seeming ridiculous that a true revolutionary is guided by great feelings of love."

CHE GUEVARA

"We're saying that ...it would be healthy for a man, if he wanted to cry, to go ahead and cry. It would also be healthy for a woman to pick up the gun."

PABLO "YORUBA" GUZMAN

The first time we heard about Women's Liberation our *machismo* and our male chauvinism said, "Well, these chicks are all frustrated—that's their main problem. What they really need is a good—you know." That was the thing that we were coming from.

And then this just didn't sit right with us. One of the things that's been good about us is that sometimes when we ain't so political and shit, we get a feeling. So we checked it out. We knew that there was something good and there was something bad about the different ideologies that were coming out of Women's Liberation. For example, we knew that there was something wrong with the concept of separation of the sexes. That may be practical in the white community, but for us in the Third World it is impractical because that's slowing our struggle down. We need everybody we can get, 'cause we're being eliminated.

After analyzing the concept of Women's Liberation, the sisters brought forth a concept that was absorbed by the Party, the concept of women's oppression: The thing with white women is that they have been put on a pedestal, right; however, with Third World women the problem has been that the white man has put the white woman on a pedestal, and then messed around with Third World women. The white cat has also helped turn around the brothers into a thing where to prove their manhood, to prove that they are like that white person, they go around oppressing the sisters.

Now, we can't blame this totally on capitalism; it is a thing that goes way back to the tribes. What we recognize in the Party is that there are biological differences between the sexes—a man has a penis and a woman has a womb. Right now that's a fact of life—it may change later, but that has still yet to be seen. The thing is, these physical differences should not mean the man should be in leadership and the woman should follow. That's like, "I got gray hair, you got black hair—therefore I should be boss"—that's *crap*, you know. It doesn't make no sense, it's not logical; it doesn't follow anybody's logic except the logic of an opportunist, of a jive cat, right.

Since I'm talking about sexism, the second thing that made perhaps a greater impact on us was when we first heard about Gay Liberation. That's a whole other trip, because we found out it's a lot quicker for people to accept the fact that sisters should be in the front of the struggle, than saying that we're gonna have gay people in the Party. There's this whole thing about faggots, you know, and queers, and this and that. From the time you were a kid your folks told you the worst thing you could be was gay. I was told, man, that if I turned out gay, I would be disinherited, beat up, kicked out—and my father was *big*, you know, and fear, man, it kept me from being gay. And when you think about fear keeping you from being *any*-thing, you realize there must be something wrong with it.

Now, I'm not gay, but maybe I should be. It would probably give me a better outlook on a whole lot of things. At this point, I am talking from a theoretical point of view where I feel like I understand the problem. Being gay is not a problem; the problem is that people do not understand what gay means. See, there is a biological division in sex, right—however, this society has created a false division based on a thing called gender. Gender is a false idea, because gender is merely traits that have been attributed through the years to a man or a woman. Like, the man is supposed to be strong, noble, hearty, hairy, rough, and the woman is supposed to be light, tender, pretty, fragile, crying, and weak. And what happens when you find a guy that's light, pretty and tender? That guy is obviously a "queer," right. And if you find a woman who has the gender traits of the man, then that woman is obviously a "lesbian." And both words are said very negatively—they're both supposed to be very fucked-up, right. In other words, a man trying to be a woman and a woman trying to be a man. Well, that's not true, you see, because in our analysis of the Gay struggle—and I like to put it in those terms, the Gay struggle for liberation—it's been clear to us that what this means is really rounding out of the person.

The time I spent in the academic world there was always talk about how you could get an education that would round out the individual. The Gay struggle really rounds out the individual, you know. Because certain traits have been assigned to people historically by society, we've actually developed as half-people, as half-real. We're saying that to be totally real, it would also be healthy for a man, if he wanted to cry, to go ahead and cry. It would also be healthy for a woman to pick up the gun, to use the gun. The gun is not the sole property of the man, you see. That's how you round out people. The Gay Liberation struggle has shown us how to complete ourselves, so we've been able to accept this and understand this.

Now, it's rough—it's going to be *very* rough, bringing this home to the Young Lords Party. But I have a lot of faith and hope in the Lords—'cause the Lords are already talking about it, and people are getting their minds blown about this. As long as people have the ability to want their minds to be blown, we will always survive as a party, we will always be able to move forward. When people start getting old minds, forget it—no matter how young they may be. An old mind is a mind that refuses to accept changes, right. If that should come down, the Party either has to get some new people with young minds, or we better find a new party.

"When you look to any group to find out who's the most oppressed, it's always gonna be the women."

DENISE OLIVER

Within the Party, one of our Thirteen Points is that we want equality for women. We oppose *machismo*, and the way we're dealing with it is by actually clarifying what it is, how we sense it as women, and how to combat it within the revolutionary struggle. It is going to be very difficult because the brainwashing has been so heavy. Women have been brainwashed into believing that they are weak, that they are not fighters, that they are not capable of picking up guns—in fact, they're supposed to be afraid of guns, afraid of anything mechanical.

Our role is to educate sisters so that they can be a vital part of the revolution. Since we see the struggle in this country as basically being one of urban guerrilla warfare, the woman must take a major role because of the mobility she has—a much greater mobility than a man's. The fact is that pigs are male chauvinists, so they may not be as inclined to shoot a woman walking down the street with her children, a pocketbook, and some bundles of groceries that may contain bombs; they may not be as brutal toward a woman when she's arrested. We have to *use* that kind of chauvinism.

We also don't want a revolution to happen *after* the revolution. We don't want to say, "Well, we want a socialist society, we want to have armed struggle," and after all that's over, still have to deal with the fact that women are oppressed.

In the Algerian Revolution, women were the carriers of weapons — they couldn't actually use them. And the position of women in Algeria today is still an inferior one. The revolution in Cuba was also one in which the woman in most cases did not play a role as fighter, and today there's a big women's liberation struggle going on inside the country.

Now, in the Vietnamese struggle the sisters are probably the most liberated women in the world. That's because all the sisters in North Vietnam are fighting, and they're fighting right alongside the brothers, and sometimes in front of them. We want that kind of thing to happen here.

The whole concept of *machismo*—that man is superior in all ways—has developed among our people because the Third World man is so oppressed by outside forces—by the system, by capitalism—that he's taught to believe that the only way he can get back at this is by being superior to women.

Machismo is a word that is used to depict a certain tendency among Latin males. It doesn't mean that *machismo* doesn't exist among white males—it's just that it's not as obvious. Among white men, their whole *machismo* thing is, like, who can make better business deals or take over a large corporation. A man is respected by virtue of the money he has. But since the Third World man doesn't have any money, he's respected by his fellows for how much balls he's got, and how much he can oppress women, and how many women he can take to bed and use and fuck over. So that although *machismo* is not just a Latin thing—and we'd like to make sure that idea gets corrected—it is more apparent in oppressed communities.

When you look to any group to find out who's the most oppressed, it's always gonna be the women. Whether it's in the bourgeoisie, or the working class or *lumpen proletariat*, it doesn't make any difference. Just look at a woman and you'll find the story of real oppression in this society. In our case, our oppression is threefold. It's first the oppression under capitalism that affects all people of the Third World; secondly, there's the oppression under capitalism that affects women in terms of jobs and things like that; and thirdly, there's the oppression that we receive from our own men.

In Puerto Rican society, the woman is taught to cater to the needs of her family, in particular to the demands of her father or husband. She's taught that she is inferior in her own ways. Like, sometimes she is taught not to enjoy sex. The man, of course, can go out and enjoy it—this is being very *macho*.

I was living with a brother who was a real *macho*, a real street cat. He had been a dope fiend, you know. He was very respected on the streets since he could fight, and all the other men looked up to him—that's how brothers judge each other, like who's got more balls and who's more down. Usually when they get into fights with each other, it's not even over a woman, it's just like a stand-off between two roosters—two roosters digging each other to see who's the king of the barnyard.

This brother's whole thing was, he couldn't stand me to go out on the street in short skirts, not because he didn't like me in short skirts, but because other men would see my legs, and I was his property. When his friends came over, I was just supposed to sit there and look pretty while the rest of them had the conversations—every once in a while I could nod my head or smile or put some little comment in, but usually it was ignored. Most of my time would be spent making coffee and bringing it in and serving it to people, and then his friends would leave, and he would go dig the TV, and I'd have to do the cleaning up. He used to insist on my going to visit his mother all the time, so that I would see what kind of a woman he wanted me to be. His mother never went anywhere. She was a slave in the home.

Now, supposedly this brother liked liberated women, but I think this just meant *sexually* liberated women. A woman was still supposed to be a slave in all the other areas of the relationship. His whole idea of what was good in a woman was for her to be attractive, to be sexy (but not really sexy), and then to know how to cook and sew and eventually have a whole lot of children.

Whenever we'd walk down the street together, I was supposed to walk a little bit behind him to show that I was his property, and that nobody else should either say anything to me or touch me or look at me in a funny way—not because this would offend *me*, but because it would insult his *machismo*. If anybody looked at me in the street, that was taking his balls away. He wouldn't get into a physical thing in the streets because that made him look like what he considered to be a punk—so he would wait until we would get home, and then the fights would start. He would feel free to hit me because nobody else was around. That's a *macho* attitude—that women are physically inferior, so if they're not doing what the man thinks is the correct thing, they should be beaten up. And, like, a lot of women are just getting tired of getting their asses kicked.

You see a lot of women with a black eye or scars on their face, and you know what's been going on at home—their husband or their old man has been beating the shit out of 'em—and there's nothing that they can do. You can't complain to anybody—nobody else is gonna stand up for you, because that's supposedly the code of the streets. It's something that we're gonna have to educate our sisters and our brothers out of.

One of the things that I've noticed in most Puerto Rican homes is that the mealtime's really a drag. The woman cooks all day long for the family. Naturally, the first person she serves is her husband—she may even serve him better food than everybody else, 'cause there may not be enough meat to go around. Okay, he sits down and eats a whole meal, then she serves the kids and whatever relatives are hangin' around and friends. A lot of times there's not even enough food left for her to eat after she's been cooking since maybe two o'clock in the afternoon, or if there is, she eats by herself, and then she has all the dishes to do. Meanwhile, everybody else has gone out to watch the ball game or out on the streets.

I rebel against that when I go to people's homes, and the woman is up there serving me. I tell her I'm not gonna eat unless she sits down too at the table. It seems like a petty little point, but after day after day of doing that, the woman starts hating the people that she's feeding. Frankly, I wouldn't blame her if she started poisoning the family. The whole attitude is that she's some kind of hired hand in the home. She's just there to be used, not only by her husband but by her sons. (A lot of women that don't have husbands, you know, are told by their sons when they can go to the movies, when they can go out. And they won't set foot out of the house without one of their sons.)

I think that a revolution—a socialist revolution—will break down the family structure as we know it now. The woman, being freed from her menial position, either as the lowest-paid worker or as household slave, will be out of the home more. She will be freed from the major responsibility of rearing children—because we feel that that should be the responsibility of the man as well as the woman. And if neither is going to be in the home that much, there should be some kind of day-care setup. Revolutionary day care centers will be necessary in a Socialist society.

The concept of marriage will change, because marriage right now is a kind of slave contract. You get auctioned off by how pretty you are. You get bought, and you spend the rest of your life slaving for your purchaser. There'll be no more of that buying of a person because both the male and the female will be looked upon as equals in the society. Probably, in the future, marriage itself, as a contract, will not exist. It will just be a head thing between two people who want to relate to each other at a certain point, and then if they don't want to relate to each other anymore, they'll just split up. It won't be necessary for people to pay money to some city hall, or get some priest to say a few words over their heads to join them forever until death do them part, 'cause that's a lot of bullshit. People will have the freedom to relate to each other as humans, to enjoy each other intellectually, sexually, and whatever else.

I don't see where there are any great advantages to the nuclear family at this point. Actually the concept of two individuals living together off somewhere is selfish and non-Socialist. Under capitalism it has been very useful to have that nuclear family because one person goes out to work, and the other person in the group stays at home and performs another kind of work—housework, which is shitwork, and raising of children. When you change to a structure of socialism, in which all people are equal in work and working in the society, you no longer have that thing where one person is a prisoner in the home.

We see the struggle, the national liberation struggle, coming as a two-person force—brothers and sisters fighting for their national liberation together. What we're trying to do is point out to the brothers that they've gotta start accepting us as people who think and feel, and eventually we'll be able to deal with each other as *compañeros* and *compañeras* and there won't be this inferiority feeling.

Now in the Women's Liberation Movement, you have different women from different classes (although primarily from the middle class) some of whom are very reformist, some of whom want to turn the tables and just be the capitalist oppressors of everybody else, and a large number, really, who are revolutionaries.

We say right on to any women who are revolutionaries. They're getting their shit together, they have to deal with the white man, who is probably at the top of the heap in terms of being a capitalist oppressor, and they've got a heavy battle—they've got to fight their husbands and their fathers. We support them, and they should support us in our struggle.

But we do have some different views. For one thing, we feel we can't have a dogmatic position on abortion. It would be incorrect for us to either be completely in favor of abortion or completely against it. You see, we're very much aware of how genocide is practiced on Puerto Rican people and all Third World people through birth control programs, population control programs, and abortion programs. We could certainly not support any kind of abortion program which meant that if you wanted to get your welfare check, you'd better have an abortion and not have any more kids—that if you wanted a government subsidy of some kind or food stamps you had to limit the amount of your children because you didn't get paid enough money in your job at the factory to be able to support more than a certain number. The Kennedy family can afford to have as many children as they want because they can support all of them. Only if you're a capitalist can you have a large family, and this is one of the inequalities in the system that is constantly being pointed out.

We have to have the kind of society where a woman can determine for herself whether or not she wants to have a child—not on the basis of whether that child will eat, because all children will be eating and will be well-clothed and well-educated, but just on the basis of how many children she feels like having at that time. Also, in a system such as ours, where abortion is kind of a forced thing—sisters have to have abortions in hospitals where they may die. Carmen Rodriguez, one of our sisters, was the first woman to die of an abortion after the abortion law was passed in New York State. She died in Lincoln Hospital because she was operated on in the supply room in a hospital overrun with garbage, filth and decay, where the electrical wiring is all hanging out loose. She died because the doctor that did the abortion has to do too many a day—so that after doing several he's very overtired, and very fuzzy about what he's doing. This is the kind of thing that happens under a system where health care is not taken care of, in a system that gives individuals totally unequal treatment.

We have decided that we say, "Yes, we support abortion under a system where abortion is not forced, under a system where there is community control of abortions, of health services, of all institutions." One of the problems we have in the Party now is that the sisters in the Party cannot even stay pregnant. We have so many miscarriages—Puerto Rican women as a whole have more miscarriages and deformed births than the rest of the population—that we've always said that this is gonna be the last generation of Puerto Ricans if we don't look out. They're trying to wipe us out any way they can. If the pigs don't kill us on the street, they wipe us out in other ways—physically and emotionally and mentally. So we say, "End all genocide. Abortions under community control."

An individual woman, you know, has the right to control her own body. Obviously, any kind of control over your own body, by physical means or through things like forced abortion, on the one hand, or not allowing women to have abortions, on the other, is a form of slavery. But if we're gonna talk about that kind of liberation, I think that before a woman can really control her own body, she has to liberate her mind—and before a woman can liberate her mind, both brothers and sisters have to have their minds liberated.

The basic criticism that we have of our sisters in Women's Liberation is that they shouldn't isolate themselves, because in isolating yourselves from your brothers, and in not educating your brothers, you're making the struggle separate—that's again another division, the same way that capitalism has divided Blacks from Puerto Ricans, and Puerto Ricans from whites, and Blacks from whites. This sort of division has kept a revolution from taking place a long time ago. Racism has to be eliminated, and that whole division of male from female has to be eliminated, and the only way you can do that is through political education. I don't believe that a group of women should get together just to educate themselves, and then not go out and educate the brothers.

When the Party got started, there were very few sisters. It was mostly brothers, and those sisters that were in the Party got vamped on constantly. We didn't have a chance to contribute politically, we weren't growing or developing, we were not in leadership positions at all. We were relegated to doing office work, typing, taking care of whatever kids were around, being sex objects. When a new sister would come in the door, all the brothers would crowd around her and say, "Hey, baby, what's happening? You really are fine, wow!" and all this stuff. We objected to that. We saw that we really weren't gonna be able to do any kind of constructive organizing in the community without sisters actively involved in the Party, because most of the people that we're organizing are women with children, through the free-breakfast program and through the free-clothing drive and the health care programs. So, we brought this up to Central Committee and it was decided that a women's caucus would be formed for our own political development, and because a lot of sisters were not at the point where they could discuss a lot of the things that bothered them in the presence of brothers, and they needed that kind of solidarity with other sisters in the Party for strength.

From the caucus, we developed an awareness of what Women's Liberation is all about and the role of the woman in the revolution. As we began to grow and develop politically, we started to force the brothers to deal with us within the Party. One thing we realized was that although the Thirteen Point Program said, "We want equality for women. *Machismo* must be revolutionary and not oppressive," *machismo* was never gonna be revolutionary. Saying "revolutionary *machismo*" is like saying "revolutionary fascism" or "revolutionary racism"—it's a contradiction. And so, through our political growth and development, that point in the program was changed.

We also started correcting and disciplining the brothers for their male chauvinism, because then we understood it wasn't just about a brother beating up a sister, but that in a political party it could be much more subtle. For example, the Defense Ministry was made up only of brothers, even though the Party said that the Defense Ministry is not to be looked upon as a goon squad; it's not about how many muscles you have—it's about how sharp and intelligent, quick-thinking, fast-acting you are, how well you can deal with strategy and tactics. So through Women's Caucus there are now sisters who play a major role in Defense.

After a while, we were faced with a real contradiction. Here we were growing in the Women's Caucus and getting much more political and jumping on brothers who didn't understand a lot of times where we were coming from. A lot of brothers in the Party are off the street, and they don't know about male chauvinism from a hole in the wall. They were getting very uptight behind the fact that they were getting disciplined every time they opened their mouths. So that one of the things that we pushed for was the establishment of the Men's Caucus to correct that. Now the men in the Party meet at the same time that the women do. They discuss the fucked-up things that society has put in their heads. They're dealing with "What is a man?" After several months of having separate caucuses, we're now having brothers and sisters meet together at each branch to discuss sexism, because we were tending toward a separation that we didn't want.

You know, I don't believe in the concept of just a liberated woman; I believe that there has to be a liberated man too—that a liberated woman without a liberated man is not gonna be a liberated woman, that men have to get away from this whole hangup on their masculinity being their penis. 'Cause that's not what it's about—there are very few differences between male and female, other than biological ones, and we have to get to that level of understanding.

Yes, there is still male chauvinism in the Party—it's a difficult struggle for a man to liberate himself after twenty-three or twenty-four or twenty-five years of being a *macho*. But there is a new man evolving, just like there is a new woman evolving. It's not just the women who are pointing out male chauvinism, the men are even disciplining other men because of it. It's gonna be very gradual, but I can see it, it's happening.

I remember when I first joined the Party, the Central Committee and the officers would give a lot of speeches, and whenever they would be talking to people in the community, they would say, "And you *brothers* must be warriors! And we *men* must struggle together in the revolution!" You know, sisters were never mentioned. When any of us would point that out, we would get, like, jumped on. They would say, "Oh, that's that Women's Lib stuff," you know.

As we developed our own strength, it got to a point where the blatant things were wiped out, but then we couldn't recognize the very subtle forms of chauvinism that go on in the Party. But we're reaching that level now. Now we're getting into questions like brothers who insist on relating to a couple of different sisters in the Party, but on the other hand, the sisters, or the sister that they're living with, can't relate to anybody else. The whole concept of jealousy, the whole concept of monogamy—we're exploring new ideas about these kinds of things. We know that we have to educate ourselves before we can educate the people in the streets.

Like, the whole thing of prostitution—we're trying to break down attitudes toward that. Being a prostitute has nothing to do with sex. These sisters are not sluts; they're women who are forced by their condition to have to sell their bodies to men to make a living. But once a woman in our community has that label, she's like a piece of shit, nobody'll go near her. Actually, both our men and our women are forced to prostitute themselves daily—they're forced to prostitute themselves in factories, they're forced to prostitute themselves with bosses, they have to grovel and shuffle. That's prostitution.

You know, every time I go to the Museum of Natural History, I dig the skulls and the bones of those Neanderthal men, and I dig the people sitting there laughing at them, like, "Aha, look at those stupid cavemen, with their thick skulls. They were really like animals." I think that maybe two hundred years from now, people are gonna sit and look at skulls of present-day people, and they're gonna laugh and think what kind of animals we were, because we still kill, we still hate, we still have a hell of a lot of animal instincts that we have to grow out of. And the only way that we can do that, of course, is through structures that liberate people—because, until people are liberated from having to work all their lives and to die, having done nothing and not having grown, until the creativity of the human being is released, you will not have communism. The first step toward that is allowing over half the population in the world to become released to be creative.

"Revolution means change from the top to the bottom, and that includes the way we deal with each other as human beings."

RICHIE PEREZ

Male chauvinism is a problem that every man has by virtue of being raised in this society. In our community *machismo* is something that is a particular problem. It's one of the trademarks of Latin culture. It is that exaggerated sense of manhood that constantly must be proven in a number of different ways.

Because of the frustrations that Puerto Rican men have gone through under the capitalist system, a lot of them have turned their anger inward upon themselves and the women in their lives. A man says, "Well, I can't control anything else in my life, but in my home I'm gonna be the king. And that means my wife does everything I say, my daughters do everything I say, my girlfriend does everything I say—and nobody dares question me." We put women into the roles of wife, mother, girlfriend, sexual partner, housekeeper, all-around clean-up person—really preventing the sisters from developing because we put them in these roles and will not let them out.

Machismo also can be the thing of brothers in the street saying, "I'm a man —I'll kill anyone that messes with me, except a policeman." Brothers are ready to fight, ready to kill each other, over slights on each other's manhood. But when it comes to our real oppressors—police, or greedy businessmen, or landlords, or politicians—no one is ever very ready to fight them.

We're all frustrated and we all have aggressions inside us, but what we've got to do is focus these aggressions on the people who have caused them. Our sisters are victims of the same oppression. If we're gonna have a revolutionary army, our sisters must develop and grow, just as we have to. And if we come on with a thing that all the leaders have to be men and all the responsibility and dangerous jobs are gonna be given over to men, then we're not going to make the revolution.

When people come in off the street they have to deal with their own self-image and how they relate to sisters before they can deal with these concepts. They find it very hard to change their heads. One of the things we've found is that brothers can't change their heads by themselves.

We have been having a weekly male caucus to discuss the oppression of our sisters not only in the Party, but in our community in general, because we recognize *machismo* as one of the biggest problems in making our revolution.

It turned out to be very interesting, because even those brothers who felt that they were liberated turned out to be into a very heavy male chauvinist thing—it was so deeply rooted in all of us. It was very painful for people to begin talking about their own private lives, 'cause, like, one of the things we all have is that we don't want anyone to know our deep, dark secrets. And when you begin to talk with a group of thirty people or more about your attitude toward sisters and your sex life and your emotional problems, you get afraid that people are gonna laugh at you and think you're less of a man. For instance, we had a situation where one of the brothers said that he had met a sister, and they just spent the entire evening talking with each other and getting to know each other —like they slept in the same bed and they didn't make love. He found it very hard to tell us this, because he was afraid that everyone would laugh at him. And a lot of the brothers, coming out of their own male chauvinism, did think that he was a fool for that. See, if you're in bed with a woman, there's only one reason you should be there—to make love, because a woman is a sexual object, she's not a human being that you talk to, and learn about and get to know.

The brother went through a lot of changes to tell us, but then the people who laughed at him were put through a lot of changes themselves—because they had to examine how *they* were looking at the sisters they were relating to. What they wanted to relate to was getting down to business. A lot of people when they were told, "Well, you're just looking at a sister as a piece of meat," got very uptight about it. They said, "Well, it's a natural thing, that's the way men look at women and women look at men."

We've talked about all kinds of things, like the fact that brothers don't know how to talk about sisters. Words like "broad" and "chick" are negative terms—again, they take away the humanness of the people that you're applying them to, and make them into objects. Of course, no brother would like to be referred to as, "That's my stud," or something like that. Instead of saying "manpower," we're trying now to use the word "peoplepower," 'cause we're not only talking about men—we're talking about brothers and sisters. This isn't an organization of just men. At first, people said, "Well, it's just words. Terminology doesn't mean anything, you know, it's how you really feel." We had to break that down. Words do show an attitude, and if you want to change that attitude, you have to begin by changing the words that you're using to describe people.

Another thing we talked about was

how you relate to sisters honestly. You know, if you want to go to bed with someone, how do you let them know that? Do you give them a whole rap about how much you love them and how much you want to spend the rest of your life with them, or do you tell them honestly, "I dig you, and let's go to bed"? So we rapped about that, and then we went from one extreme to another where brothers who used to have this long, complicated, bullshit rap, started coming on to sisters—like, they'd meet a sister and three hours later they'd be telling her, "Yeah, I dig you. Why don't we make it?" which was, like, again, not what we're talking about.

One of the greatest problems in this country is how dehumanized everything is. When the brothers deny the humanity of the sisters, they also deny their own humanity.

We live in a system where your position in life is determined by how much you own directly, or how much you control directly, or how many people you can manipulate or control. Those people who own a lot, who possess a lot of material things, who can control other people on their jobs and within their families, are said to be successful. Madison Avenue tells our people "You've got to have this, this and this. ... If you do, you're a groovy person, you're a swinger. If you have a new car, you're gonna make it with a lot of girls. If you use a certain perfume, you're gonna be able to entice a lot of men."

Our people strive to be successful in those terms, but every time they try to move forward toward that apple that's being held in front of them, they're blocked. And you know, they don't understand that it's all a sham, that it's only Madison Avenue—plastic America selling its products to people by telling them "You're not good as a human being unless you possess all of these things." So, our people work hard and, like, they'll never make it—because the system isn't constructed for that kind of mobility.

A sense of self-destruction begins to build up—people striking out at each other because they can't put their finger exactly on what's wrong, but they know that there's a lot of things that they're supposed to have and they don't have them.

This is one of the things that we're trying to educate people about, that all of this anger and frustration that we feel, like the sense that we're nothing, have no power over our lives, are not successes in the sense that America defines success—it's not because we're not worth anything, which is the way a lot of people begin to feel.

We're trying to tell our people that this is not happening to us because of *us*—this is happening because it's all planned, it's been done consciously. Those Madison Avenue people are very smart, man, and they study psychology, and they know how to make people want something. This system is constructed in such a way that we're supposed to strive as much as we can because the system benefits from us working as hard as we can even though they know that they're not gonna let us make it.

A lot of us came into the Lords and we had been exactly that type of person, where we were into impressing other people. Many of us who worked used to spend our entire salaries on going out and spending money, living very quickly with our money trying to prove something we weren't even sure of. It isn't until you begin to get political that you understand exactly what you were doing and what you were trying to prove, and begin to analyze why you felt frustrated, why you could party six days out of seven, and go out with a lot of girls and wine and dine, and it would still be very empty—you know, you would still have the feeling that you were drifting, and not having any roots in anything.

When I first came into the Party, I was into a lot of partying and into, like, a very heavy male chauvinist, deceitful, and lying thing. I was into a whole ego trip about how many sisters I was relating to at the same time and how beautiful they all were, and how they all cared for me. I was this big lover, Don Juan-type cat.

When people started talking about male chauvinism, at first I didn't want to relate it to myself at all. I said, "Well, I'm not a male chauvinist, man—that's not me that they're talking about." And as we got deeper into it, and as I got more involved in the Party and left my job and was relating to the Party full-time, I had to begin to deal with my male chauvinism because it was sort of interfering with my work—like, people were beginning to pull my coat about my attitude toward sisters.

When we began talking about things at the male caucus it was the first time I had ever talked to a big group of people about my personal life. I began to really examine my own attitude toward sisters and understand that, as a male chauvinist, as soon as a sister would walk in the door, the first thing I would think about was, you know, can I rap to this sister? Is she pretty? Is she pretty enough for me? I wouldn't think, as I should have, is this sister gonna be a good revolutionary? The first thing I began to be more conscious of was the way I was thinking and the attitude that type of thinking was coming from.

I've been in the Party now for, like, three-quarters of the year, so I'm sort of on the way to dealing with the male chauvinist shit. But a lot of the other brothers are just beginning.

From this point on we're gonna be having a joint caucus of brothers and sisters. We are all gonna sit down together and begin to talk about how to relate to each other inside the struggle, so that we don't have to stop our revolution to deal with this problem. See, one of the things that we understand is that because we're oppressed people we have a lot of neuroses to deal with. It's no use making revolution if after we make it and take state power we're as fucked-up as the people we replace. We not only have to change the political structure of this country, we've also got to change everything else. Revolution means change from the top to the bottom, and that includes the way we deal with each other as human beings.

"We're trying to make a society where opportunity is the rule for everybody."

PABLO "YORUBA" GUZMAN

Really what the Young Lords Party is about is a very fast process of growing up. Let's say you're in the Young Lords Party six months—those six months are like five years spent in a normal life. A day in the Party is like a week. Like, I came into the Party when I was eighteen and I'm twenty now—and there are times I've gone through so much, I feel like I've gone through two other people's lifetimes. That's what we're all about. We're not so much about political takeovers and coups and military maneuvers, but about a very fast process of maturing that goes on inside the Party, of having to deal with problems that are on a very high level—so that when you're thirteen you learn how to deal with people in their twenties and thirties.

Suppose you have to work on the breakfast program, right. You have to deal with how you handle twenty kids at the same time—little kids can be a pain in the ass, you know, at nine o'clock in the morning. You gotta keep 'em happy, keep 'em swingin', get 'em to eat and then get 'em out, and do it so that you don't become like a nursery school, you don't really want to be their teacher. You know, when a Lord goes through this kind of thing, it's the best training there is for dealing with life and trying to change it.

Being a Lord is not about *accepting* life—that's what we've been taught, to accept life, to accept shit the way it is, because we ain't got the power to change nothing. Being a Lord is about saying, "Now that I know where things are at, I'm equipped to go out there and change the motherfucker. Go out there and meet it head on, and take it, see, and defeat it." The main thing that motivates you is that you know you can win, you know you can do it.

Media people often ask me, "Well, where do you plan to go? Where is the revolution gonna go?" And it's hard to explain to them that I know where it's gonna go just by looking at the Young Lords Party. I look at the Party, and I see the drug addicts who stop taking drugs and start dealing with trying to build something, deal with discipline, deal with taking their push-ups. The most individualistic people in the world are the people who have to come up off the street. 'Cause on the street, you're taught to look out for number one, and number one is you and fuck everybody else. When those people start looking out for other people, they start saying, "We have to think about the collective," you know where the revolution is going, you know what socialism's about. You know that somehow the Young Lords Party has created—I don't like to use the word "refuge," because we don't take shelter in it and bury our heads in it, and divorce ourselves from reality—it's created for us a working alternative to what happens under capitalism. And that alternative is not the kind that says, "Well here it is, we've got it, let's live in utopia." No, that alternative lives in the middle of a whole lot of shit, and because it's in the middle of a whole lot of shit and we can still smell it, that alternative makes us want to go out there and make everything smell sweet.

We're talking about creating individuals who are *selfless*—or as close to being selfless as possible, since, you know, we're not into sainthood. To do that we have to turn around the order of things, the capitalist order of things, and create a socialist order. So that we say, "First there is my nation, and last there is myself." And people don't understand this. We're brought up to be individuals who look out solely for themselves. In school we're taught that the first law of nature is self-preservation. We say that's bullshit—the first law of nature is preservation of the group, because as long as the group exists, as long as your nation exists, then you exist.

See, people often run the line down to me, "Well, you know, you've got some brains—you could make it." Yeah, I could make it, I could—me, myself, Pablo "Yorúba" Guzmán. I could be into law, I could be into public relations, a number of fields I could have gone into, right. But that same thing does not hold true for my people. I become the exception rather than the rule, and we're trying to make a society where opportunity is the rule for everybody.

We say we want our nation to be first, right. As long as our nation exists, we exist. We want the Puerto Rican to be number one because the best thing in the world to us is a Puerto Rican. However, in addition we say that there's room for everybody else to be number ones. We say the best thing in the world is an Asian, the best thing in the world is a Vietnamese, the best thing in the world is a Cuban, the best thing in the world is Jewish people, Polish people, Irish people, Italian people. We say *everybody*, right. And we're struggling to put everybody up there.

What the Party is leading to is true socialism—an entire re-evaluation of the whole traditional system of how we relate to people—ethics, mores, codes. It can be hard.... Let's say you're walking up a flight of stairs to get to the Lords' apartment and you have something to eat. Do you finish everything you have before you get up there—kill it quick before you've got to share it with everybody else—or are you willing to share what you got? If you examine the thing itself, it's a little thing, but coming from the motivation, that's what's happening inside the Party.

I believe that when you start digging at what motivates people, what makes them move, what makes them tick, then you can get down to the basis of economic and political systems and the rest of it. Because simultaneously with your political and economic, cultural and religious, and whatever revolution, you also have to make a revolution within the minds of people. If you can't do that, then chalk it up, 'cause you gonna have some socialists who got capitalist minds—and then you gotta start your shit all over again. And that's how come Mao had a cultural revolution long after he took power. That's how come in Cuba they've had some problems. And because we learned from the past, right, we don't have to go through that same thing. We're trying to become more efficient by having that revolution now, rather than going through it after we take the power of the state. That's the beauty of the American revolution that's going on now, that's the beauty of the Young Lords Party.

When I first got involved in a street action and I saw this old lady throw a bottle at a pig, I mean, that did it—that cemented my commitment to the revolution right there. I said if this old woman can throw that bottle, then look out, they've had it. I had this flash, you know, that it's inevitable we're going to win. See, before that, when I used to read Mao, I used to say what the fuck's he talking about that it's inevitable we're going to win—he ain't over here, he did his shit forty years ago, easy for him to write that. But I know what he means now. I know when I see it inside the Party. I mean, when I see brothers off the block, hustlers, you know, talking about, "I got to deal with my male chauvinism," when I see that—man, I feel like we can do anything.

THE PARTY

"If our people fight one tribe at a time, all will be killed. They can cut off our fingers one by one, but if we join together we'll make a powerful fist."

LITTLE TURTLE, MASTER GENERAL OF THE MIAMI INDIANS, 1791

"The price of imperialism is lives."

JUAN GONZALES

What is a colony? Essentially, it is a nation controlled in all facets of its life by another nation or group of people. It is a nation that does not have the same right to govern itself that a country like the United States or Britain has.

Puerto Rico is probably the oldest colony in the world. For 500 years it has been controlled by one nation or another. It was discovered on Columbus' second trip, in 1493 (this was before the European countries began to build their colonial empires), and for about four hundred years it was controlled and dominated by Spain. Spain did not use Puerto Rico primarily as a colony to extract wealth from, but mostly as a commercial way station or a sort of military base, where the riches extracted from Mexico and the rest of Latin America could be shipped to Europe.

The Taino Indians were the original nation that inhabited Puerto Rico, but as the Spaniards tried to enslave them they began to die off. So finally, the Spaniards were forced to import Africans, mostly from the Yoruba nation on the west coast of Africa. By the thousands, they were kidnapped and brought to Puerto Rico, where *they* were enslaved. That continued pretty much throughout the rest of Puerto Rican history.

The majority of the people on the island, according to the earliest census-takers, were Black, then the second largest population were Indians. The whites were always the smallest part of the population. The percentage of whites diminished very quickly, since the Spanish brand of racism, unlike the American/Anglo-Saxon brand, allowed a lot of intermarriage. So the pirates and the vagabonds from Europe raped the Black and Indian women and over the years we had a situation where, little by little, the Puerto Rican developed as a cultural personality.

This personality wasn't really expressed until 1868, when we had the first major uprising on the island against the Spaniards. This uprising—our first rebellion—occurred in the town of Lares, and it was led by a Black Puerto Rican, Ramon Emeterio Betances. Even though it failed and was crushed by the Spaniards, at least one concession was granted because of it—slavery was abolished in 1873.

In 1897 we were granted autonomy from Spain because by this time Spain was fighting two wars—against Puerto Rican revolutionaries and against Manuel de Cespedes in the Cuban independence struggle. Autonomy is about as close as you can get to independence without being independent.

But the United States had been looking at these islands for quite a while—ever since the establishment of the Monroe Doctrine, and the concept of the superiority of the American race, and things like Manifest Destiny and all that other bullshit that was coming out of the American leaders at that time. In fact, we discovered a letter from President McKinley to General Miles, military commander of the invading force, saying that the U.S. wanted Puerto Rico as a safety valve—a place to which American Blacks could be exported in case they got too troublesome back home. That was the same reason they ripped off Hawaii and the Philippines—two more safety valves.

By 1897 American investments had already begun to move into Puerto Rico and Cuba, so the United States concocted its Spanish-American War. It's amazing how they pull this stuff off, the Americans.

They've done this a number of times. They create some sort of event which they then use to convince the people that a war has to be fought. One recent example was the Gulf of Tonkin incident, which was used as an excuse to escalate the Vietnamese war. Throughout American history, excuses have been used—and when they weren't available, they were created—to enable the United States to move against countries it wanted to move against. The mysterious bombing of the *Maine* in Havana harbor allowed the United States to start the Spanish-American War.

So here was Spain caught in three battles—the battle with the United States, and the fight against revolutionaries inside Cuba and Puerto Rico. Under that pressure Spain lost, and a peace treaty was made in Paris that included everybody but the countries that were involved. And Puerto Rico and Cuba were *given* to the United States. That started our second period of colonialism, this time under the *gringo*. Until 1900 we were ruled by the American military.

Up to then the island had been more or less self-sufficient. It was a small, agricultural colony that pretty much got along. Tobacco was the main product. Most of the people who worked in the center of the island were small tobacco farmers (they were *jibaro*—a mixture of Indian and Spanish).

But the Americans didn't need tobacco from Puerto Rico because they were getting it from the South. What they needed was sugar. In 1900 the United States passed the Foraker Act, which established civilian government. Then they immediately began making plans to change the whole agricultural make-up of the island. They revamped the whole economy—divided the land into large sugar-cane plantations—destroying the whole social fabric of Puerto Rico. A small tobacco grower, you know, has an entirely different mentality than an agricultural field worker, employed by a plantation, which is like a large corporate structure.

In 1917 the United States *imposed* citizenship on Puerto Rico. They didn't ask the Puerto Rican people whether they *wanted* to be Americans (in fact, the only elected Congress of Puerto Rico protested against the imposition of citizenship). What they did instead was say, "Anybody who *doesn't* want to be an American citizen must go to the nearest courthouse or the nearest municipal government, and declare himself opposed to American citizenship." So what they had, in effect, was a list of all the "subversives"—in their words—all the anti-Americans who were really just all the Puerto Ricans, in the country. And then these people were subjected to repression and harassment. Even so, thousands of Puerto Ricans refused to accept American citizenship.

From 1917 on was probably the darkest period in the history of our country. Puerto Rico was just a hellhole. The economy fell apart. Poverty and hunger, for the first time, became part of our daily lives.

Then they started to send in American teachers—large numbers were recruited from places like Columbia and Harvard to come and change the language of the island. The language was officially made English, right, and English was taught in the public schools. Now, I don't know how the hell you can expect that people are going to overnight change their language. I don't know. But it wasn't until about 1932–1933, during the Roosevelt administration, that they realized that people weren't learning English. So they changed the official language back to Spanish, rewrote all the textbooks in Spanish, right, and made English the secondary required language.

In addition to trying to destroy our language, they tried to rewrite our history. In most history books Puerto Rican history stops in 1898. Nobody talks about what the Americans did afterward—none of the books deal with that. Everybody talks about how the standard of living of the island was raised, how this happened and that happened, when all that happened was that sugar cane became the main product of the island and certain American companies developed—like the South Puerto Rico Sugar Company, which is owned by Rockefeller and the Aguirre Sugar Company—and those were the people who were making all the money.

In the 1930s things got even worse. All of a sudden the great system collapsed, and all over the world there was a depression. Of course, the ones who felt it the most were the fringe areas of the world, the colonies, where unemployment was fantastically severe. It was in that period that Albizu Campos built the Nationalist Party in Puerto Rico. For the first time since 1868, there was a revolutionary movement that proclaimed that Puerto Ricans were going to be independent.

In 1920 the Nationalists participated in the colonial elections, which were obviously all American-controlled, and were defeated. After that they were through with elections. They said, "From now on, the only way that we are going to fight for liberation is like the Americans fought for theirs." Anybody who is slick gets their liberation by fighting for it. And so, led by Albizu, they began the Second War of Independence for Puerto Rico. Essentially, the Nationalist Party's tactics took the form of armed struggle. They would get attacked by the police, they would fight back, and then they would either kill some policemen or be killed.

That went on into the forties, ending up in 1950 with the Revolution of Jayuya, another revolt led by the Nationalist Party. Again, a revolution in Puerto Rico was crushed. A lot of the facts about this one are not generally known. It's not generally known, for instance, that the Americans brought in planes to bomb Jayuya, or that over 2,000 Nationalists were arrested after that revolt was put down, and that over thirty or forty leaders of the Nationalist Party were sentenced to up to 480 years apiece for their participation. Most of them were put in American jails. Albizu Campos himself spent twenty-five years of his life in American jails. He was only released in 1965, near death, and he died a few months later. Over 100,000 people attended his funeral. It was the largest single demonstration in the history of Puerto Rico—for a man whom the Americans called a madman, he had a lot of "mad" supporters.

There were failings in the Party—they never really organized masses of poor people, and as such, they were never able to mobilize into an organized revolutionary force—although there was a lot of nationalist sentiment. To this day the Nationalists are feared and respected by the people because they stood up for their principles and for their ideals.

Back in the thirties and forties the United States saw the nationalist movement building up very quickly, so what they did was bring the New Deal to Puerto Rico. They got this Rexford Tugwell, who was a leftist Social Democrat, to be Governor of Puerto Rico. He was a liberal, right, and he made all these programs to change the island. In effect, what he was trying to do was just keep capitalism running. And Rexford Tugwell got himself a little pupil that he dug up somewhere in the village, a guy named Muñoz Marin who had been the son of a sellout Puerto Rican way back in the early 1900s. The United States always does this; whenever it has a country that's giving it trouble, it goes somewhere in the village and gets somebody who'll take over—like Diem and Syngman Rhee. In 1948, they made Marin the first elected governor.

Now, Marin was shrewd. He organized something called the Popular Party, and the Popular Party organized the people under the slogan: "Bread, Land, and Liberty—Independence." He started out with this slogan, but once he got into power, his method of getting bread and land was through the liberal social programs of Roosevelt and Tugwell. Of course, independence was forgotten.

In 1952 Marin was elected again, this time as the first governor of something that was called the Free Associated State of Puerto Rico, and a constitution was written. Now, the Free Associated State of Puerto Rico is sort of like the Holy Roman Empire. The Holy Roman Empire was neither holy, Roman, nor an empire—and in the same way the Free Associated State was neither free, associated, nor a state. It was a colony, with a different name put on it.

Now, most people are upset by the word "imperialism"—they think it's the rhetoric of the left. But imperialism is very real to us. I'll give you a simple example of imperialism. Our people eat *bacalao* a lot, *bacalao* is codfish, right? Now, Puerto Rico is in one of the best fishing areas of the world, but where does the codfish that we eat all the time as part of our diet come from? It comes from New England, because Puerto Rico is not allowed to have its own fishing fleet, or to fish in its own waters. So we have to buy all our fish from American fishermen. We're not allowed to import food from any country except the United States. We're not allowed to have our own army, we're not allowed to have our own postal system, or our own court system. None of the laws governing trade, economics, etc., are made by Puerto Ricans, but by the United States Congress.

Another example is Puerto Rican rum. Rum is one of the only imports to the U.S. that's taxed. That's like New York taxing Florida oranges. So that Puerto Rican rum, the one product that could be making a lot of money for our country, becomes very expensive and can't compete with the whiskey products of the United States or other countries.

The United States has tried to convince both our people *and* Americans that Puerto Rico could not exist as an independent country. We have a population of two and a half million, right? But I don't know how many countries in the world have even smaller populations — little countries like Switzerland, which has no natural resources, countries like Liberia and Lebanon, somehow manage to exist. And yet Puerto Rico, with two and a half million people and with much more fertile land, somehow can't be independent.

It was discovered in 1950, you know, that there were copper deposits worth something like two and a half billion dollars in the center of the island. Well, for years, Muñoz Marin kept it quiet. He was very slick, he knew he couldn't get away with selling those copper deposits to American companies, although he wanted to. But, now we have this new governor—Luis Ferre. Now Ferre is not only the Governor of Puerto Rico, he is also the richest man in Puerto Rico—he made his money out of cement. He's a stone capitalist—he doesn't give a damn about what the people think or what they need. So, he quickly sold the rights to the copper for very little money to the two big American copper companies. Now they're going to exploit the copper resources, but they're going to use open field mining, strip mining—which is just ripping the earth open and taking the copper out—so that large amounts of land will be polluted and destroyed, instead of using more expensive methods that would drill deep into the land. But after all, it's only Puerto Rican land, and they don't have to be concerned about it. And historically that's been the case, throughout our island, that our economy has been distorted to fit the needs of the United States, not the needs of our own people.

You know, American business has tax exemption in Puerto Rico. If you are a corporation, and you don't want to pay taxes in the United States, you can start your company in Puerto Rico, and for seventeen years be tax exempt. Then, at the end of seventeen years, you can close your business and open up under a different name—another seventeen years to go on your tax exemption.

Eighty-five per cent of all the business in Puerto Rico is controlled by the United States. Now what does that mean? Well, let's say you live in New York, and you walk up and down Fifth Avenue and all the businesses you see there are owned by Germans. The soda you drink is made by a German company, the cars that you ride in are all Volkswagens—and you knew that all the money that you paid for that stuff didn't stay in your country, it went to Germany, and Germans got rich off of it. Now that's imperialism.... Americans don't understand that because they aren't controlled by anybody. America controls everything, and that's why it's so hard for Americans to understand what imperialism means—'cause they suffer less from it than any other country.

You know, you can always tell when a country is dominated by American imperialism—if it's famous for its whores. Saigon is now a famous whorehouse for Vietnam, just like Havana used to be the famous whorehouse of the Caribbean, where all the American businessmen and all the labor groups would hold their conventions. After the Cuban Revolution, everything switched to San Juan. So now Eastern Airlines and all the others have their advertisements about how San Juan is the paradise that every businessman dreams of. And the tourist business has grown, and the dope business has grown on the island.

You have no idea what it is for a people never to have known what it is to run their own lives—the terrible spiritual effects. Like, oppressed people don't relate to any kind of organization. Because the only types of organization that they have known are school and the factories. And they see both of them as instruments of their oppression. So when you try to organize something, or plan for something, or when you bring out a book, they automatically think of the oppressor, who has always planned their lives out for them. Our people don't *believe* that they could control and plan their future—they live for the moment, for this day.

After a while that sort of absolute control by a system or society works on the mentality of people. That aggression, that hatred they feel because they can't control their own lives, is turned against their own—so we kill each other, we knife each other, we steal from each other, right? We form gangs to fight each other, because of that absolute contradiction between a human being who thinks and feels and wants to run his or her own life, and a society that's structured not to allow that human being to do that. It's that contradiction where a woman can work in a factory and in one day make fifteen dresses, and then go home and not be able to clothe her own child. It's a contradiction that's so *great*—that contradiction between the fact that a society can only run if everyone is involved and working to make it run, but that only a few people benefit from the wealth that everybody produces. And that's essentially the type of society we're living in now.

When Frantz Fanon talks about the colonial mentality of oppressed people, it's very true, as he says, that what happens in a revolution is that each individual realizes that he alone can't control his own life, but that if he joins with other people, it is possible that they can say: "This is the type of life that we will have, because this is the type of life that we want." That sort of contradiction, then, between what one wants and what one gets, is eliminated. And that kind of knowledge—that you have that power, or that you *can* have that power, is the most important thing that a revolution accomplishes.

Essentially, what revolution means then is that a group of people, or a nation, or a class of people, make their own history—they decide their own lives. They don't have their history written by somebody else for them—they make their own. They seize their own destiny and they shape it. This is a hard thing to get to, because people don't believe that they have power. They don't believe that they can make the society run, and that without them it couldn't run in the first place. And building that sort of consciousness is the most important thing in a revolution.

"Free Puerto Rico Now" has become a slogan for the Young Lords Party. What it means to us is that Puerto Rico must be liberated immediately. The power to determine the destiny of Puerto Rico has to be put in the hands of the Puerto Rican people. We don't say "independence" because there are lots of countries that are independent in a legal sense, but are still controlled. Algeria, for instance, had a long revolutionary struggle, and in Independence Plaza in Algeria there's a big monument to the independence struggle—and then all around the plaza there are First National City Banks and Chase Manhattan Banks and all the other American banks. So they have independence, but they don't have freedom. And the same thing with all the former Spanish colonies—they got free of Spain, only to be controlled by the United States. We want liberation for our people. We don't want Puerto Rican businessmen to replace the American businessmen—we don't want businessmen. We want economic organizations, social organizations, political organizations, cultural organizations—controlled by the people. That's what socialism means to us.

The price of imperialism is lives. That's what imperialism is all about—money over lives. Fidel said that at the Second Declaration of Havana in 1962: "*The summary of this nightmare which torments America from one end to the other is that on this continent of almost two hundred million human beings, two thirds—Indians, mestizos, and Blacks—are discriminated against. On this continent of semi-colonies, about four persons per minute die of hunger, curable illness, or premature old age; 5,500 per day, 2 million per year, 10 million each five years. These deaths could easily be avoided, but nevertheless they take place. Two thirds of the Latin American population live briefly, and live under constant threat of death. A holocaust of lives, which in fifteen years has cost twice the number of deaths as World War I—it still rages. Meanwhile, from Latin America, a continuous torrent of money flows to the United States; some 4 thousand dollars a minute, 5 million a day, 2 billion a year, 10 billion every five years. For each thousand dollars which leave us, there remains one corpse, that is the price of what is called imperialism—a thousand dollars per death, four deaths every minute.*"

"The chains that have been taken off slaves' bodies are put back on their minds."
DAVID PEREZ

Cultural genocide is the destruction of a people's awareness of themselves—as a nation, as a people. It also means the destruction of those physical things that represent a people's culture, such as their food, their language, their music, their poetry, their history. It's very necessary for an oppressor to destroy a people's ability to communicate among themselves. In this country, for instance, one of the first things that was done with African slaves was to separate people from the same tribe so that they couldn't get together and build a resistance movement to the slave traders. Language is one of the ways that people are able to communicate and to build a way of fighting back against the enemy—to maintain those ties of identity and therefore strengthen themselves to fight. Destroying the language, as the Americans did with the African slaves and with our people in Puerto Rico, is the initial step to breaking down the people's connection with one another.

To support its economic exploitation of Puerto Rico, the United States instituted a new educational system whose purpose was to Americanize us. Specifically, that means that the school's principal job is to exalt the cultural values of the United States. As soon as we begin using books that are printed in English, that are printed in the United States, that means that the American way of life is being pushed—the American way of life with all its bad points, with its commercialism, its dehumanization of human beings.

At the same time that the cultural

values of America are exalted, the cultural values of Puerto Rico are downgraded. People begin to feel ashamed of speaking Spanish. Language becomes a reward and punishment system. If you speak English and adapt to the cultural values of America, you're rewarded; if you speak Spanish and stick to the old traditional ways, you're punished. In the school system here, if you don't quickly begin to speak English and shed your Puerto Rican values, you're put back a grade—so you may be in the sixth grade in Puerto Rico but when you come here, you go back to the fourth or fifth. You're treated as if you're retarded, as if you're backward—and your own cultural values therefore are shown to be of less value than the cultural values of this country and the language of this country.

What all this does is to create severe problems for our people. First, it creates a colonized mentality—that means that the people have a strong feeling of inferiority, they have a strong feeling of not being as worthy as the Americans because the structure tells them that to become American is always a goal they have to attain. Now it's not easy to shed years of one culture for another—so we have people struggling with themselves to throw off the old way, instead of questioning whether it's correct to throw off the old way or not. Because it's a matter of their survival in this country. The people get a sense of frustration with themselves, because they can't change themselves as fast as is necessary.

In the Young Lords Party, we talk a lot about the colonized mentality when we're frightened of taking on responsibilities. We've been conditioned to feel that we can't lead other people. The school system doesn't develop an individual's initiative and creativity. It develops your ability to follow, it develops a worker-employer mentality, which is suited to this country—the teacher is the employer and the students are the workers.

Puerto Ricans here and in Puerto Rico are taught three things: Puerto Rico is small and the United States is big; Puerto Rico is poor and the United States is rich; Puerto Rico is weak and the United States is strong. Sort of a national inferiority complex. These things are constantly put in our heads and in this way people are conditioned to believe that independence is impossible because our country could never survive without the help of big brother United States.

In this country education is used as an extension of the American economic system. We understand as we go through school that we are being prepared for one of the various positions there are for people in America. Now, the ruling class of this country doesn't go to public school—so we can eliminate that consideration. Then there are the lackeys of the ruling class who run the businesses for them, the managers and corporation heads. The next class is a more functional class of people who are doing the actual work of running the corporations of America: they may be typists, file clerks and secretaries, or assistant managers who are just the lackeys of the managers. And last of all, on the level below that, we have people who are what used to be called blue-collar workers—who work with their hands and they don't wear a suit and tie if they're a brother, or they don't wear a dress if they're a sister, and they wash dishes, and they push pushcarts with clothing, and they do more or less the slop jobs, the unskilled jobs in society. In the schools, right from the beginning, Third World people are programmed for the lowest-level jobs. Because right from the beginning, IQ tests are given to determine where a kid is going. And the IQ tests are based on a white Anglo-Saxon norm that's established in this country, which doesn't apply to the cultural background of Third World people—so you're not gonna do good on the IQ test. Those tests have to some extent been discarded, but they've also been disguised in other ways. Now you get a reading test. Kids read shit about houses with trees and families with two cars and dogs and everybody going to the swimming pool

—and that's bullshit, man. It doesn't relate to them and therefore they don't get into it, and they don't do well on the tests. So if you don't do well on those tests, right from the beginning it shows on your record that you're a slow student.

As you move up in the school system, the guidance counselor looks at your record and says, "Well, you did so poorly in reading last year—why don't you go into a general program in high school. You won't have to do too much reading there." When you go into high school, you can either go into an academic program, a commercial program, or a general program—this is called the tracking system. Actually you have very little choice because you're simply put into a specific program, and unless you bring a lot of parental and outside pressure on the school system, you stay in that one, whether you like it or not. And our people end up in the last level, the general program—people who are being prepared to do shitwork for America. That means they're not being prepared to do anything, basically. The highest level of preparation in the general program is to be a cashier; or if you're a brother, they train you in mechanics, but you find out very soon that everything you've been trained on is outdated already, so you can't get a job. Also, if you're a brother, to get out of school with a general diploma means that you're going to Viet Nam. Students with academic diplomas get college deferments.

When we talk about cultural genocide, we have to see what it does to an individual that goes through this school system. When you raise your hand in class and the teacher, instead of listening to what you have to say, begins to correct your accent and insists that you're gonna talk perfect English, whatever thoughts are coming out are just gonna be ignored until this superficial thing is corrected according to what the system has set as a standard. We're faced with an education that isn't relevant to us. We're faced with reading books that have nothing to do with what we know to be our people's experience and what we know to be our personal experience. We're faced with out-and-out racism, not only the racism of textbooks, which ignore the contributions of the Third World to the development of civilization—but also the out-and-out racism of the teachers who instruct us, who have already been told that they have a class of slow learners and so therefore they feel that they don't have to work too hard, because we can't learn too much anyway. We have the racism that this society generates in white people that tells them that people of color are inferior, and therefore you can treat them like inferiors. We still have the vestiges of slavery, the slave trade, left over. The chains that have been taken off the slaves' bodies are put back on their minds.

Besides boredom, besides racism, we have the fact that the educational system is a mediocre system. It doesn't educate people, it doesn't provide a forum for opposing points of view, it doesn't develop the creativity of the individual. It tends to smother people, it tends to value conformity instead of originality. It tells you, "Don't be different—be like everyone else," it tells you to sit still, raise your hand if you want to go to the bathroom, you have no rights as an individual once you're in the system. Instead of developing the potential of human beings, we're putting young people into a jail—locking up their heads, locking everyone into a dead-end street.

We don't want our children to go through this school system—this is the school system that creates My Lai massacres, the school system that dehumanizes us to the point where we can watch someone killed in the street and not feel pain and not feel the need to intervene, that teaches us it's dog-eat-dog in America—that's how the pioneers lived so that's how we should live. We see a need to create our own school system, a school system based on developing each person to the fullest potential that they have, and bringing out the beauty that we know is inside our people, that's being buried in the American school system.

We have to understand that cultural genocide is being used to destroy the strength of people so that they can be used to perform certain low-level tasks in industrial society. At the point when that society no longer needs these people to do those tasks, the logical progression from cultural genocide will be physical genocide—the systematic elimination of Third World people who are no longer needed by a highly technological society. Many of our people see that our culture has been destroyed by this country, and they react in an extreme way, and become cultural nationalists—whose sole purpose in life is to revive the culture of the Puerto Rican nation and to keep it alive, to speak only Spanish, to relate only to our music, to dress the way we dressed when we lived on the island. Now, our feeling is that nationalism is important—that we have to be proud of our nation, our history and our culture—but that pride alone is not gonna free us, the ability to play congas is not gonna free us, the ability to speak Spanish fluently is not gonna stop landlords, the ability to run down Puerto Rican history like it was right from the beginning is not gonna stop the exploitation of our people on their jobs and everyplace else. We know that just going back to our culture is not gonna make it in and of itself. We have to use our culture as a revolutionary weapon to make ourselves stronger, to understand who we are, to understand where we came from, and therefore to be able to analyze correctly what we have to do in order to survive in this country.

"It's not medical care our people get, but a test tube kind of thing."

GLORIA GONZALES

Among our people there are many, many who are sick. Our mere living conditions are a health hazard because our housing is so old and decrepit and the landlords are there just to collect the money for rent—not to provide decent apartments for people to live in. Often we have no heat in the winter, so our people suffer from pneumonia, become asthmatic. Our children suffer from lead poisoning because of the cheap paint the landlords put on the walls.

When our people are sick and have to go to the hospital, they have to wait many hours before they see a doctor. Once they see a doctor, he usually doesn't bother to explain what's wrong with them—people take medication, but don't know what it's for, it's never explained whether the pill is for the stomach ache that they went there for originally or for their nerves—because a lot of our people get treated with nerve pills, they get labeled neurotic and their medical, physical condition is never taken care of. They can go on with this kind of neglect for years and years and years.

At Metropolitan Hospital we started organizing to try and change these conditions. We got together a collective of workers who were sick and tired of seeing how people were being treated and who refused to align themselves with the medical team. One of the first things the Party did was to lead a demonstration in the administrator's office to change a plan that they had for building an emergency room. This room would have been totally inadequate because everybody would just have been in the same place, whether they were children or adults, with whatever diseases. After the protest, the plans were changed. Then the organization started working with the East Harlem Health Council. This was a community group who'd been involved in trying to do something about Metropolitan Hospital.

I was working at Gouverneur Hospital, and when we heard about what the Lords had been doing at Metropolitan, we got together and said that the way that health was delivered to the people was going to have to change. They were going to have to have door-to-door programs, like testing for lead poisoning and anemia, because we saw that our people just wouldn't go to a hospital to get a check-up. Upper-middle-class people can go to a doctor once every six months and get a blood test and an X-ray in a very comfortable atmosphere, and if something is detected early enough it can be cured. Because of the way our people are treated, because of the racism in the hospitals, poor people will only go into hospitals when they feel like they're dying. If patients are Puerto Rican and can't speak English, they either have to bring an interpreter with them, or go without understanding anything that's happening, because there are no doctors or nurses who speak Spanish. And the hospital environment is so bad. It's so depressing to just sit in a hospital like Bellevue for hours and hours and hours, because the hospitals are filthy — they're never mopped, they're never cleaned. You look on the floor and there are rats running all over the places and roaches. You feel worse when you come out than when you went in, actually.

We started saying that we wanted all this to change, we wanted people to feel like they could come into a hospital, not only when they were sick and dying, but to get preventive medicine that would make them strong and healthy. So we formed the Health Revolutionary Unity Movement (HRUM) and wrote up a ten-point health program, modeled after the Black Panther Party Ten-Point Program —but more geared toward health needs. We want community-worker control of health institutions, we want lead poisoning and anemia testing, we want day care centers in all the hospitals, so that both workers and patients can leave their children in a safe place.

One of the first jobs was to unite the patients and the workers to be able to take control, because only people who are going through these problems can know what is needed. At this point the hospitals are run by businessmen. Lincoln Hospital, for example, is run by the Albert Einstein Medical College. The Medical College gets a good sum of money from the city to run Lincoln, and Lincoln provides the students with the materials—poor people guinea pigs. A patient might go in for, let's say, a stomach ailment. While that stomach ailment is being treated, his appendix will be removed, so that the student surgeon can learn how to remove an appendix. It gets more serious when they start digging into the gall bladder and the liver, just to test, and just to train their medical students. It is also very degrading. For example, when I had my first baby at Bellevue Hospital, I was going through labor pains, a very hard thing to go through, and in front of me were these twenty young people, standing there and looking at me through this glass. I was very embarrassed because there I was having a baby, and I thought I'd be there with only a doctor, maybe a nurse, and to my surprise there were twenty people just staring. Later I found out I was supposed to be very grateful because I was being taken care of not just by a doctor and nurse, but by twenty medical students. I was never asked for permission. Who's gonna ask a spic about whether these students should be there?—I had to be grateful. In actuality it's not medical care our people get but a test tube kind of thing.

The hospitals also become testing grounds for the hospital equipment companies. You'd be surprised how much money runs into that industry. If you want to invest in the stock market, it is the second most profitable industry after defense. Let's say a new type of x-ray machine comes out. Well, before they'll test it in a suburban hospital, they'll test it in Bellevue — they'll test it there because they have to test it with humans, so they'll test it on Third World people. For example, there's one injection that came out about ten years ago that was supposed to be a birth control device for the sisters—the first place that it was tested was Harlem Hospital. The first place birth control pills were tested was in Puerto Rico. These same pills have been shown to be very dangerous in their side effects—cancer, phlebitis, heart disease.

The hospital industry, like everything in this capitalist society, is interested only in making itself wealthy—it has no interest whatever in the side effects people suffer as a result of the way that they're used as guinea pigs. The interest is, as always, to get more and more profits. Ten thousand Puerto Ricans can die tomorrow, as long as the industry continues to make that money.

In the Young Lords Party we believe in complete change, no patch work can be done. The Lords have adopted the ten-point health program of HRUM and have been working with HRUM very closely. In all the hospitals in the city, workers have started talking about health and getting involved in changing the health system, because they have been witnessing the type of treatment our people get in the hospitals. The Lords have also become involved with preventive health programs. We heard about a lead poisoning kit that the city had gotten hold of, but wasn't using. They just had them in refrigerators up at City Hall someplace. So HRUM and the Young Lords went to Commissioner McLoughlin's office and we said that we wanted to put those kits to use. After many hours of discussion, they gave us one hundred kits to start working with.

When we went back into *El Barrio*, and started going door to door, we found that many children were suffering from lead poisoning. Now, lead poisoning is a very dangerous disease. Those children who don't die from it can get mental retardation—for the rest of that child's life he can be just a vegetable, a human being that's always going to have to be dependent on someone else. When we did our testing, we knew that we weren't dealing with our oppression itself, we were just dealing with the symptoms of it. But what we could do at least was show our people that we do not have to wait until some cat graduates from medical school and then comes down to aid us—we can help ourselves. So we collected urine, we tested it, followed it up and we found many children who were poisoned. Then we made sure that these children were seen in hospitals like Metropolitan, Mt. Sinai, Lincoln. As a result, the city started moving to co-opt the program. Suddenly it declared lead poisoning the number one health problem in the city. It had been the number one problem in the city for years and years, because the houses have always had the same lead paint on the walls.

We also started testing for TB—another "disease of oppression." The city has this little patchwork program, you know, to try to prove to somebody that they're doing something—in actuality it's just killing time. The TB rate among Puerto Ricans and Black people is very, very high. Most of the time when the test is given it's positive, because even if you don't have the disease itself, the germ is surely there because we live in such crowded conditions and TB is so contagious.

We started going door to door and doing the tine test, which is a very simple thing—the myth that only doctors could do it was done away with—and found again that a lot of our people were suffering from TB. Again the hospitals had to move because a lot of people just started going in and demanding that those services be given. Finally we ripped off a TB truck. We knew the city had this truck that was used in *El Barrio* only two hours a day. We wanted to use it around the clock to serve our people. They said no, we couldn't have it, that it didn't belong to them, that they had rented it. The thing was, our people couldn't wait, 'cause they were dying from TB. We took the truck and we started testing our people, and in one day we tested 1,000.

Then we moved into Lincoln Hospital. Lincoln Hospital has an amazing history. Back in 1969 the Mental Health Center of Lincoln Hospital was taken over by the Black and Puerto Rican workers, with the demand that the hospital serve the people. The Panther 21 were involved in that struggle there and it was a long one—a lot of people who were involved were arrested, some workers were fired—but nevertheless it planted the seed for the health movement in New York City.

In 1970, the Young Lords went back to Lincoln. We started to organize again, 'cause Lincoln Hospital is about the worst of the city hospitals. It was condemned twenty years ago because of its total inadequacy— and it's still there. And in that twenty years Metropolitan Hospital was built, Beth Israel's Linsky Pavilion on 17th Street was built, and a new wing was added to St. Vincent's. Lincoln Hospital used to be a rest home for slaves, for Black slaves, where they were treated after they were very old. And that's what it remains—a home for slave Third World people. There, with HRUM again, we set up a complaint table to receive complaints from patients and from workers. We started receiving all these complaints, and we saw the administration was not doing a damn thing about them.

People would come in with heart attacks, cuts, shock, whatever it was, and they'd die sometimes waiting in the emergency room. We decided it was time to move on Lincoln Hospital. About a hundred people went to Lincoln and we took it over. We had gotten the support of the workers and the patients at Lincoln. At times we'd even have to stop some patients from just grabbing some doctor's throat, 'cause the patients had just had it with this hospital. While there we wanted to set up the preventive programs, a day care program, do anemia testing, TB testing, lead poisoning screening—all those programs that are not being done in the municipal hospitals. But we were only there for twenty-four hours, a little less, because then the city moved to get us out. When you're dealing with something like the second most profitable industry, people move on you quickly. Before we knew it, the place was surrounded by police, and we had to leave.

But we came back the next day because a sister, Carmen Rodriguez, died. She was killed by the hospital's neglect. While she was having an abortion, she had a heart attack. The hospital thought it was an asthma attack, because she was also asthmatic—so they gave her an injection that made her heart stop. There again was another death, another needless death of a Puerto Rican sister. The abortion clinic had a reputation of giving totally bad care, malpractice, sterilizing sisters all over the place without letting them know, but Carmen's death just did it—it got people very furious, and the hospital workers and patients started moving, setting up watchdog committees.

HRUM—Health Revolutionary Unity Movement—is still doing a lot of the work at Lincoln Hospital, and we support them, and continue to be very involved in health, because it touches on the very essence of living.

We're saying that we want a complete change. We know that we cannot have socialized medicine without having socialism as the new system. And we know that's the change we want to move for, and that we will only get that through armed struggle. But that type of revolution has to be built—while we're getting there, we're saying we will not permit the continued neglect of our people's health. Since we've been involved there have been a number of improvements. The city moving in with lead poisoning and all those shit reform programs is like nothing—the main improvement is that more and more of our people refuse to be treated like guinea pigs, that more and more of our people go into those hospitals and demand that they be treated as human beings. So this has been a change in our people—and this is what's going to make our people strong enough to change the entire system.

"If you're poor, you stay in jail."

JUAN "FI" ORTIZ

We really became involved with the things that were going

on inside the prisons after the murder of Julio Roldan in the Tombs. After Julio was killed, we began to receive letters from inside the Tombs telling us about the things that had happened to Julio and the things that happen to everyone there. The letters detailed the conditions inside the prisons—talking specifically about the terrible substandard food, the lack of clothing, the lack of warm bedding for people in the wintertime. Sanitary conditions are very bad, and there are roaches and rats and bedbugs and lice in the prisons. There are rats running out of the toilet bowls. The guards in the prisons are sadistic and continue to beat people every time they step out of line.

We began hearing about all these things, and we began to understand that what happened to Julio wasn't an isolated incident. Julio just happened to be another Puerto Rican who was busted on a phony charge, and because he was poor and couldn't afford to pay his bail, he had to stay in jail until the court case came up. In that time he was subject to the whims of the guards who were running the place without anyone controlling them. After we saw what happened to Julio, and we heard similar things from a number of people, we began to investigate on our own. The pattern became very clear to us: Poor people are arrested on charges that a rich white person wouldn't even be arrested on. When they're taken into court, because they don't have money they don't have a lawyer with them right away, and they can't put up bail—they're put inside the Tombs or inside the Queens House of Detention, until bail money can be raised. And if they're inside the jail, there's no way of raising bail money. Usually the bails are very high, so that we wouldn't be able to get people out of jail anyway. Carlos Feliciano was originally held on a hundred thousand dollars bail, and there's no way in the world that a Puerto Rican family can raise that. Carlos was accused of being a member of MIRA, and was snatched away from his family and thrown into jail without any way of getting out. So the bail then becomes not bail, but ransom instead.

Once inside the jails, all of your rights are taken away—your right to freedom of speech, your constitutional rights to privacy. All of a sudden you have no rights. You're treated like an animal, you're thrown into a cell which in physical terms is, like, too small for human beings to live in. You're kept in the cell, you're told when you can bathe, you're told when you can urinate.... One of the things we saw after the takeovers in the prisons was that while Third World politicians like Shirley Chisholm and Herman Badillo had supposedly intervened, after they snatched the headlines, the brothers inside the jails were still subject to reprisals, including a forty-day lock-in—for forty days the brothers were locked in their cells and not allowed to bathe or come out, not allowed to do anything but try to find something for their minds to do besides go crazy.

One of the other things we see is that the city and the city officials keep talking about how outraged they are about the conditions inside the prisons. All of a sudden they discover that there are rats and roaches in the food—but this is something that we know has been going on for a long time. Someone sent us an article from 1965 that told about the fifth Puerto Rican so-called suicide in the Tombs, and the city was astonished at *that* point. And this year there have been nine people dead in the Tombs, and the city is still astonished. At one point the line that the politicians and medical people were putting out was that Puerto Ricans tend to commit suicide when they're isolated because of their tight family structure—it just blows their minds, and they kill themselves. We know that's bullshit.

Going back to the specific conditions inside the jails, we see that there is not enough medical care—there is one doctor for many too many men. Inmates aren't allowed easy access to lawyers. There's no watchdog committee, there's no outside group that could go in, a group that has no political ties that could go inside the prison and assure that the basic human rights of the people there are being guaranteed.

After Julio was killed in the Tombs, two other brothers were killed. And right after that another brother was killed, and then two other brothers. So, the whole thing is continuing. We're saying that the prison system is another form of genocide that is being perpetrated on poor people, because if you're poor, you stay in jail—it's very apparent that in the New York City prisons, approximately 90 percent of the prisoners are Black or Puerto Rican. All you have to do is check it out to come to the conclusion that there's one standard of justice going down for one class of people, and another standard of justice going down for our people. And when the city government begins to talk about justice, what they're really talking about is burying people away from the public eye so they can't raise too much of a stink. Right now, the Women's House of Detention is gonna be phased out and all the women are gonna be transferred to Rikers Island, because the Women's House of D is the only prison in New York City that's in a residential area, so that every time there's shit going on inside there, the people in the neighborhood can hear.

Everything that we have seen so far has shown that the city establishment is gonna continue to push the line of genocide in the prisons, they're not gonna clamp down on the sadists that are running the prisons, the politicians are gonna use the prisons to make political points for themselves. At the same time, liberals are gonna cry about how bad it is, but not do anything. And meanwhile, people are still gonna be beaten to death and tortured. With all of this going on, we see clearly that there is no way that we can depend on anyone except ourselves, the people, to begin to change the situation.

When we took the People's Church for the second time—we had two demands. First, we wanted to have a legal defense center set up inside the church to coordinate and document cases of brutality inside and outside the prisons. You see, Third World people are in prison, even on the outside—it's just that the security has been made minimum instead of maximum. The second demand was that an impartial investigation of the prison system be conducted by clergy—because we felt that everyone could relate to clergy going inside the prisons and checking out exactly what was happening, and being allowed to go into the cells, into the laboratories, into the shower stalls. Naturally, the City Board of Corrections didn't want to hear about it, they didn't want anyone to go inside. Obviously they had something to cover up. When we made these demands, we felt our people's lives were at stake, and we wanted to lay our own lives on the line. That is why we took the church with guns.

After a whole lot of dickering with the city administration—at one point they said yes, the clergy could go in, at the next point they said no—it's still in a limbo stage. Some clergy have been allowed in, and selected newspapermen have been allowed in—but it's still not open to the people. Now, pressure is still being increased. We're saying that we have no choice, that by any means necessary, we have to open those prisons up, so that the people of this city and of every city can see what goes on in there and regulate what type of prison treatment is being given.

"Before people called me a spic, they called me a nigger."

PABLO "YORUBA" GUZMAN

People always look for the beginnings of the Party. We started the Young Lords because we just knew something had to be done. If we didn't find or create an organization that was gonna do something then everybody was gonna get shot, see, because it would have gotten to the point that people got so frustrated, they would just jump on the first cop they saw, or just snap, do something crazy.

At first the only model we had to go on in this country was the Black Panther Party. Besides that, we were all a bunch of readers, when we first came in we read Che, Fidel, Fanon, Marx, Lenin, Jefferson, The Bill of Rights, Declaration, Constitution—we read everything. Now there ain't too much time for reading.

We also felt that the potential for revolution had always been there for Puerto Rican people. If we had gone into the thing from a negative point of view, we wouldn't have made it, right. 'Cause a lot of times when things were really rough, it's been that blind faith in the people that keeps us going. The problem has been to tap that potential and to organize it into a disciplined force that's gonna really move on this government. Puerto Ricans had been psyched into believing this myth about being docile. A lot of Puerto Ricans were afraid to move, a lot of Puerto Ricans really thought that the man in blue was the baddest thing going.

Things were different in the gang days. Gang days, we owned the block, and nobody could tell us what to do with the street. Then dope came in and messed everything up, messed our minds up and just broke our backs—dope and anti-poverty. Anti-poverty wiped out a whole generation of what could have been Puerto Rican leaders in New York City.

For example, in '65, the time of the East Harlem riots, we held East Harlem for two days. We had the roof-tops, the streets and the community—no pigs could go through. It was like back in the old days. A lot of people really tripped off that, a lot of the junkies who had been in gangs remembered that shit. To end it they shipped in anti-poverty. They brought it in full-force, and they bought out a lot of the young cats who were leading the rebellions. A lot of dudes who were throwing bricks one day found themselves directors of anti-poverty programs the next, or workers on Mayor Lindsay's Urban Action Core.

So we had no leadership, and we had no people—our people were dying from dope. But we knew that it was *there*, man, 'cause we knew that the fire was there. Those of us who got together to start the thing, we knew we weren't freaks—we didn't feel that we were all that much different from the people. There's a tendency to say "the people" and put the people at arm's length. When we say "people," man, we're talking about ourselves. We're from these blocks, and we're from these schools, products of this whole thing. Some of us came back from college—it was like rediscovering where your parents had come from, rediscovering your childhood.

Our original viewpoint in founding the Party was a New York point of view—that's where the world started and ended. As we later found out, New York is different from most other cities that Puerto Ricans live in. But even in New York, we found that on a grass-roots level a high degree of racism existed between Puerto Ricans and Blacks, and between light-skinned and dark-skinned Puerto Ricans. We had to deal with this racism because it blocked any kind of growth for our people, any understanding of the things Black people had gone through. So rather than watching Rap Brown on TV, rather than learning from that and saying, "Well, that should affect me too," Puerto Ricans said, "Well, yeah, those Blacks got a hard time, you know, but we ain't going through the same thing." This was especially true for the light-skinned Puerto Ricans. Puerto Ricans like myself, who are darker-skinned, who look like Afro-Americans, couldn't do that, 'cause to do that would be to escape into a kind of fantasy. Because before people called me a spic, they called me a nigger. So that was, like, one reason as to why we felt the Young Lords Party should exist.

At first many of us felt why have a Young Lords Party when there existed a Black Panther Party, and wouldn't it be to our advantage to try to consolidate our efforts into getting Third World people into something that already existed? It became apparent to us that that would be impractical, because we wouldn't be recognizing the national question. We felt we each had to organize where we were at—so that Chicanos were gonna have to organize Chicanos, Blacks were gonna have to organize Blacks, Puerto Ricans Puerto Ricans, etc., until we came to that level where we could deal with one umbrella organization that could speak for everybody. But until we eliminate the racism that separates everybody, that will not be possible.

What happened was, in 1969 in the June 7 issue of the Black Panther newspaper there was an article about the Young Lords Organization in Chicago with Cha Cha Jimenez as their chairman. Cha Cha was talking about revolution and socialism and the liberation of Puerto Rico and the right to self-determination and all this stuff that I ain't *never* heard a spic say. I mean, I hadn't never heard no Puerto Rican talk like this—just Black people were talking this way, you know. And I said, "Damn! Check this out." That's what really got us started. That's all it was, man.

We started by trying to pick something that would introduce us to the community. It had to be an action. See—it was summer, it was hot, the people were just, like, sweltering in the heat, nobody was doing nothing. For four years there had been no action. Puerto Ricans hadn't had a good riot since 1965, not even a good fight, a good brawl. Something had to happen that would stun the community. It had to be something with a sense of drama, and a flair, right—but it also had to be something that was real, so the people would know that this wasn't just a bunch of young punks messin' around.

The best thing to hook into was garbage, 'cause garbage is visible and everybody sees it. It's there, you know. So we started out with this thing, "Well, we're gonna clean up the street." This brought the college people and the street people together, 'cause when street people saw college people pushing brooms and getting dirty, that blew their minds. It also got us out of our shyness. When we began, people said, "Well, what are you doing with those berets?" and "What are you doing with those buttons?" and "What does 'All Power to the People' mean?" and things like that. The bolder ones in our group would get out there and yell to people, and everybody else would jump with shock. It was frightening, man, to go on the street and to walk up to some strangers and just start rapping, and give 'em a leaflet—that's frightening shit. And we just forced ourselves to do it, and it got to a thing where nobody wanted to be the one who didn't talk that day, because everybody else would criticize you.

At first some people thought we were part of Lindsay's Urban Action Task Force, and some thought we were just a gang that was trying to be a social club. People couldn't figure us out, man. If we said, "All Power to the People," some of them who read the *Daily News* right away said, "Well, those are the Panthers, and they're Communists." A lot of people thought we were the Panthers, and to that we got a bad reaction, 'cause they were afraid of us. But some people just came out and looked.

This is all we did for the first two Sundays—clean up the street, make it look nice, and put the stuff in garbage cans. We picked Sunday 'cause that was one of the few days when everybody could get together. Some of the members of the Party got pissed. We'd have general meetings and they'd say, "I didn't do this for this *shit*, to clean up no garbage. I came here to off the pigs"; they were comin' from that, right. So, it was hard, man, 'cause we had a bunch of crazy people who just loved fighting, loved getting into shit. And cleaning garbage was not where it was at, so it was a kind of discipline for us, to go through that and learn patience. We didn't realize that what we were doing at that time was building the proper conditions for struggle. I mean, we could have gone underground and started blowing shit up—the thing is, nobody would have understood where it was coming from. Those people who didn't think it was the pig, would think it was some lunatics, and they'd probably be right. So we were just getting ourselves known.

By the second time around, everybody said, "Hey, here they come again! Here come these nuts!" They were calling their friends out—"Look at these fools cleaning off the street!" It was a big thing. They were coming from blocks around. We cleaned 110th Street from Second to Third to Lexington.

By the third Sunday we did something we had learned from what we had read about the Chicago group, and that was to get the people involved through "observation and participation." This time we got the people to clean the shit up with us. We knew somehow we would take them through some kind of a struggle, we didn't know where the hell we were going, but we had to get them involved.

And then came the Sunday of July 27, when we had a lot of people and not enough brooms, and we went to the Sanitation Department.... Now understand this—for the Young Lords Party, this July 27 is probably a historical date. It was a Sunday, right? When four of us went to pick up some brooms, they told us, "Well, you can't have any brooms." And we said, "Why?" and they said, "Because it's Sunday." Now the sanitation cats are just second cousins to the cats in blue, 'cept that they wear green. This fool at 106th Street which was the nearest branch of the department asks us, "What area are you cleaning up?" So we tell him 110th between Second and Third. He says, "That area is serviced by 73rd Street and York." So we had to go about a mile and a half outside where we were, when there was this place four blocks down. And the dude at 73rd and York says, "Well, you can't have any brooms." So, we were pissed, you know. We had gone through all the legal machinations, and now we were pissed. We were looking for a rationale for what was going to come next.

In the car on the way up, the four of us said, "Look, we're going to take the garbage and throw it in the street and that's all there is to it—we're just going to dump it." And that's what we did. We blocked Third Avenue to traffic, right. The people, they went and blocked 111th Street and Third Avenue, blocked 112th, and what was developing was a riot situation. When we saw that happening, we set up a line of garbage cans at the end of 112th Street and we set up a line of Lords and said, "We ain't lettin' nobody through." There was this one cat who said, "Let's go! Let's take it all the way up to the Bronx!" This cat was freaking out, and we were saying, "No, you ain't going noplace—we're stoppin' right here because if we keep going, this is what the pigs want, they just going to pick us off. You ain't got no guns, you know." And this guy kept saying, "No, no, let's go! We got all these people here!" 'Cause people had come out, they came from all over East Harlem for this, they moved a truck into the street, they turned cars over, they were ready to go crazy, The pigs showed up and didn't do nothing, 'cause the pigs believe that Puerto Ricans are docile, you know. We didn't know what kind of reaction we'd get. I mean, all we were doing was throwing some garbage in the street, but we saw that it turned the people loose, it was what they needed, it just set them going. So, we had a quick rally and signed up some recruits, and we said, "Well, we're gonna do this again next Sunday."

When we went back the next Sunday, more people came but it was a different thing. This time it wasn't "Here come those nuts..." but "Here come those people who started the shit last Sunday—let's get together." And people were just, like, waiting, waiting like this on the corner, waiting for us to throw the garbage so they could get involved in the shit.

The next day, Lindsay's office called a meeting. Gottehrer and all those dudes came down to East Harlem to this poverty place. That's when we found out what poverty pimps were really about—they're like outposts in Indian territory, like Fort Apache and Fort Savage, they are the eyes and ears of the mayor of any city. And they're supposed to keep the savages down, right. In this case, we weren't working with the poverty pimps. This was coming from the people, and the poverty pimps are far removed from the people. When they couldn't explain to their masters what was going down in East Harlem, they said, "Well, we have this under control... there are these leaflets that are going around...."

We found that a lot of people thought we were there just to throw garbage in the street. They couldn't understand that we were really there for a Socialist revolution, we were really there to off the government of the United States. They just couldn't deal with that, you know. So we tried setting up political education classes.

I remember a lot of those being really funny. Juan had become Deputy Minister of Education, because he knew the most, he had the clearest mind. Juan was dealing with books, right, but, like, ain't nobody could read the books, and then those who could read, let's say something like Che on *Man and Socialism*, threw the book away and said, "This is boring." Juan could not understand how Che Guevara could be boring. But these cats said the dude was boring. You know, it blew his mind. We had to try to find some way of reaching brothers and sisters who did not dig school, the concept of school or the classroom. And how the hell were we gonna do this? This is a problem we're still dealing with. We tried everything, man, from jokes to getting high together, everything to try to bring the point across.

Then there were other problems like people's commitment. Like, "Well, how come you wasn't here last Sunday?" "Ah, man, you know, my mother told me not to come," or, like, "I was out late Saturday night, and I just wanted to sleep...." I mean, how do you build up discipline? If you were going to divide fifteen people into three groups that could block an avenue at a given time you needed discipline. How could you cool out cats who knew nothing but fighting and say to them, "Listen, this is not when you hit this pig—you do not hit this pig now."

It was very difficult, it was very hard to do....

Well, after the First Offensive, the Garbage Offensive, all Puerto Ricans in New York knew about us. Then it was the People's Church Offensive that put us on a national level in terms of the United States and Puerto Rico. This was through the correct use of the media. We said, "Look, you know, the media is gonna have to be used. Until we can put out the *Daily News* regularly, until we have a TV station and a radio station, chalk it up. Everybody on welfare got a TV set, everybody got a radio, everybody buys the *Daily News* and *El Diario*, so as long as the people already got access to these things, we might as well use them to the best of our advantage."

It was December 28 that we took the church and during the eleven days we were in there we learned a lot of things about the media. The first day there was this quick press conference on the steps of the church. That night I saw myself on TV, and I didn't like myself, you know. I came across as this stereotyped image of what a militant was supposed to be—the Afro and the shades and all this. I was up there talkin' all kinds of shit about this, that, and the other. And it was so routine and blasé, I said, "Damn," you know. I didn't dig myself. So the next day we had the press conference indoors behind a table. It was a relaxed atmosphere, I had my clear glasses on, so people could see my eyes, and as the press was settling down, I said, "How you doing?" introduced myself and got into raps. All the time we were in that church we had something to give the media people every day, that's how we had 'em going, 'cause they had no other news going on at the time. I got to know 'em, I know everybody in New York City in the media, you know, and we developed a kind of rapport, 'cause they understood they could talk to me, and that meant they could talk to the Party. I learned a lot of things out of that. I learned that a reporter could be your best friend, you shouldn't classify a reporter immediately as being a pig, especially now that they are letting a lot of Black and Puerto Rican reporters in. The real enemy is up on top—management levels. I had some good people, man, who wrote some good things for us—the editors came and hacked the shit up, and it was nothing like what they put in, and they proved it to me, 'cause, like, at first I distrusted them also. There's that whole Movement orientation toward distrusting and watching out for the media—a lot of times, man, the Movement people come up there and treat the media people like shit, you know. Then they say, "Well, they put me on the air bad." *Of course* they put you on the air bad, you came across like an idiot.

And TV gets into somebody's house, man. You know, when you're on the screen in somebody's crib, you better not be saying things that come out with a lot of blips on the screen, 'cause you're gonna turn off whole families like that. You should understand what you're doing. The whole thing is to forget the person behind the mike that's asking the questions and imagine that you are talking to 300 of the most assorted kind of Puerto Ricans in the world in one room, in one little room—just do it like that, and as long as you keep the people in your eyes, you've got it.

Too many people tend to get into arguments with reporters. There are some reporters that come in there red-baiting—what you gotta do is use that, and that's where a little humor doesn't hurt. You can turn things around to make them look like jackasses and expose their game to the people right there on TV or radio. The people dig an underdog, that was the great appeal of the Mets at one time, and you have to understand that that's exactly what we are, underdogs. Once the people can start digging us for that, we can tell them, "Dig yourself for that."

When we're standing up there tellin' the pigs off—they dig that, man, whether or not they're of the same political persuasion. When the chips are falling down for us, a lot of times there have been Puerto Rican reactionaries that have defended us—sometimes *before* the Puerto Rican liberals, because at least they realized that one thing they can never say about us is that we are against the nation. We know for a fact that because of the way we've used the media, people dig our audacity, they love us, they feel like we're their grandchildren.

There was a period in our Party from July of '69, when we first started, to about August of 1970 or July of 1970 when we ran really on the personal magnetism of the leadership. But as we started to grow we said, "Look man, there ain't no way you can get a party going on that—you can't build a national liberation movement on the charisma of five or six people." 'Cause that would mean they would always have to be traveling everyplace to keep the whole machinery together. And if you want to keep a thing together, you've got to lay down certain principles that people can pick up on and go to town with—like the Thirteen Point Program and Platform. We have also developed our own political analysis. Right now we are going through a whole big thing of teaching ourselves to think in scientific terms, to study the theories of other revolutionary philosophers — people like Marx, Lenin and Mao.

Actually, we have made *two* analyses because we have to think of two struggles which are interrelated and at the same time not related—like the law of opposites. In other words, we have to make one analysis for the Puerto Rican nation that includes Puerto Rico, the island and the mainland; then another one for the Puerto Ricans who are struggling in the United States.

Within the Puerto Rican nation, there have been many groups who have been struggling for a long time, and our analysis has shown that the correct method of bringing about revolution is to isolate the enemy to as small a number as possible and unite the greatest number of people. Our major goal at this point is defeating the U.S. enemy. Right now we work with anybody who has the same goal. We're trying to work with the greatest number of people. In doing this, one of our most important concepts is that we are humble before our people, and vicious before the enemy. If you read *History Will Absolve Me*, you will see Fidel was *very* good at isolating the enemy into this little clique. See, when people think the enemy is this big mass, it wears away at the will to fight, but when people see that the enemy is just this bunch, right—this *Tame* Bunch—people begin to move.

The first segment of our people that will join, work with, and support the revolution is the *lumpen*, the street people: prostitutes, junkies, two-bit pushers, hustlers, welfare mothers. That's the group that got the Party through its first two years. Marx and Lenin said the working class would be first, right. But we have to examine the Puerto Rican reality. The street people come into the revolution because they've got nothing to lose. And it's a law of revolution that the most oppressed group takes the leadership position.

After the *lumpen* come the lowest classes of workers. For a long time in America, for a lot of reasons, the importance of the worker has been underrated, and when people have said "Power to the people," they have talked about only one segment, and have sort of isolated everybody else. In the phase we are entering now, we are pushing very strongly for a *lumpen*-worker alliance as being the basis for the revolution within the Puerto Rican nation—an alliance of working people and street people, which will build and see this revolution through to the end.

We're going very heavily into worker organizing while we continue the organizing of street people, and we will continue to create situations where the two can come together because this system has created an antagonism between the working people and the street people of the same nation. In the ghettos of the city you have poor working-class people living in projects, and poor street people living in the tenements. And the people in the projects always think that they're better than the people in the tenements, and the people in the tenements can't stand the people in the projects. I mean, there are junkies ripping off the working people when they come home from the subways with their paychecks, and then the workers want to get together to form vigilante groups.... So we have gone out into the community to end this antagonism. This is one of the things that came out of the Second People's Church, this alliance. We know this will bring on a lot of repression from the enemy, because that's been one of their greatest games—like racism, like sexism—to keep the lower classes fighting each other, because they have the greatest revolutionary potential.

The group that comes in between the *lumpen* and the worker is the student. A student is this weird thing—a student actually could be classified as *petit bourgeois*, because the student, see, doesn't have much to do, the student is not working, has nothing to support except himself or herself. The student just has to worry about term papers and grades and scholarships. Once the student gets over that hangup, the student then begins to join the struggle. But the student doesn't have the same kind of gut commitment that the *lumpen* has, or the same kind of overall response coming from prolonged pressure that the worker has.

Many of us in the Party were students. But after checking it out, we saw that we were the children of workers or *lumpen*, so this prevented us from tripping out into a real *petit-bourgeois* vacuum.

Among *petit-bourgeois* people—lower-*petit-bourgeois* people like teachers, certain poverty pimps that ain't gettin' too much bread, middle-class professionals—there's almost a fifty-fifty split in the time of revolutionary struggle. Some will join, and some go against, there's a left-wing *petite bourgeoisie* and a right-wing *petite bourgeoisie.*

When you get to the ruling class, you'll find very few of our people there. And very few of the people who are actually a part of the elite in Puerto Rican society are going to join and support our struggle. Anybody who comes along is considered a bonus.

When we talk about our role in terms of creating the American Revolution, we are not saying we are going to take Puerto Rican people and ship them back to Puerto Rico. We are saying that we have been here in this country for two generations—in some cases, maybe three generations—we've been here for so long, right, that it would be too convenient for us to move back now, and just create a revolution there. We're saying that we want pay back for the years that we have suffered, the years that we have put up with cockroaches and rats. We had to put up with snow, we had to put up with English, we had to put up with racism, with the general abuse of America. And we are gonna hook up with everybody else in this country who's fighting for their liberation—and that's a whole lot of people. We know that the number-one group that's leading that struggle are Black people, 'cause Black people—if we remember the rule that says the most oppressed will take the vanguard role in the struggle—Black people, man, have gone through the most shit. Black people, along with Chicanos and native Americans, are the greatest ally we can have. So we must build the Puerto Rican-Black alliance. That is the basis of the American Revolution for us. Actually, the first group in America that we had a formal coalition with was the Black Panther Party. Also we must further the Latino ties, especially as we move west, and here in New York City, we must work with Dominicans—to further eliminate the racism that has deeply divided Black people and Spanish people.

We are also coming very close together with the struggle of Asians in this country, Asians who have been disinherited from the land that was theirs. Hawaii, for example, was made a state. One of our immediate struggles is to prevent that from happening in Puerto Rico. The Asian struggle is, like, twice as hard, because now they have to free a state, which is different from freeing a colony, right. That's actually going in and busting up part of a union.

Now the time has come for the Young Lords Party to begin organizing on the island. I mean, that's inevitable—we're not fighting just for Puerto Ricans in the States, we are fighting for all Puerto Ricans, you know, and in turn, we're fighting for all oppressed people. In the fourth point of our Thirteen Point Program and Platform, we say we are revolutionary nationalists, not racists. That also means that we recognize the struggle of white people.

One thing we always say in the Young Lords, "Don't ever let any particular hatred you have prevent you from working. Always take it into you and let it move you forward. And if it's strong, change it, because it stops your work." We tell all Puerto Rican youth to listen to this. High-school-age Puerto Ricans are into a *big* thing about whitey, and we tell them, "Man, it's not white *folk.* What we are trying to destroy is not white people, but a system created by white people, a capitalistic system that has run away from them to the point that it is now killing white people, too." And in fact, in that struggle, we're gonna hook up and we're gonna be allies with white people, like the Weatherpeople. The fact that the Weatherpeople rose is important to us because for a long time it was very theoretical talking about white allies. Every time we talked about it with somebody, the brother or sister would say, "Well, where are they?" And it was a good point. You know, where was everybody when Fred Hampton was killed? So that the emergence of the Weatherpeople—their beginning was very shaky, but it's a good, solid, steady group now—has given us a lot more trust and has helped us a lot in relating to other white people.

You know, when we meet somebody from the Third World, we immediately call them brother or sister, right. And then they have to prove to us through their practice that they are not our brothers or sisters—like Gene Roberts, who infiltrated the Panther Party. We view white people, when we first see them, with mistrust and suspicion, and then they have to show us by their practice that they are really our brothers and sisters—and that is the difference in the two.

It would be totally naive for us to openly embrace white people, even if they are in the Movement, simply because they're supposed to be revolutionary. We've gone through too many frustrations with white people in the Movement to have that happen. 'Cause you really want to hope that once you get into the Movement there ain't no more racism. But that's a joke. In many cases racism becomes sicker than what you see in the so-called "straight" world, because it's kind of like a psychopathic hero-worship. You know, everything the Panthers do is right simply because they're Black, the Young Lords are fantastic because they're Puerto Rican. That's ridiculous. The Young Lords make mistakes, and if we make mistakes we want our white *compañeros* and *compañeras* to criticize us. If they really love us, that's what they'll do. That's one of the weaknesses of the Movement, you know, that people do not want to criticize the Panthers because the Panthers are Black. But in doing that they do more harm to the Panthers than they do good.

We try to encourage honesty in our relationships with white people. I think that we've gone a long way toward eliminating a lot of the shit in the Movement. And I think a lot of people get good vibes when they're around us. I think a lot of people in the Movement dig us because of that.

The Young Lords Party today is the fastest-moving group of people inside the Puerto Rican nation. We're moving faster than anybody else, and this means that all the contradictions that exist among our people are much more highlighted among us, that things come out much more quickly. That's why you have the Young Lords arguing about male chauvinism, female passivity, racism, Viet Nam. People on the street ain't talkin' about all those things yet, you know. We try to take that word "vanguard" and give it a new definition, because the definition that it has now is that the vanguard is some elitist group, that they're better than everybody else, and they tell all the other groups, "Go fuck yourself." Like, to us, the vanguard means that we have a great responsibility. It means that we are in front of the people and show the people the way, but at the same time we are among the people, because we are the people. We are also in back of the people, you know, because sometimes you got to lay back to check the people out. And that's where we get our strength from.

We're here because we are trying as best we can to take the power of the State and put that back in the hands of the people who for so long have been denied everything. It's a very deep, emotional thing, you know, for people who've been told for so long that they're fucked up, that they're niggers, spics, that they ain't worth shit, to be doing this.

We are showing people an alternative to living under a capitalistic society—an alternative to the tenement, to the street, to the workplace, to the *fanguito*. Each generation that comes up is taught that this is the only way things can be done, this is life, right. It's a fact of life that you're poor, that there are some people on top, and that most people are on the bottom. It's a fact of life that this is a dog-eat-dog world, and if you want to make it you got to make it by yourself. But we're gonna take them facts of life and turn them around. We're saying that it is gonna be a new fact of life that what counts first is not so much the individual but the group, and in order for the individual to survive, the group, the nation, has to survive.

There's a whole new way to live, you

know, if the people together are planning where their nation's gonna go, how their government is running, how much they're going to produce, who's going to produce what, and what they're gonna do with it once they get it. In cold, scientific terms this means that production and distribution get put in the hands of the people. That's a phrase that everybody can sing by rote, but if we think about it and if we understand it, it's a whole mindblowing concept to oppressed people, because we've never been shown that we can succeed in anything.

You know, there was a way that the people used to walk in the street before 1969, before the Young Lords Party began—people used to walk with their heads down like this, and the pigs would walk through the colonies, man, like they owned the block. They'd come in here with no kind of respect in their eyes. They'd *walk* through, they wouldn't ride through. See, when a pig *walks* through the street that means they got less respect than if they gotta ride. But after the Garbage Offensive and the Peoples' Church it was a whole new game.

As these things started to happen, as each one came, it was like boom, boom, boom. You and the enemy are standing there like this, right, and the enemy's been kicking your ass. But suddenly you throw up a couple of blocks, right, and you land a couple of solid ones, and people start digging this, and they see you're landing more solid ones. You're fighting toe to toe and, like, you're takin' some shit, but you know you can take his best. For 400 years, you've taken the best that this motherfucker could throw at you, and now you're gonna deal. So now, what's he gonna do? He wants to land his haymaker, he wants to round everybody up—you know that's coming. But we are a tempered people, we have been tempered like the blade of a knife by years, man, of living under this shit. When fascism comes, people gonna be ready for it. It's gonna blow the pigs' minds, right, but we ain't gonna give up. Because the people have seen that there's a way.

At the Second People's Church, we brought guns out into the open, and these guns were definitely illegal, they were unregistered, right. But because we had our people with us, Mayor Lindsay had to say the guns were legal. He had to hold his police back, because the white racists in the department wanted to kill us, you know, and they couldn't. And when people saw this, people said, "Wow!" We took the guns out of the church and we showed them—like we say in the street "we showed our shit" and got away clean. We still ain't been popped for that one.

Now, when they catch us, when they start rounding up the first bunch of Lords, they're gonna throw everything on us. But the point is the people now have hope. They can round me up, they can round up the Central Committee, but they're gonna have a hard time. First of all, the explosion that's gonna come if they touch anybody on the Central Committee will be tremendous. We already know what happened when they tried to take our Chief of Staff, Fi, and that was months ago. The main thing is that they can take any Young Lord now, because now they've got to kill an idea. Like, we have a second-, third-, fourth-level leadership. This is one of the greatest things we've done. Ain't nobody done this in the Puerto Rican nation—build something that's gonna live on. The Nationalists tried and failed because they were centered around this one cat—Albizu Campos.

Our people have been taught to believe that when they rounded up Albizu Campos and two thousand members of the Nationalist Party they broke the back of the Nationalist Party. But now the people can think about Albizu and all of a sudden it seems like the Nationalist Party has just been going through different kinds of changes for twenty years. "Well, man, we thought you all lost—it looks like we're gonna start winning." And, like, the concept of winning, right, that is the number one contribution of the Young Lords Party—that is what we are, man, the concept of winning.

One thing about us I really dig is that we don't get so hung up in theory that we don't move. We can still jump out into the street, we still do battle with the pigs, we still haven't lost our heart. That may sound like a whole big *macho* thing, but it's not, see, because it's important that we understand that the thing that kept the Puerto Rican nation intact, the thing that made us was the soul and strength of our men and women. That's what did it. When people would get put up against the wall, it wasn't because they had read Marx or Mao, it was because deep down inside there was this basic nationalist feeling that said, "Get off my back, you don't belong here—you ain't got no business bugging me. Get the hell out! And if you don't, I'm gonna punch you in the mouth!" This is the thing that is in our core, this is our nationalism.

Now, there are some people who would say that there's a contradiction in being a revolutionary nationalist—in fact, they say you can't be a Nationalist and a Socialist at the same time. Well, that's wrong. See, for these people I would quote Mao, where he says that loving your people and your country and fighting to liberate your people is the best way to aid the struggle of all peoples around the world. It's ridiculous to say you're an internationalist and you're going to struggle for all oppressed people, without picking a particular segment of people you're gonna work in. Because the people, you know, are divided along nation and class lines, and we have to recognize both. In this country, for example, racism is like a stick that the pigs are clubbing you on the head with. Now you got to grab the other end and hit them back with it—and the other end of the stick is nationalism. And if you do it righteously, if you do it with the interest of the people and with the backing of the people, then it becomes revolutionary. Now that's revolutionary nationalism—that is the kind of nationalism that says, "Yes, we are proud to be Puerto Rican, we are proud to be number one—but we want everybody else to be number one too, and we're gonna help everyone else be number one." See, 'cause the other kind of nationalism is reactionary nationalism—where you say, "Well, I'm number one. Fuck everybody else."

We've seen how the Black colony in America has been divided in terms of culture versus politics. We don't want to see the Puerto Rican colony divided that way. We don't want to create divisions where there need not be any. So that we do promote interest in the culture of the nation, right—but we only want to take from the culture what has been good. We're not gonna go into a trip glorifying the *pava*, which is a straw hat, or the *guayabera*, which is a kind of shirt, 'cause there ain't no hat or no shirt gonna free anybody. But the fact that our people, when put up against the wall, have managed to kick ass for centuries—that is good, that is part of our culture, right. That's why we say that the most cultural thing we can do is pick up the gun to defend ourselves.

Culture, see, is the gun—as long as we understand that it is not the gun that should control us, but the Party that should control the gun. That is a rule that our Minister of Defense has made very clear. And that was the whole lesson of the People's Church. It can be said that the Second People's Church, when we took the church with guns, when we armed ourselves in our own defense, was probably one of the most cultural events in the history of the Puerto Rican nation—on the same level with the uprising at Jayuya in 1950, and *El Grito de Lares* in 1868. The only cultural form that's gonna go beyond that is armed struggle.

We are not nihilists, you know, we're not just destroy, destroy, destroy. We're saying to our people, yes we've got to destroy, but we have a new system that we're already starting to build, right. Taking the whole Puerto Rican nation into account, we're a small group, but inside that small group we're dealing socialistically with one another in a very human manner, and as we move, that influence is gonna spread out in many ways.

PALANTE
YOUNG
LORDS
PARTY

PHOTOGRAPHIC ESSAY

ROOTS
REVOLUTION
THE PARTY

A “FANGUITO,” FAJARDO, PUERTO RICO, DECEMBER, 1970

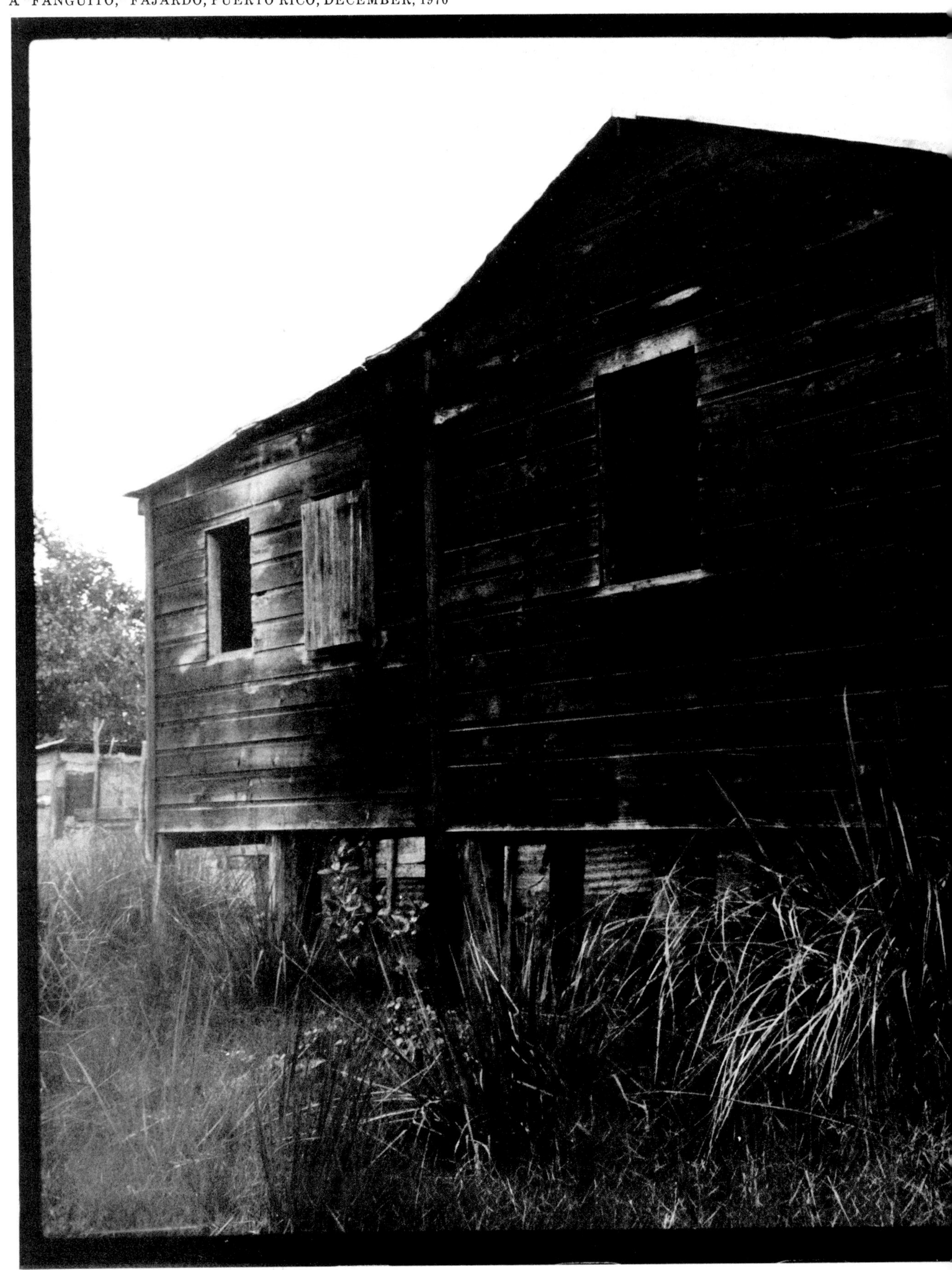

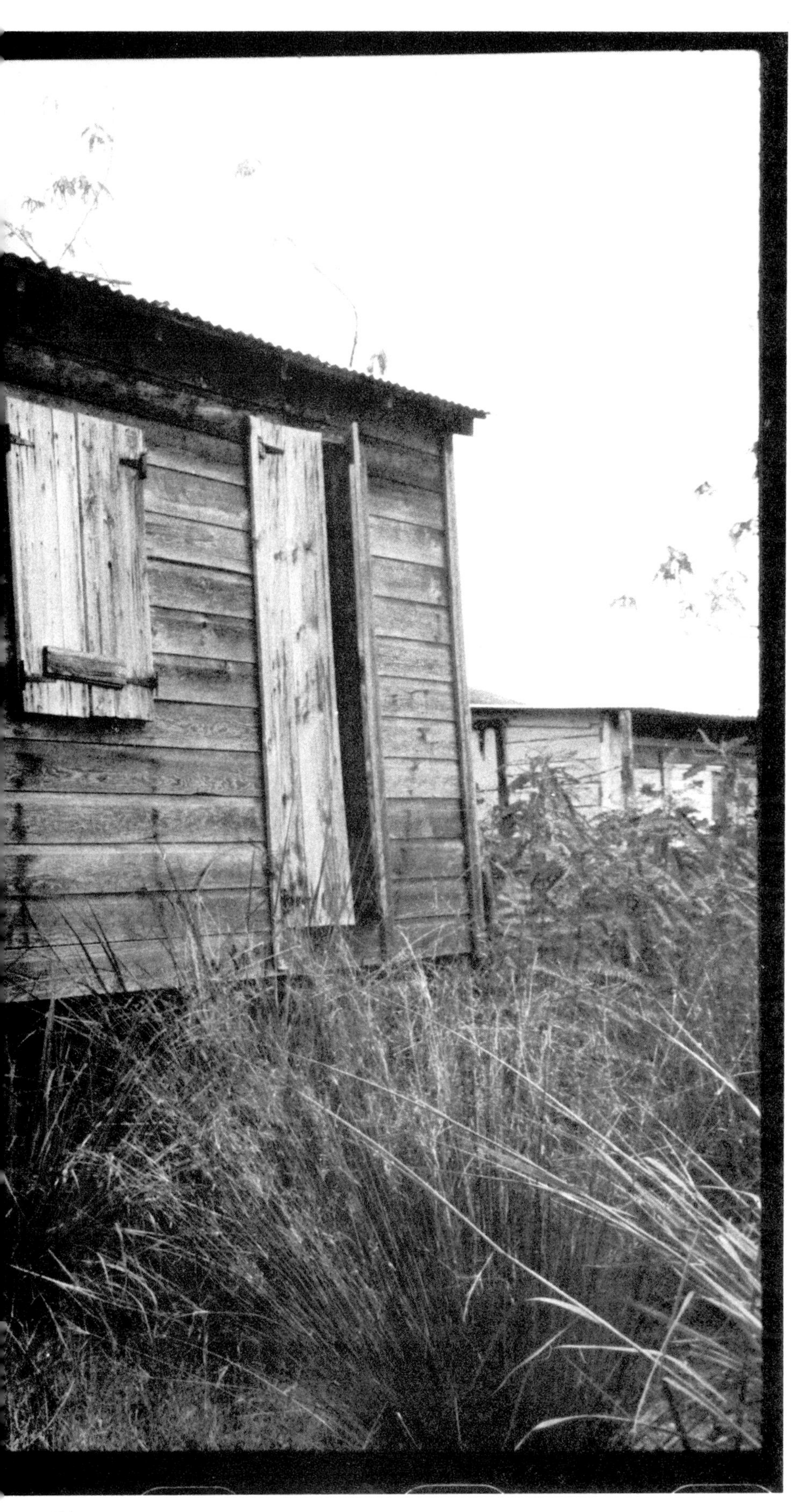

"In most history books Puerto Rican history stops in 1898. Everybody talks about how the Americans raised our standard of living–when all that happened was that sugar cane became our main product and certain American companies were the people who were making all the money."

SAN JUAN, PUERTO RICO, DECEMBER, 1970

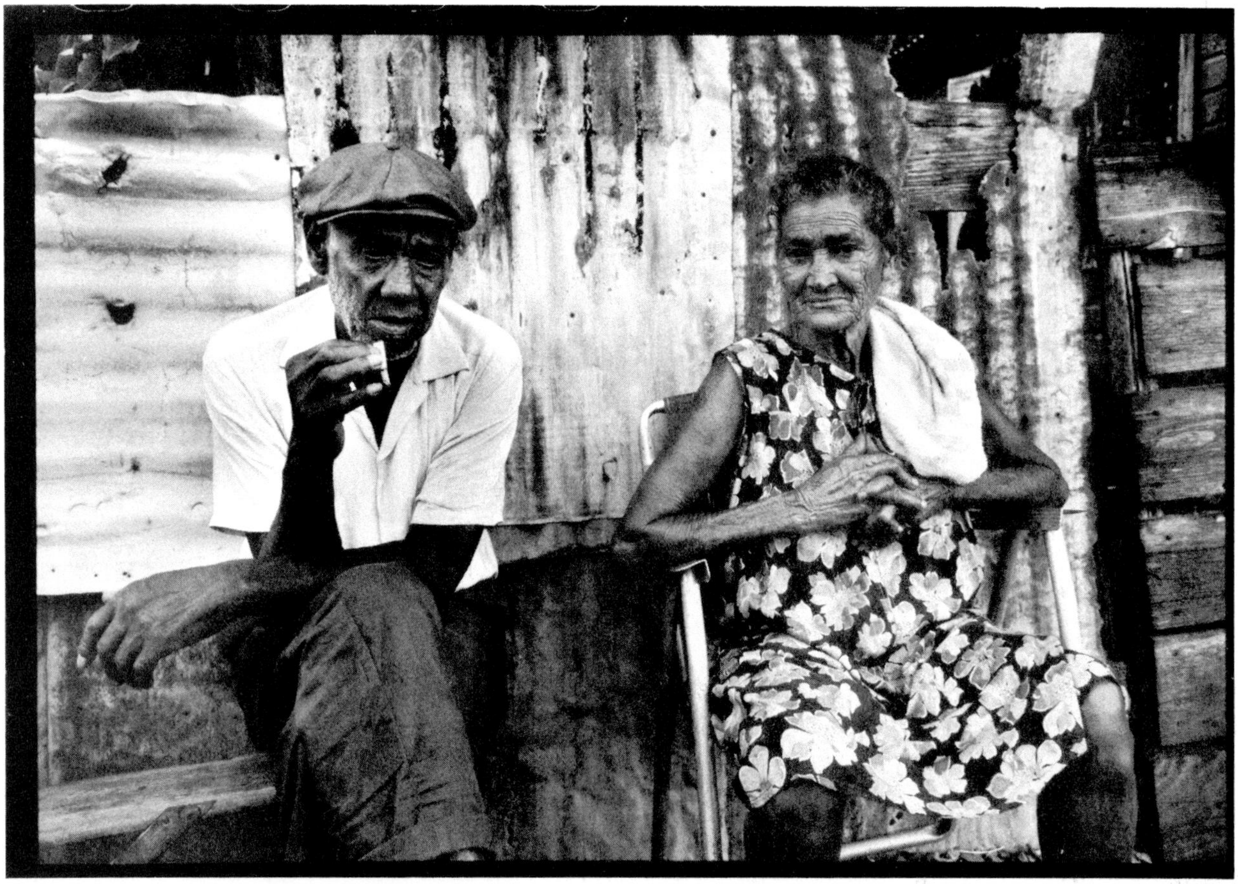

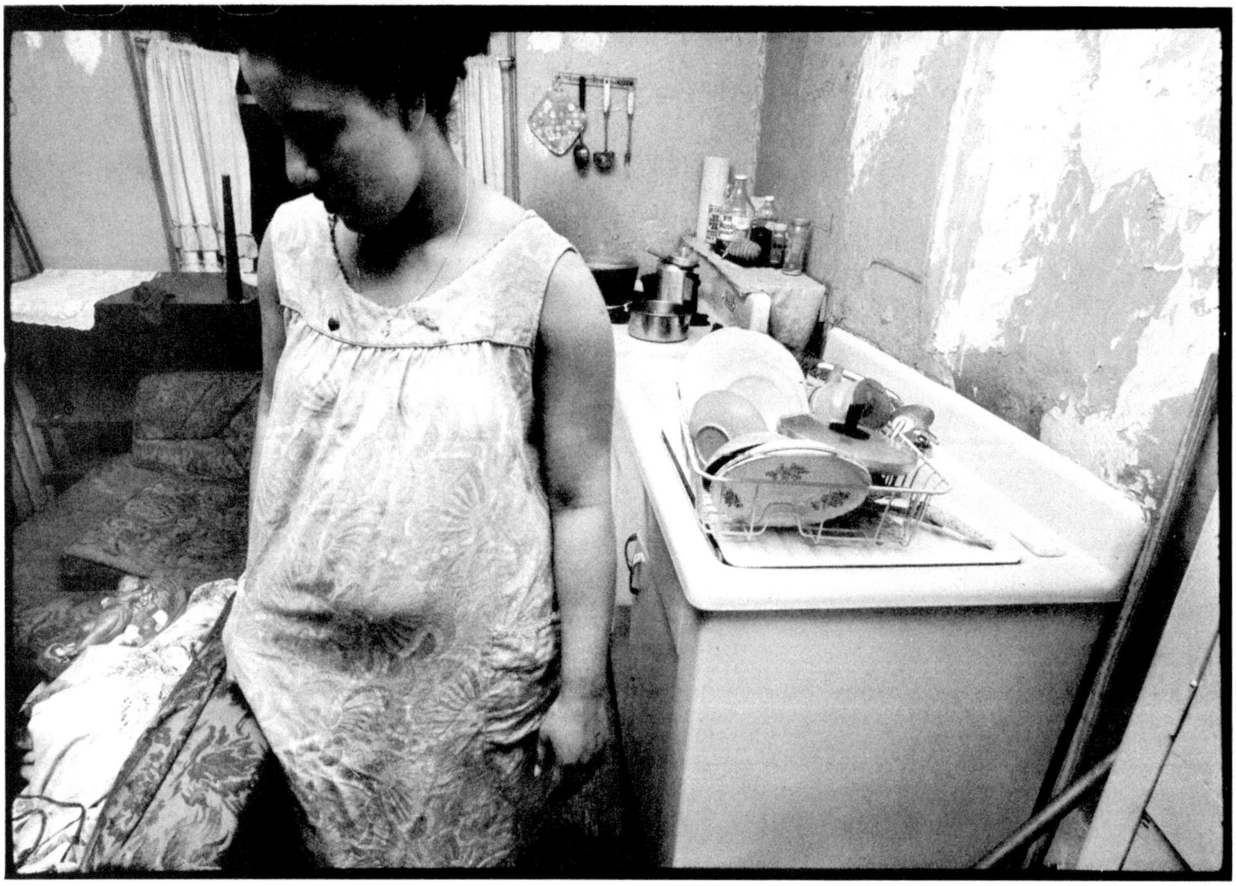

CAULDWELL AVENUE, BRONX, NEW YORK, NOVEMBER, 1970

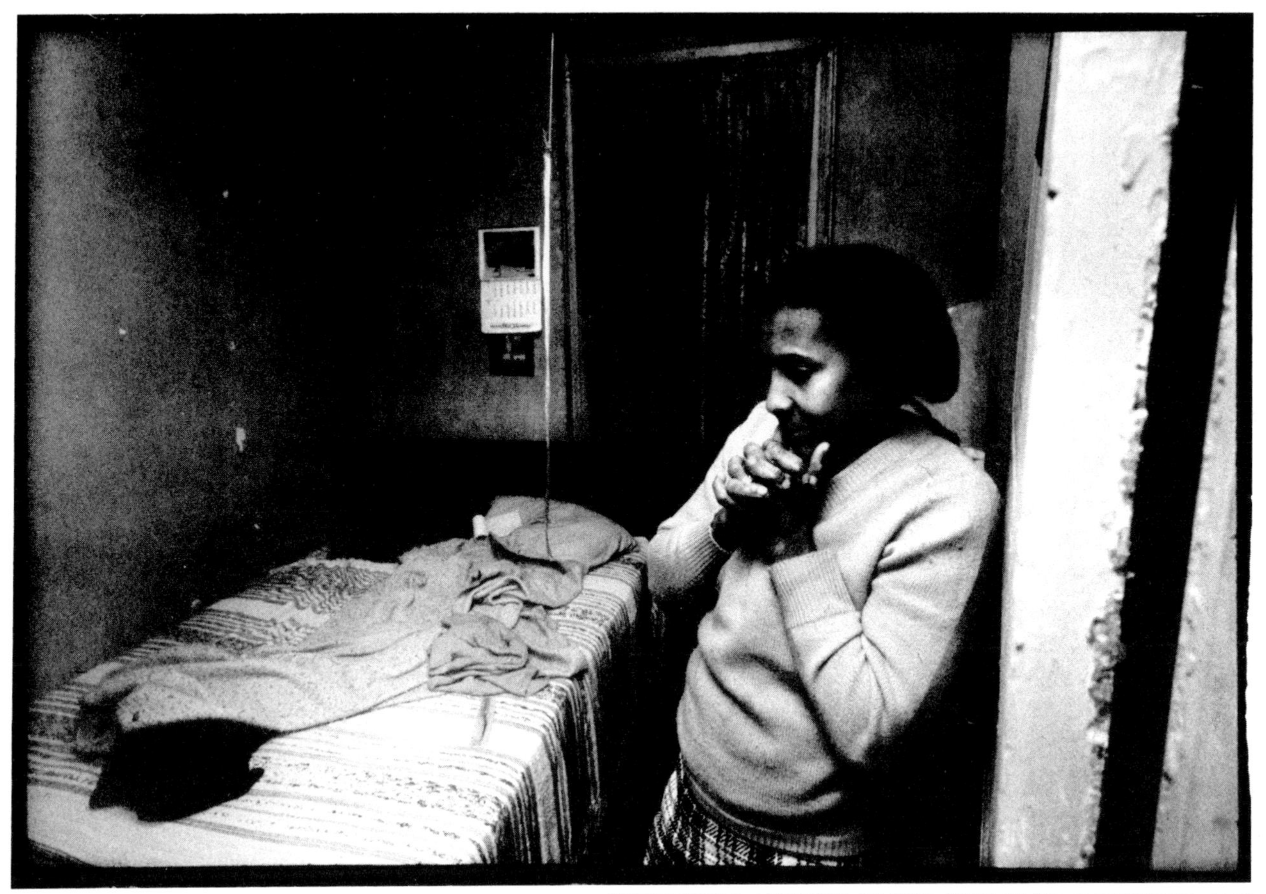

CAULDWELL AVENUE, BRONX, NEW YORK, NOVEMBER, 1970

"Bullets and bombs aren't the only ways to kill people. Bad hospitals kill our people. Rotten, forgotten buildings kill our people. Garbage and disease kill our people."

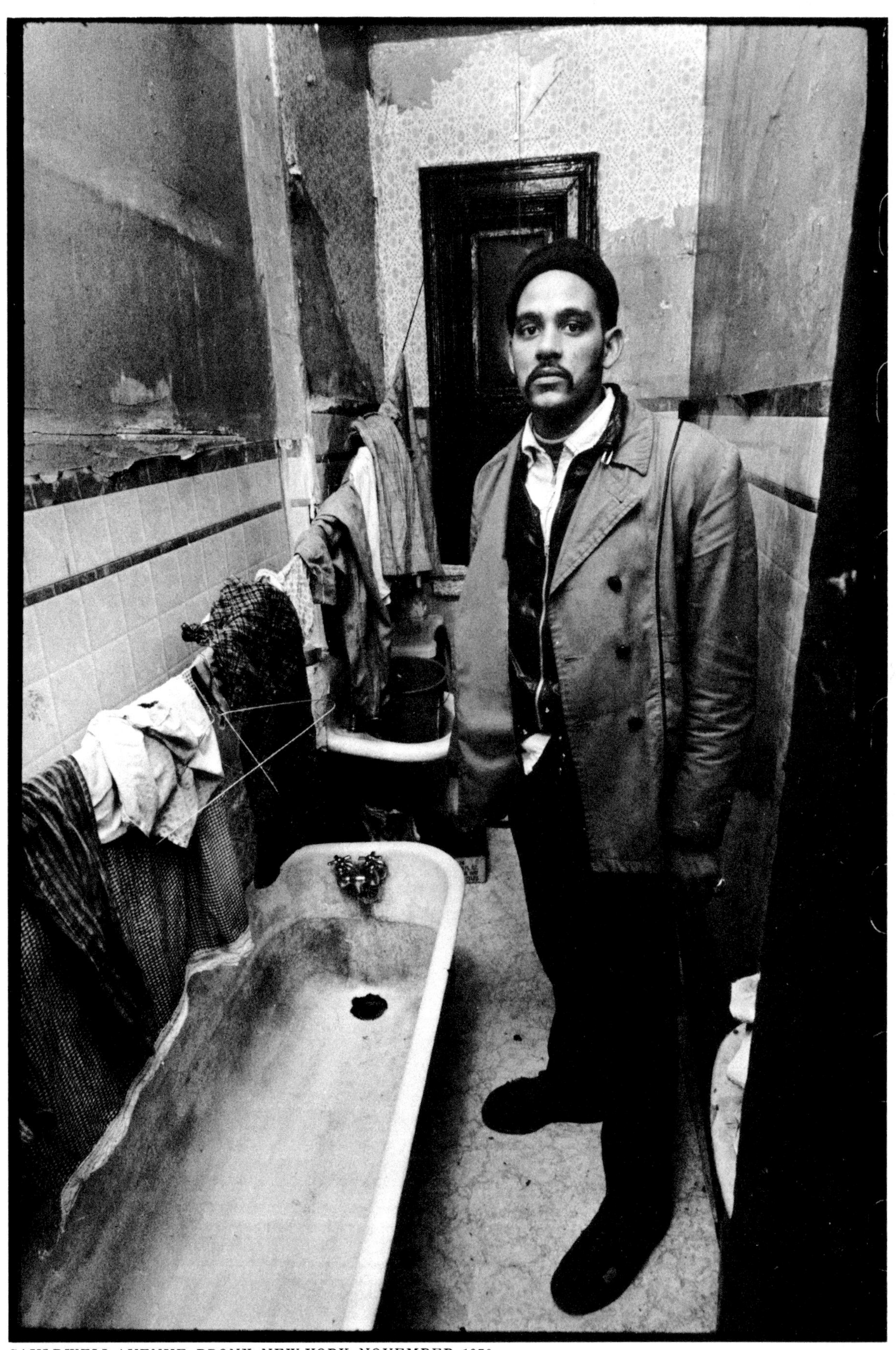

CAULDWELL AVENUE, BRONX, NEW YORK, NOVEMBER, 1970

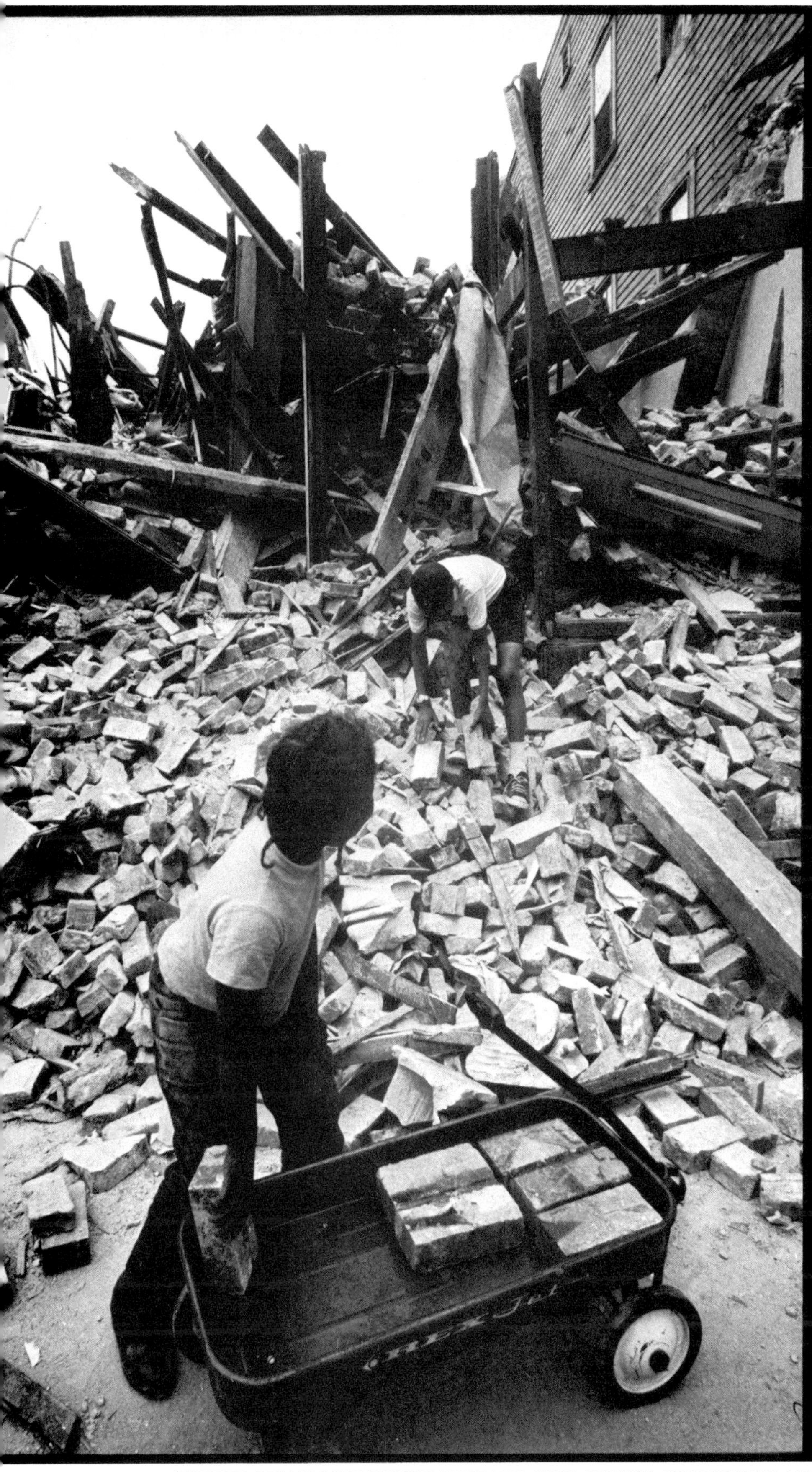

"... the nervous
breakdown streets–
Where the mice live
like millionaires–
And the people do
not live at all..."

PUERTO RICAN COMMUNITY, NEWARK, NEW JERSEY, SEPTEMBER, 1970

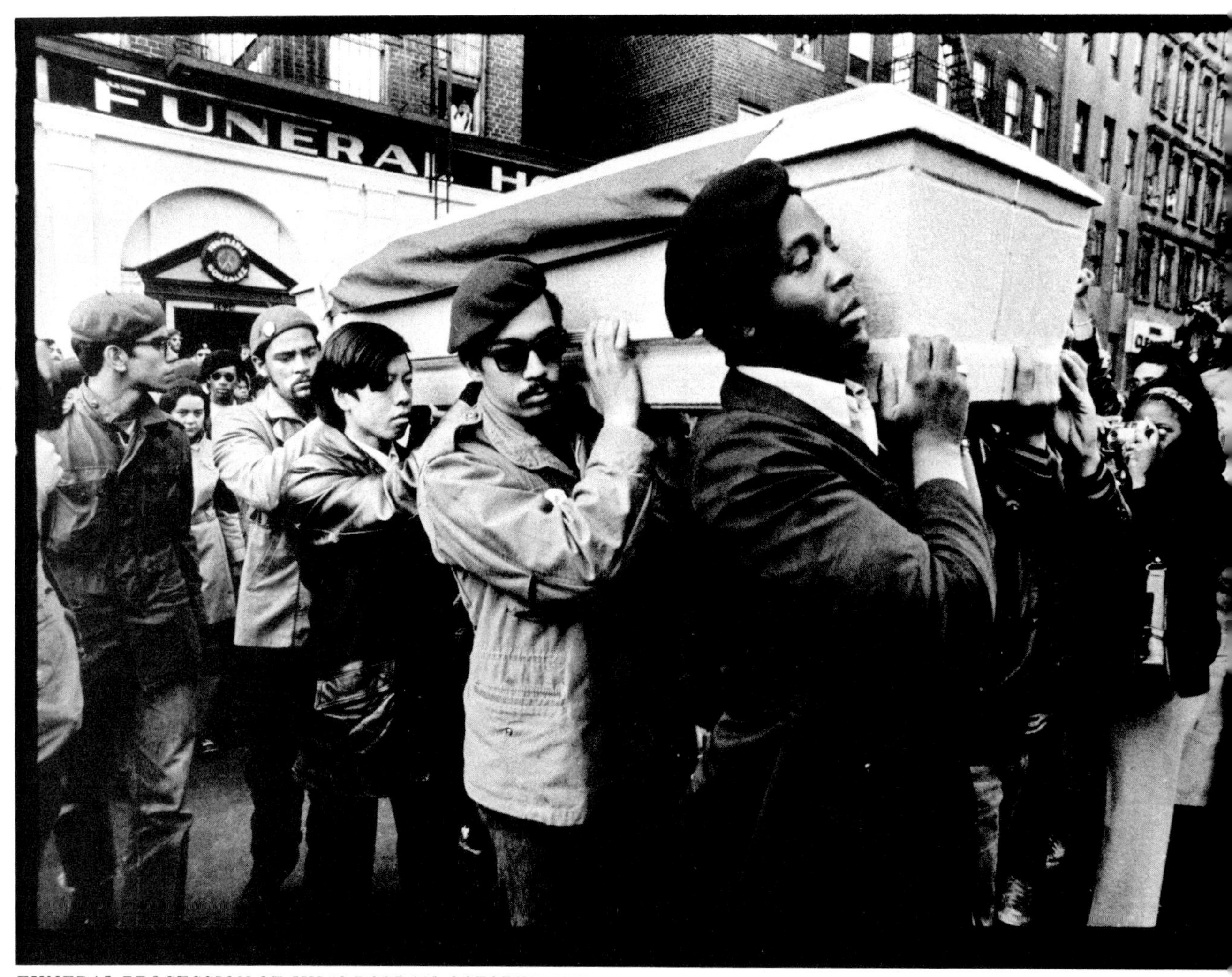

FUNERAL PROCESSION OF JULIO ROLDAN, OCTOBER, 1970

"No revolutionary hangs himself.
No revolutionary kills himself.
Julio was a revolutionary.
He lived for his people, he lived
every day striving for a revolution.
He loved life, he had no reason
to die other than in battle
for his people and his island."

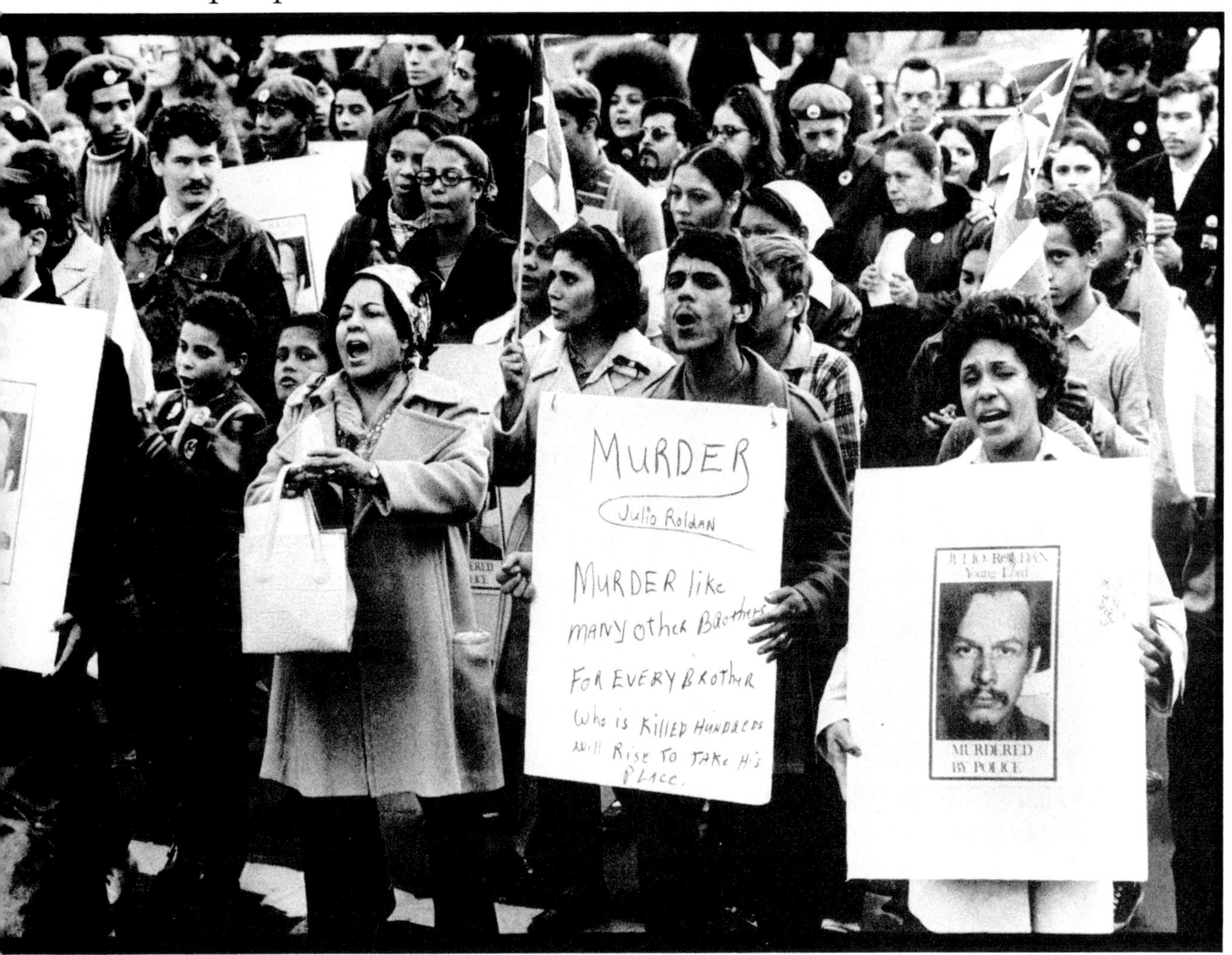

FUNERAL PROCESSION OF JULIO ROLDAN, OCTOBER, 1970

"We were not born violent. We do not enjoy killing. We just want peace and freedom. But our daily lives are violent. This country is violent. The enemy leaves us no choice. Either we sit by, saying 'ay bendito' as our nation dies, or we stand up, organize, prepare for the revolution we know is coming."

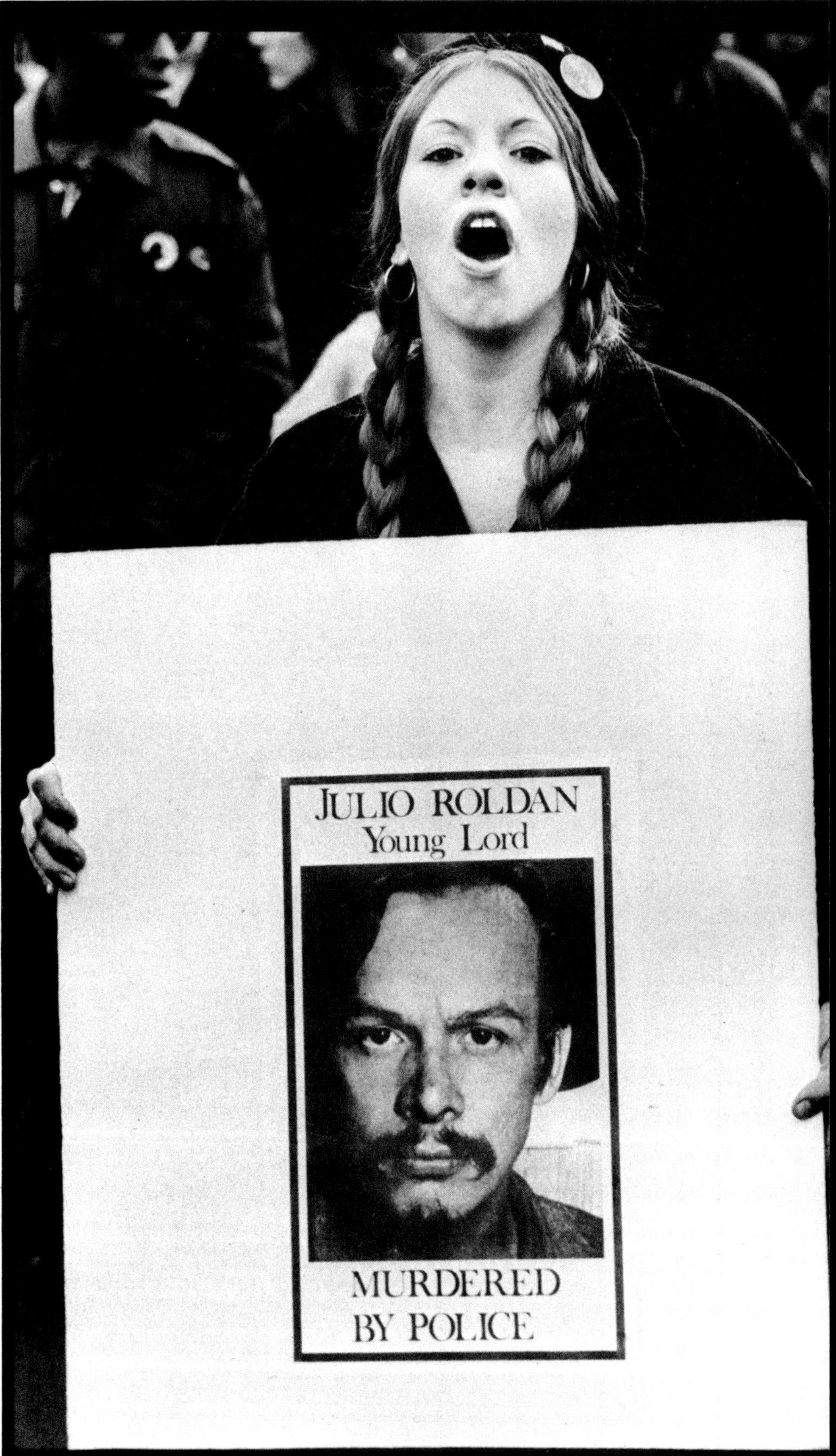

FUNERAL PROCESSION OF JULIO ROLDAN, OCTOBER, 1970

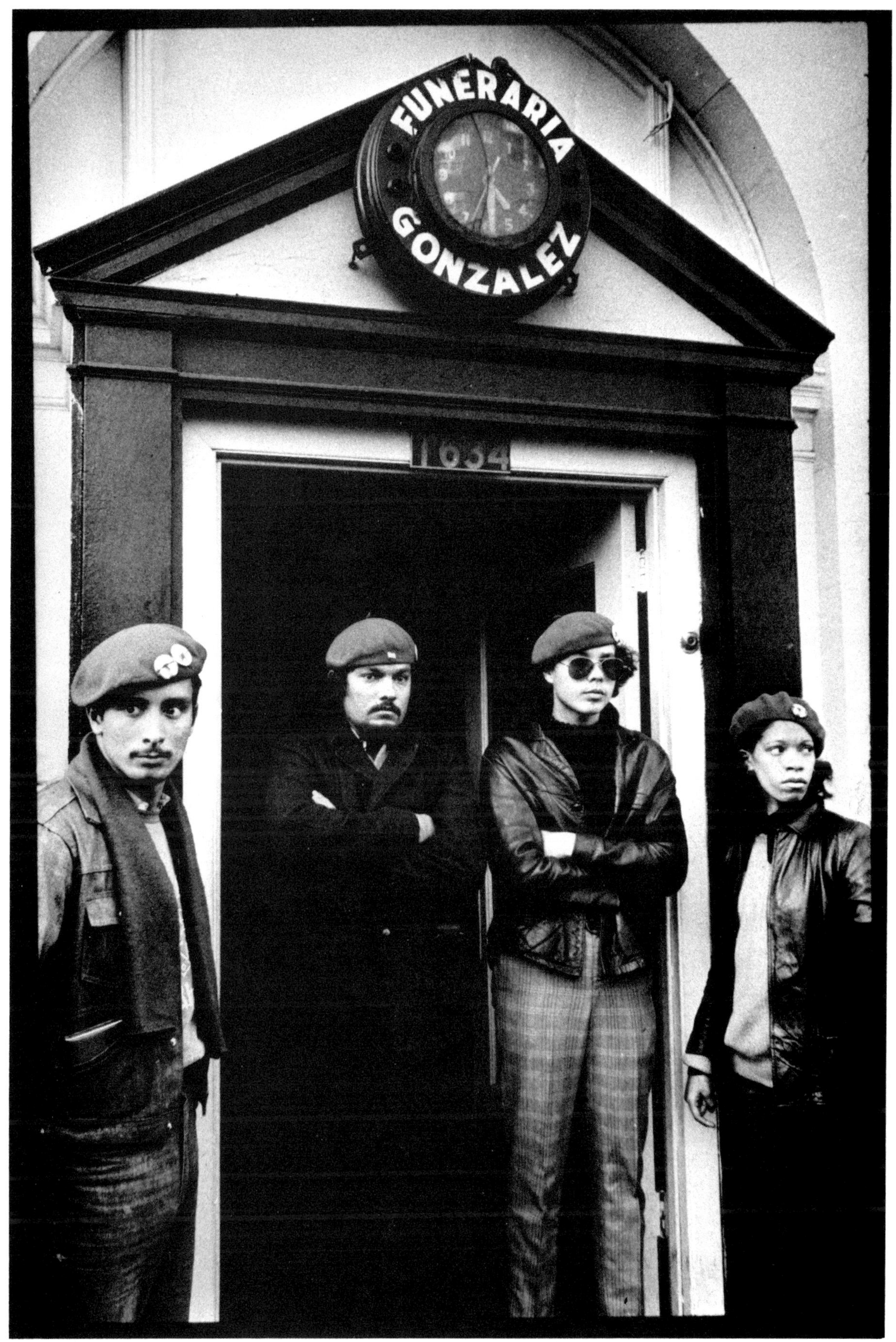

VIGIL OUTSIDE GONZALEZ FUNERAL HOME, OCTOBER, 1970

CONGREGATION OF THE SECOND PEOPLE'S CHURCH, OCTOBER, 1970

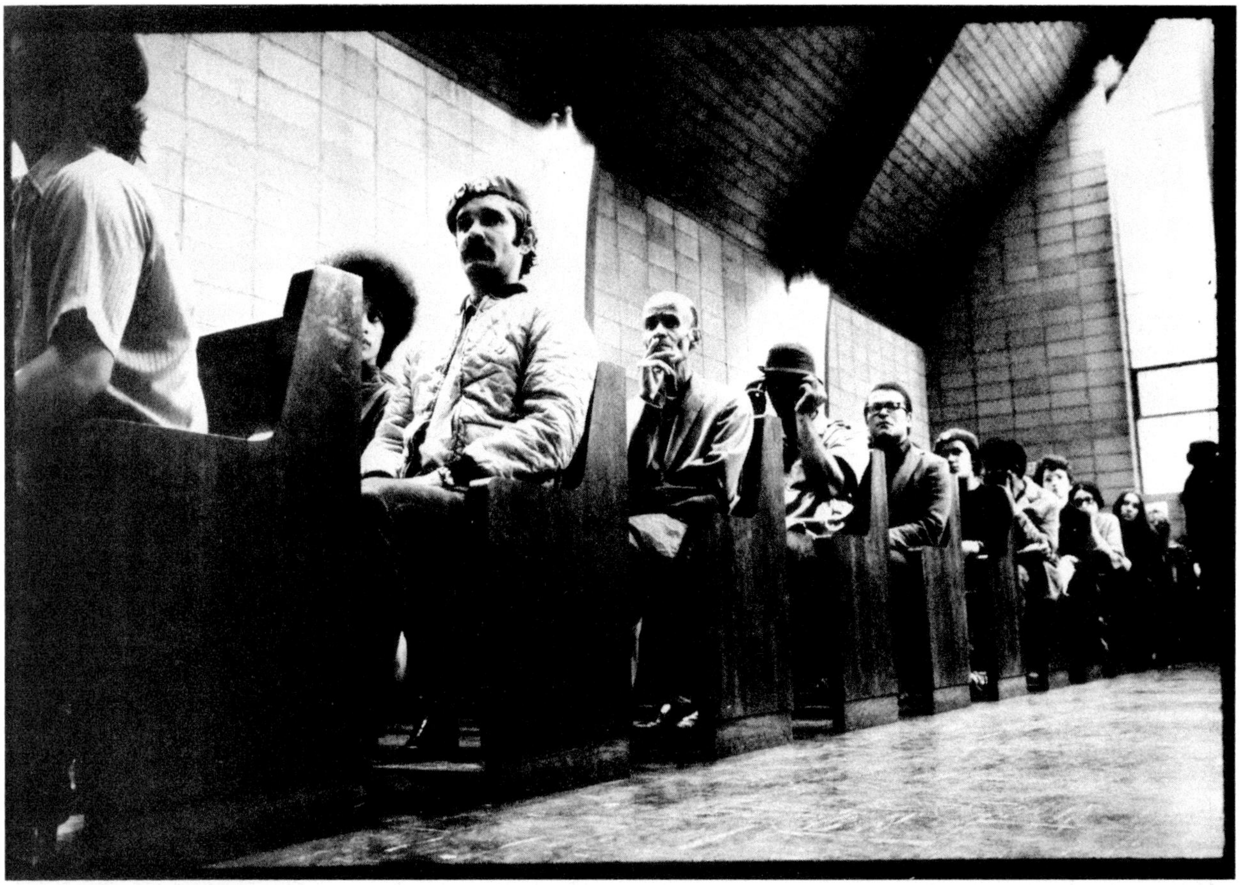

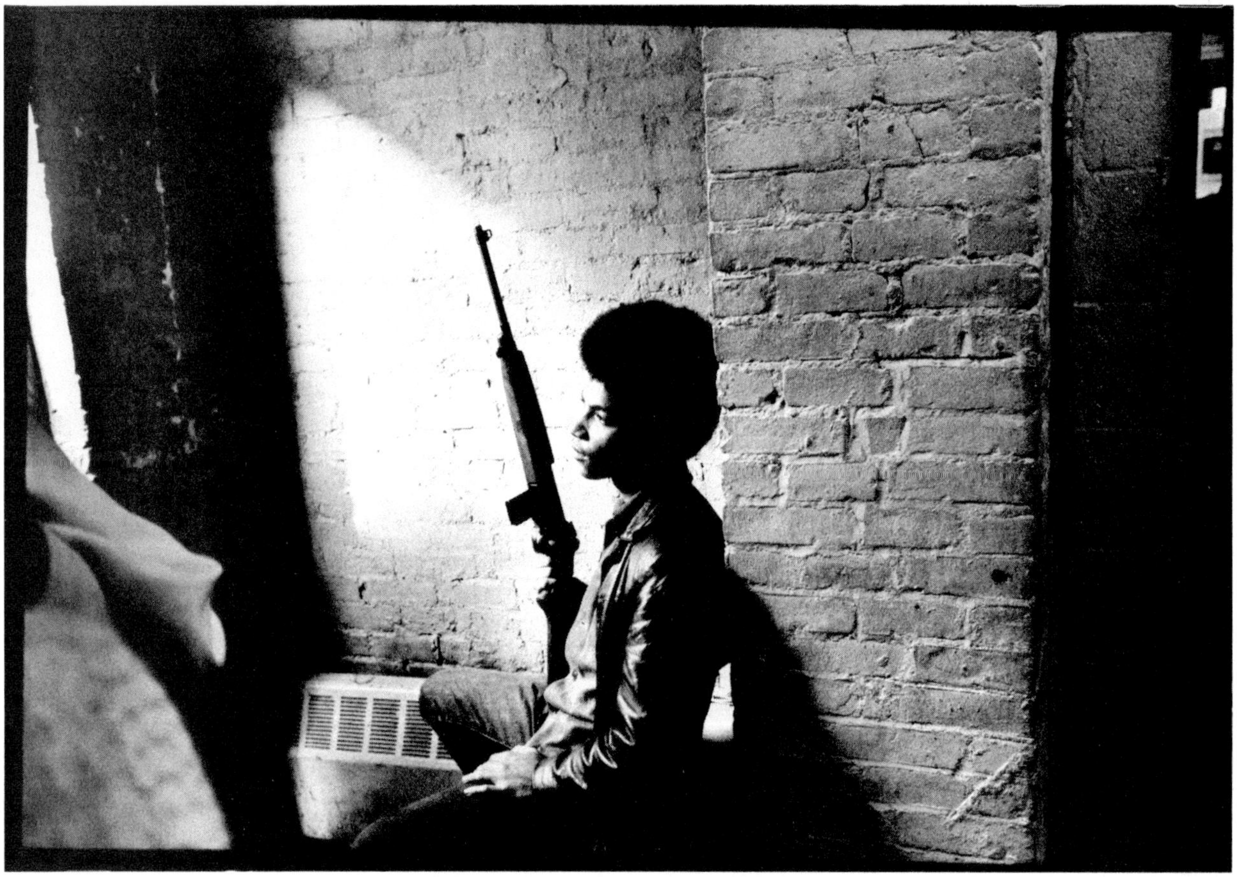

A YOUNG LORD GUARDING THE ENTRANCE TO THE SECOND PEOPLE'S CHURCH, OCTOBER, 1970

LAST RESPECTS FOR JULIO ROLDAN, OCTOBER, 1970

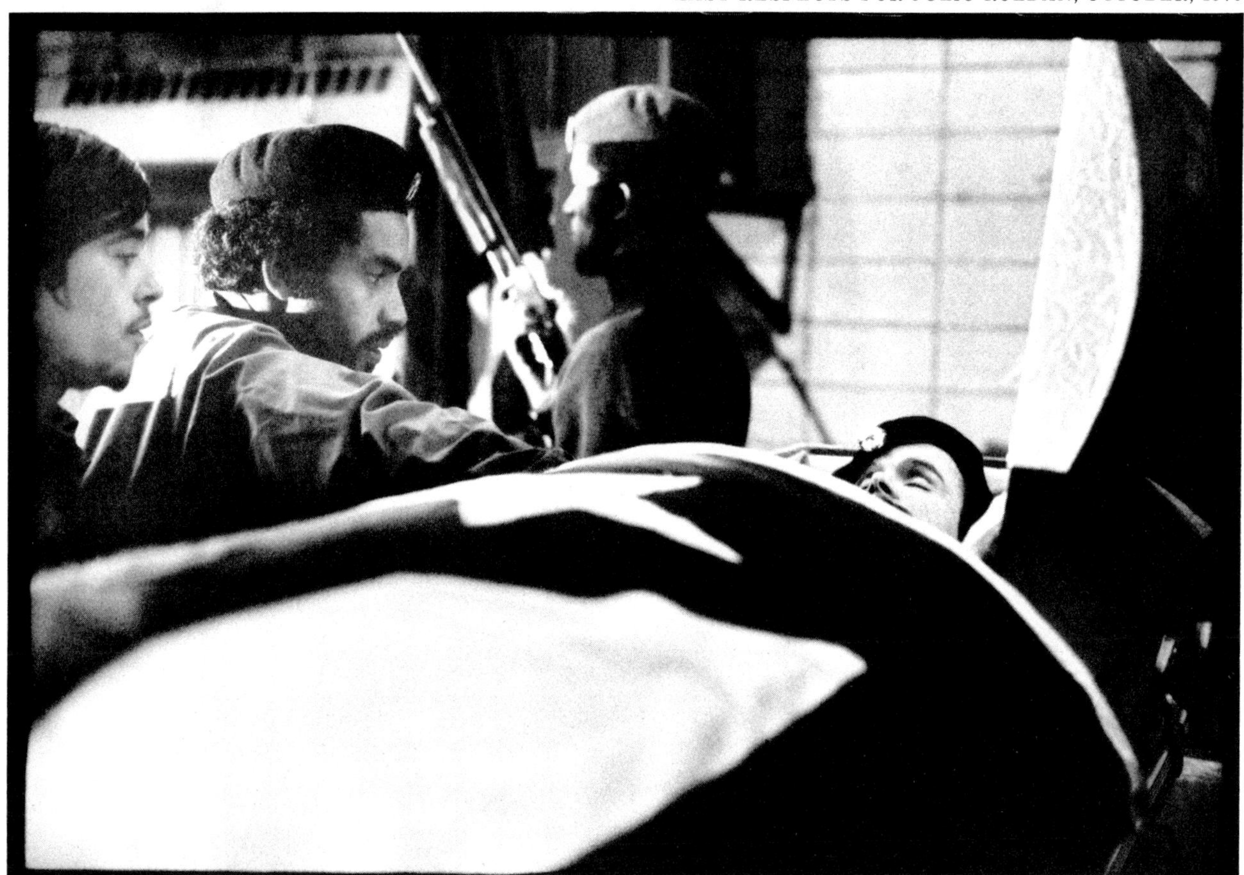

"We have liberated the People's Church again, and this time we are armed. We know that our demands are righteous, because they come out of the needs of our people. We are armed because we have seen that the government won't hesitate to kill Puerto Ricans fighting for their rights. We are armed because we must defend ourselves."

"All over the world, the people know that the streets are ours, the moon is ours, the future is ours, man, it's all ours! All of it! And we here today will not rest until it's won and placed firmly in the hands of the people."

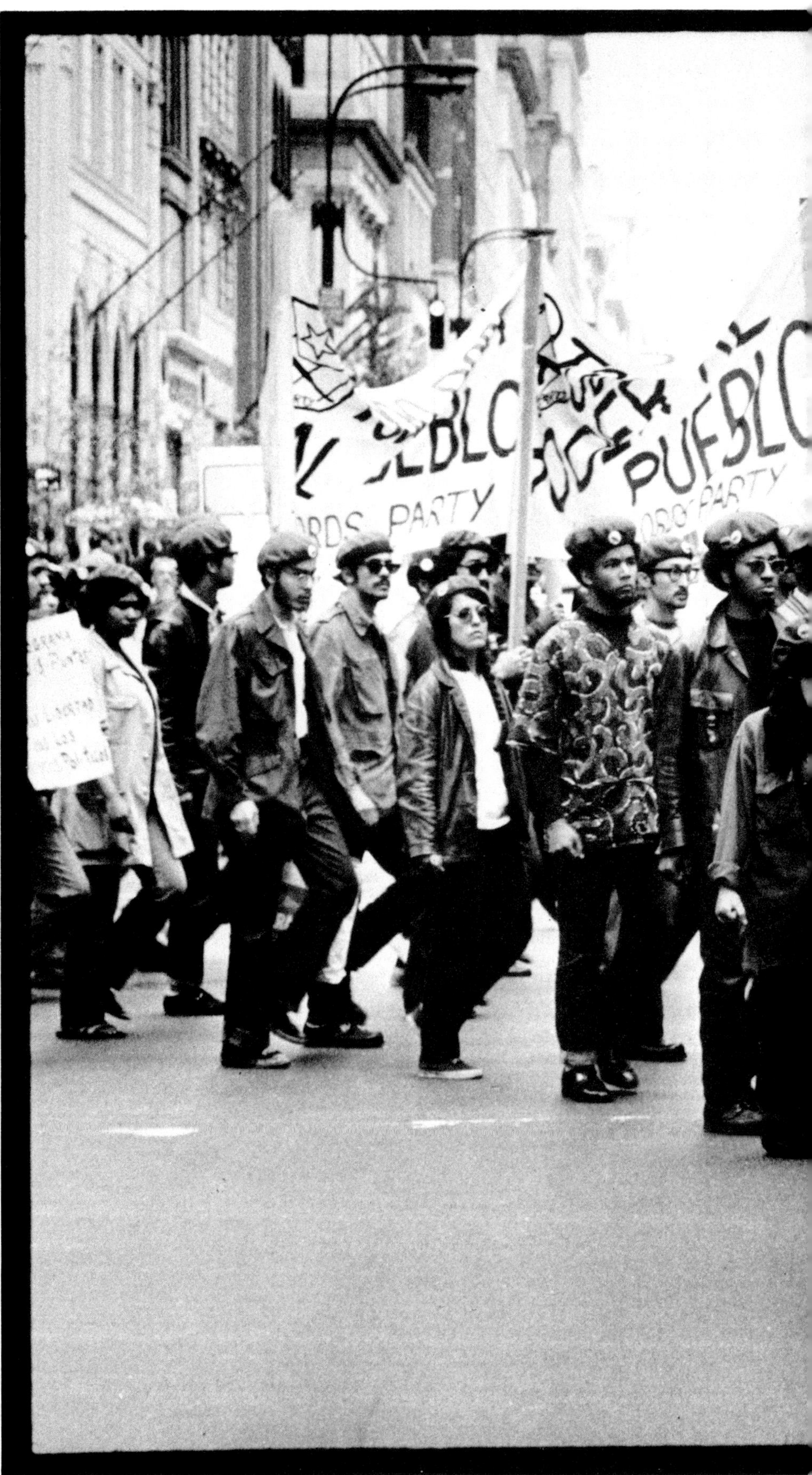

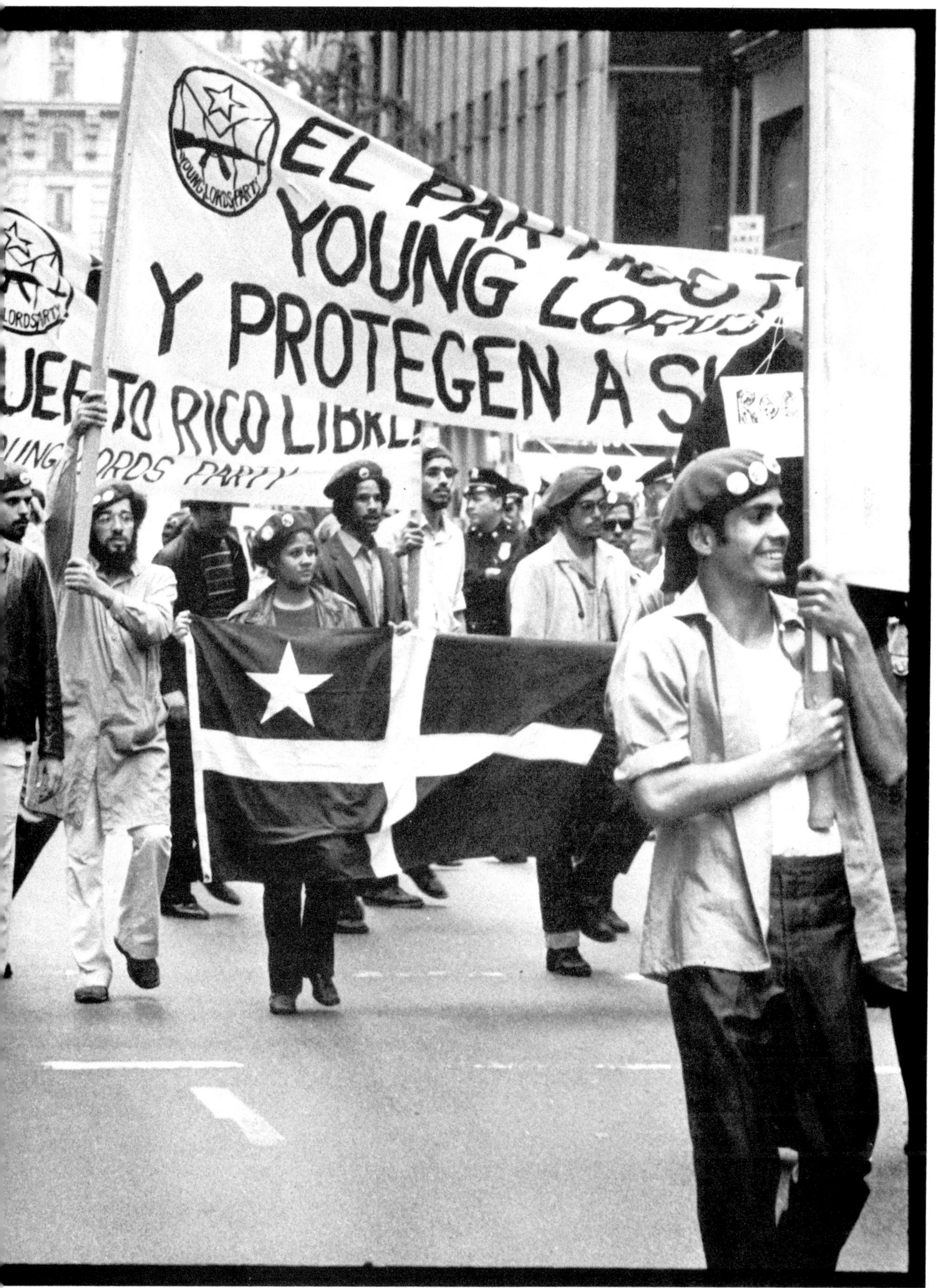

PUERTO RICAN DAY PARADE, JUNE, 1970

MARCH TO THE UNITED NATIONS, OCTOBER 30, 1970

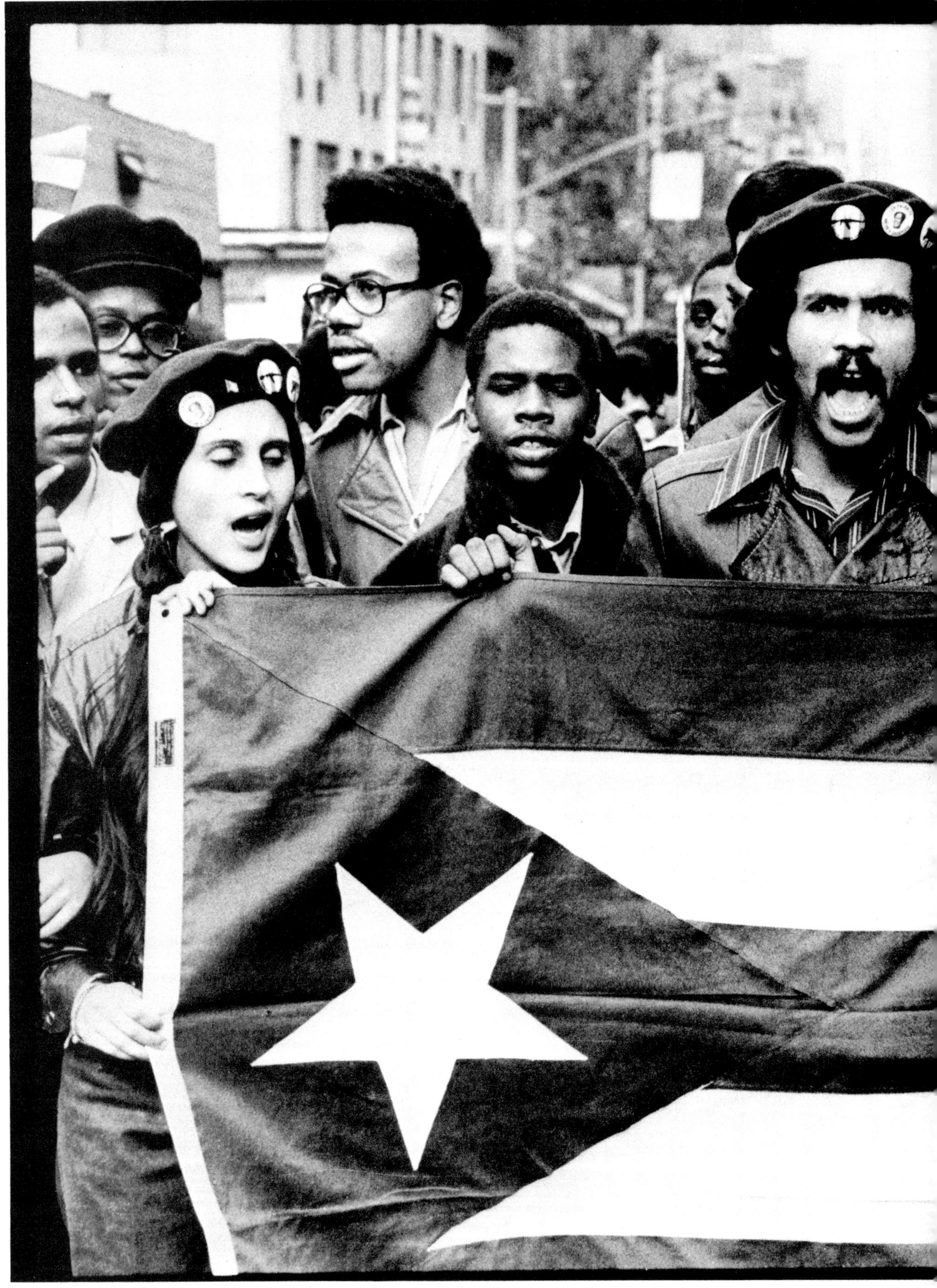

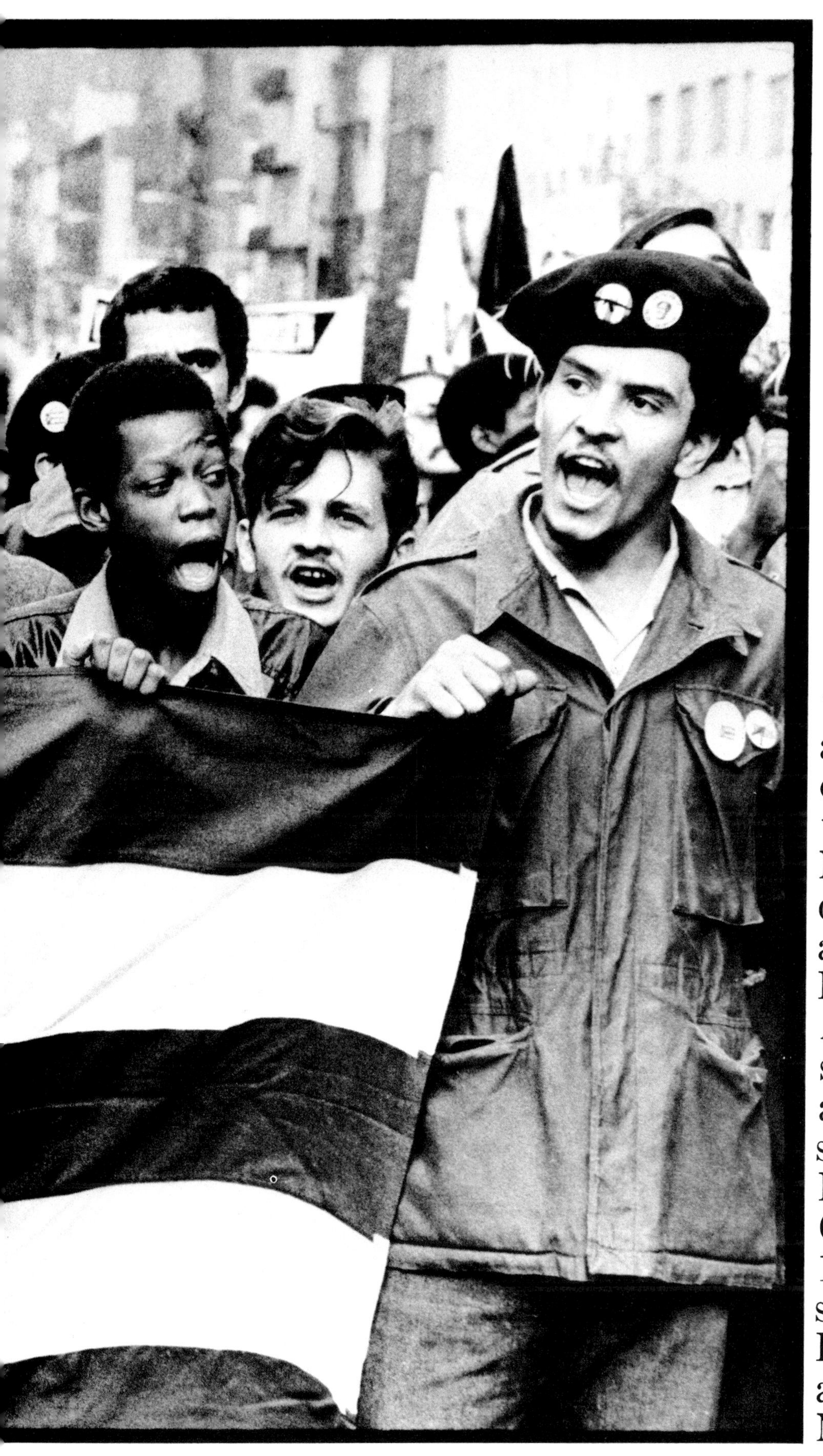

"A year ago, to be an 'Independista' or 'Nacionalista' was to be crazy. Now you go to a dance and the bands are saying, 'Viva Puerto Rico Libre!' At weddings, in the streets, the people are beginning to say, 'Viva Puerto Rico Libre!' On October 30, 1970, 10,000 people shouted, 'Viva Puerto Rico Libre!' at the United Nations."

RALLY ON STEPS OF PEOPLE'S CHURCH, JUNE, 1970

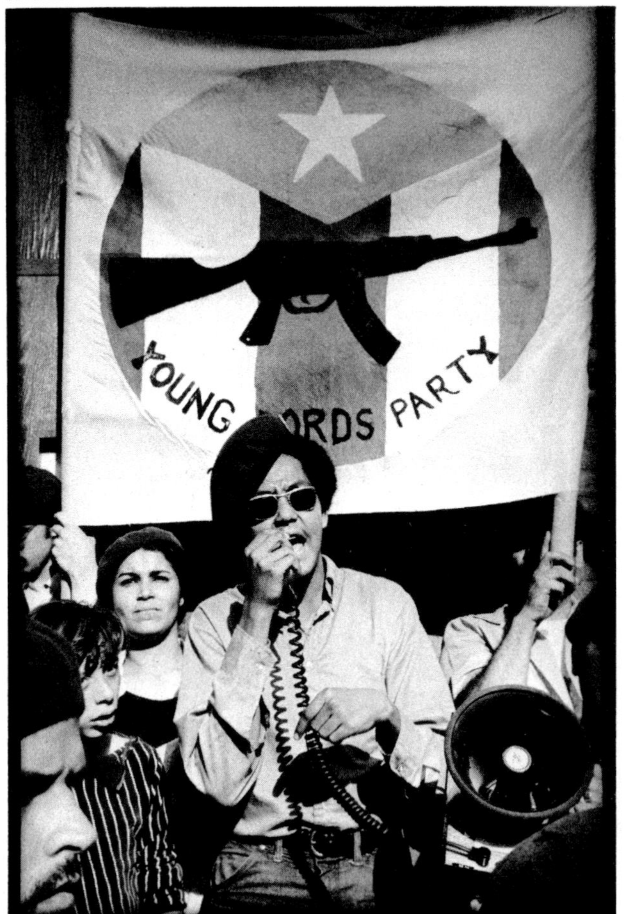

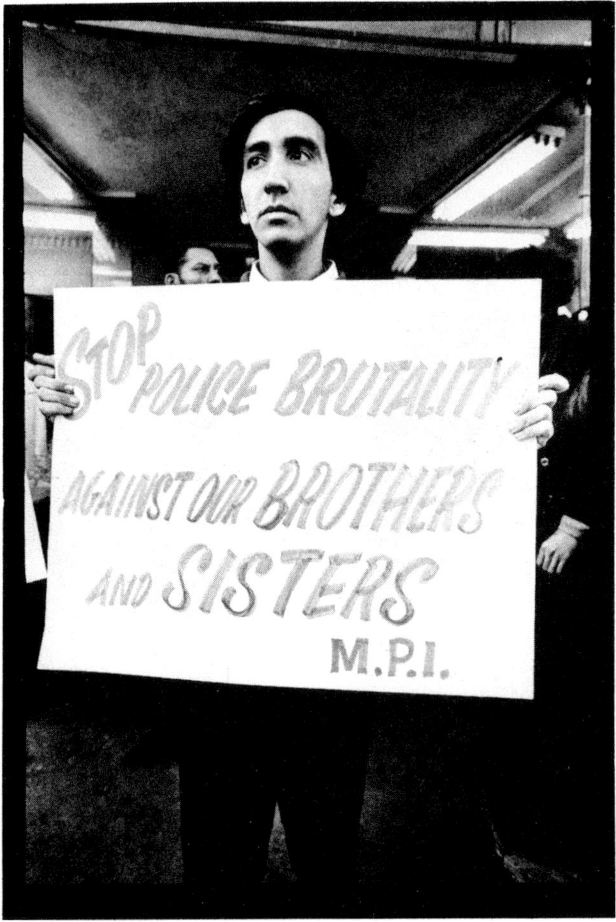

YOUNG LORDS RALLY, OCTOBER, 1970

"For centuries
we have been taught
that we are a small,
quiet, insignificant,
shuffling people who
cannot even govern
ourselves and who
are very happy having
outside governments
control our lives.
We are taught that
revolution is the
work of maniacs and
fanatics and has
nothing to do with
nice, docile spics. Yet we
have not been quiet."

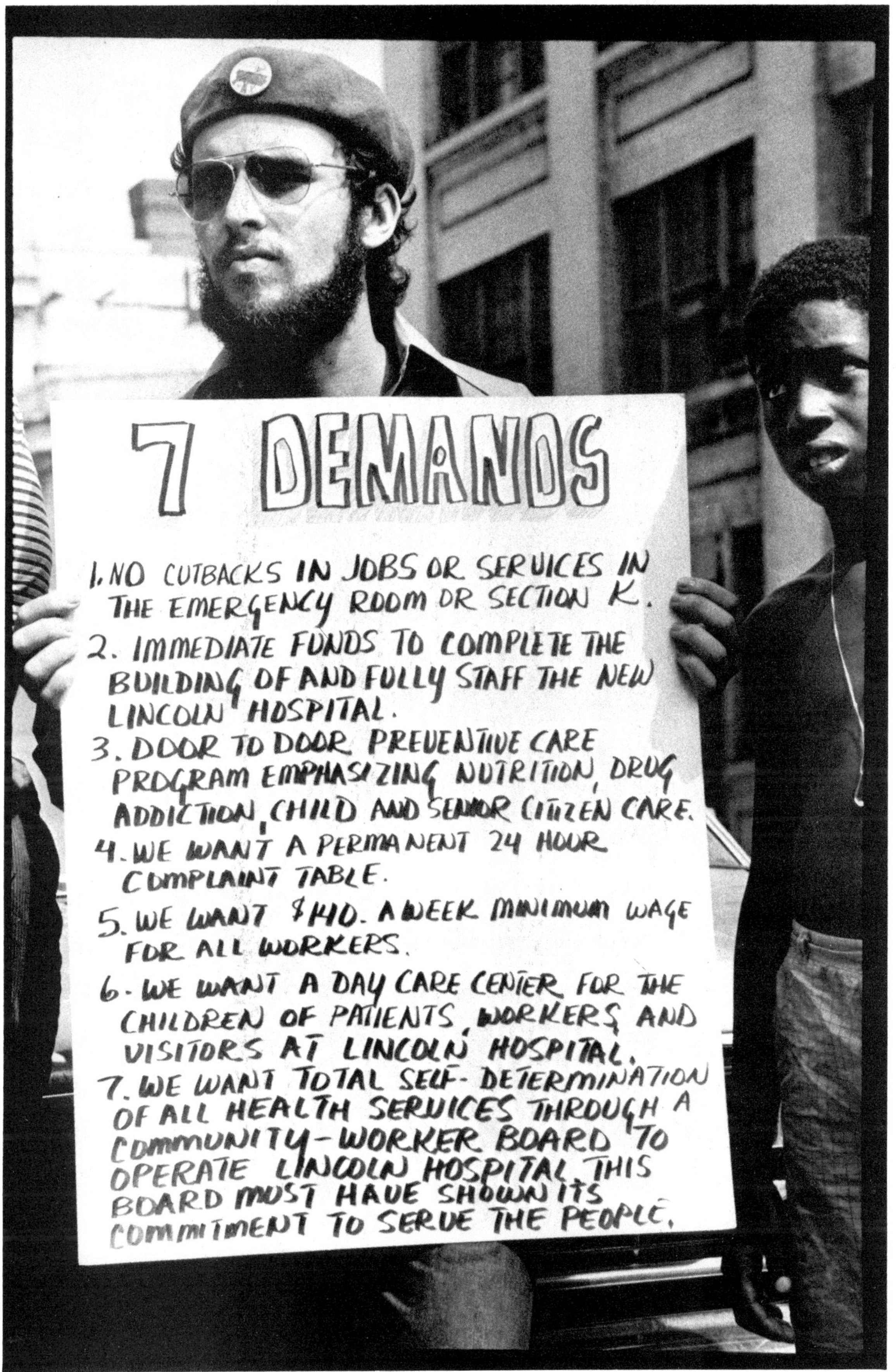

RALLY OUTSIDE LINCOLN HOSPITAL, BRONX, NEW YORK, JULY, 1970

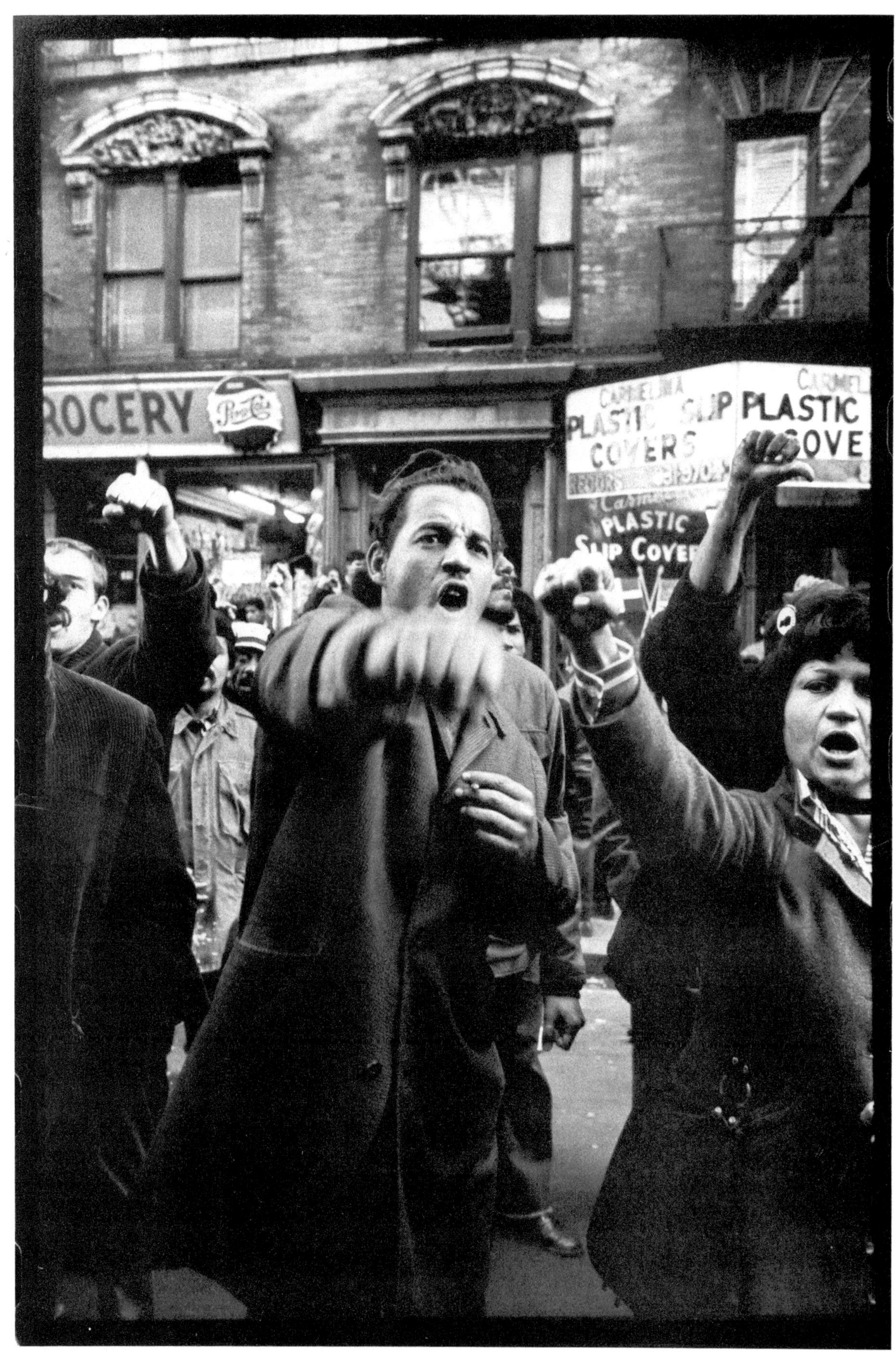

DEMONSTRATION OUTSIDE POLICE PRECINCT HOUSE, SEPTEMBER, 1970

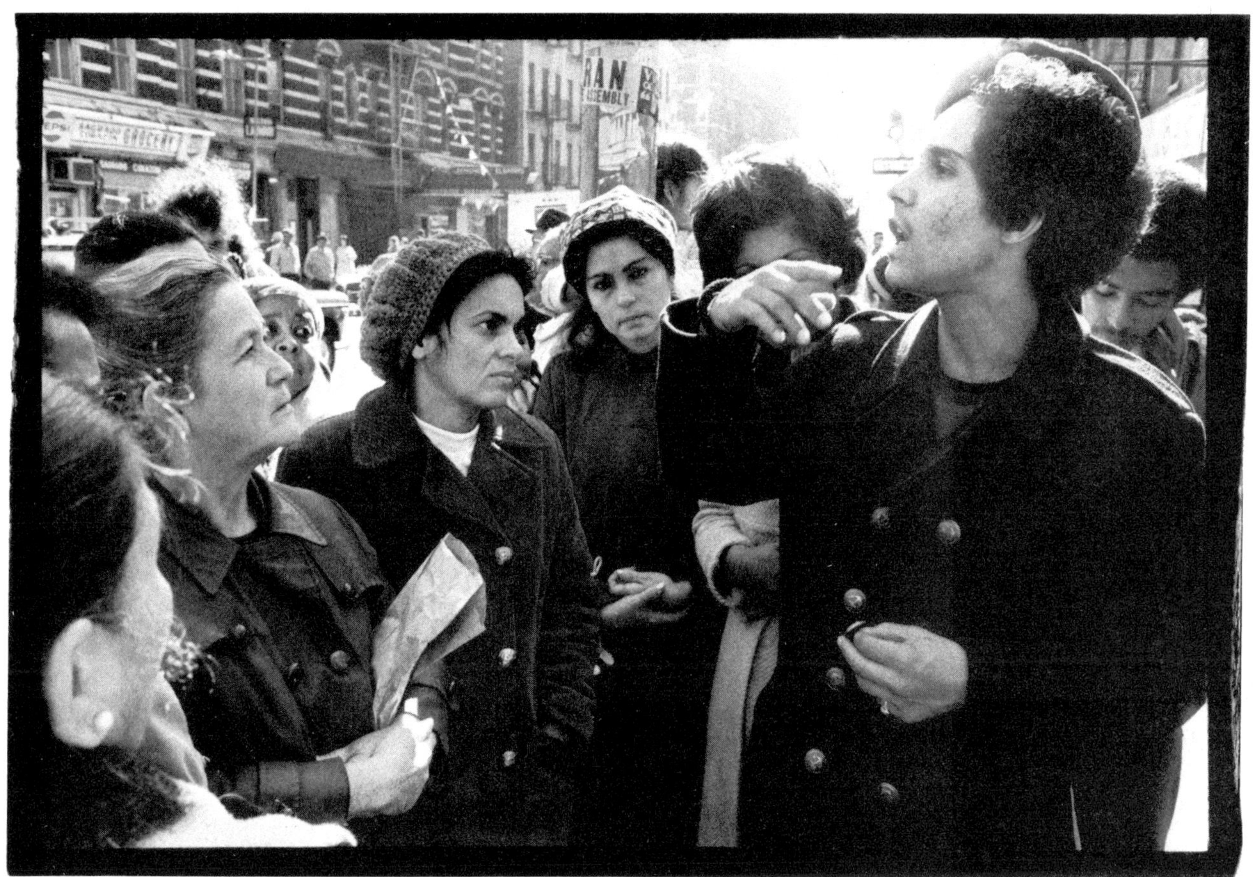

EXPLAINING THE ARMED SEIZURE OF THE PEOPLE'S CHURCH, OCTOBER, 1970

"Our people have a sense of no worth. The oppressor is everything and we are nothing. And on that basis, it is very hard for people to take hold of their destiny, to take hold of their own future, and to say that we are going to make our own history."

"The concept of winning, that is the number one contribution of the Young Lords Party– that is what we are!"

YOUNG LORDS SUPPORTER—
MARCH TO THE UNITED NATIONS, OCTOBER 30, 1970

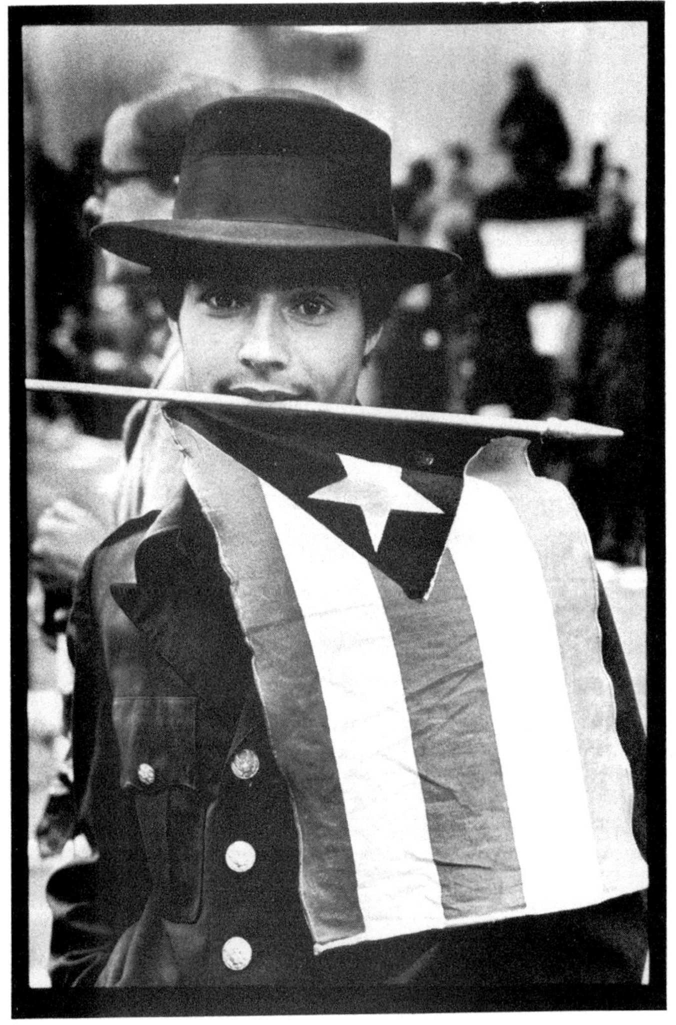

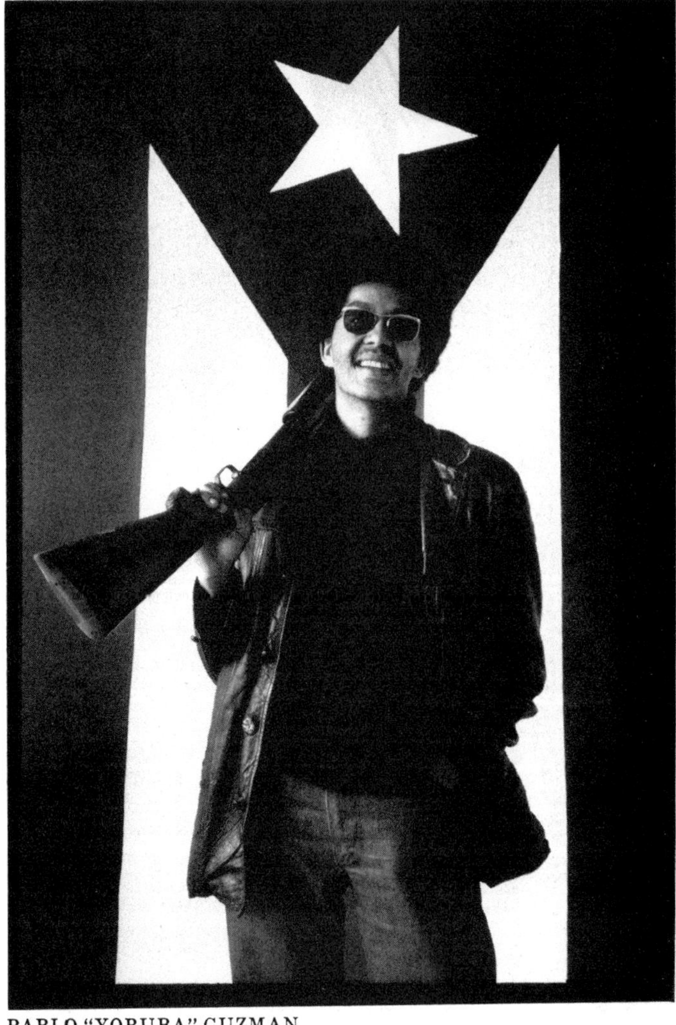

PABLO "YORUBA" GUZMAN

MEMBER OF PUERTO RICAN STUDENT UNION, OCTOBER 30, 1970

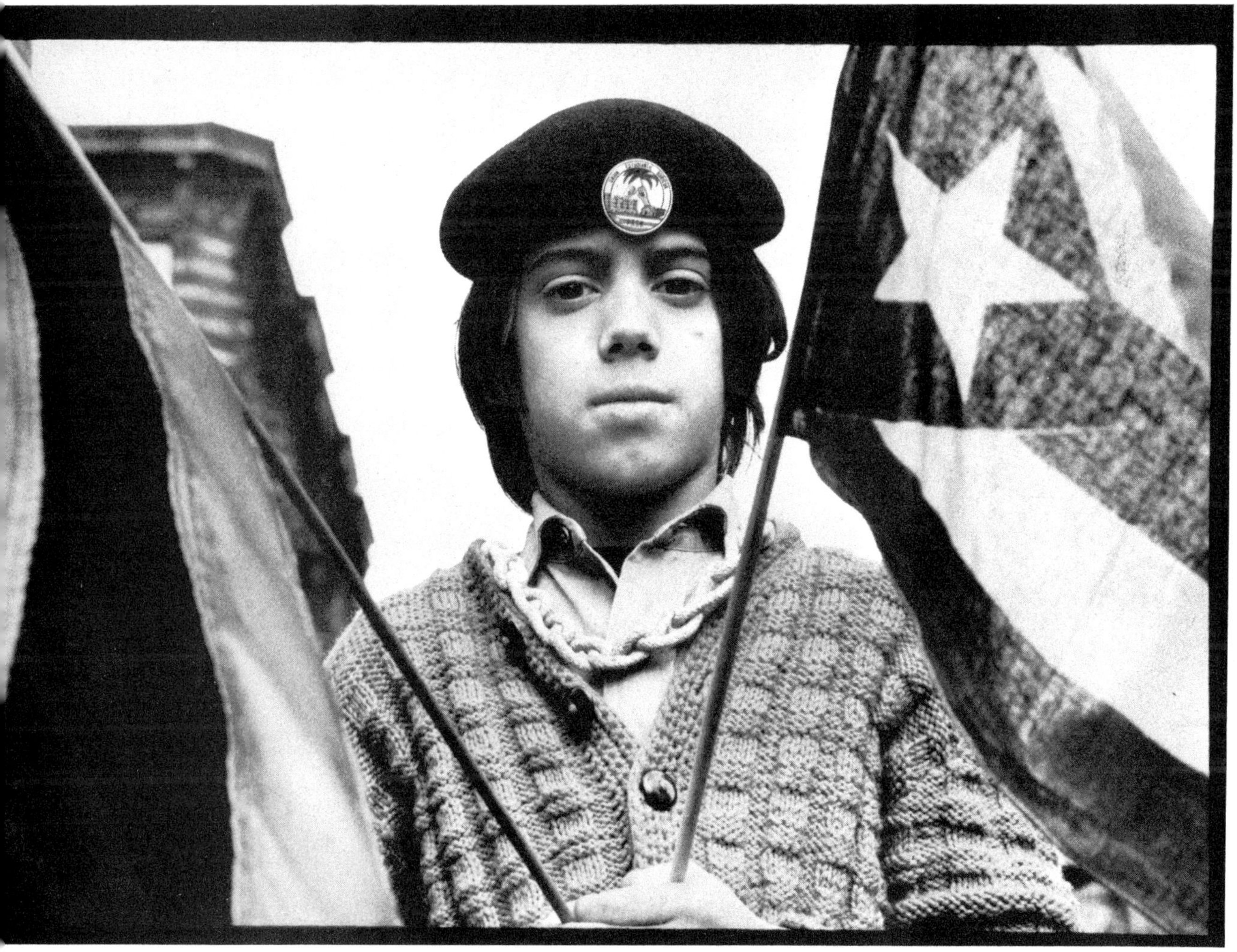

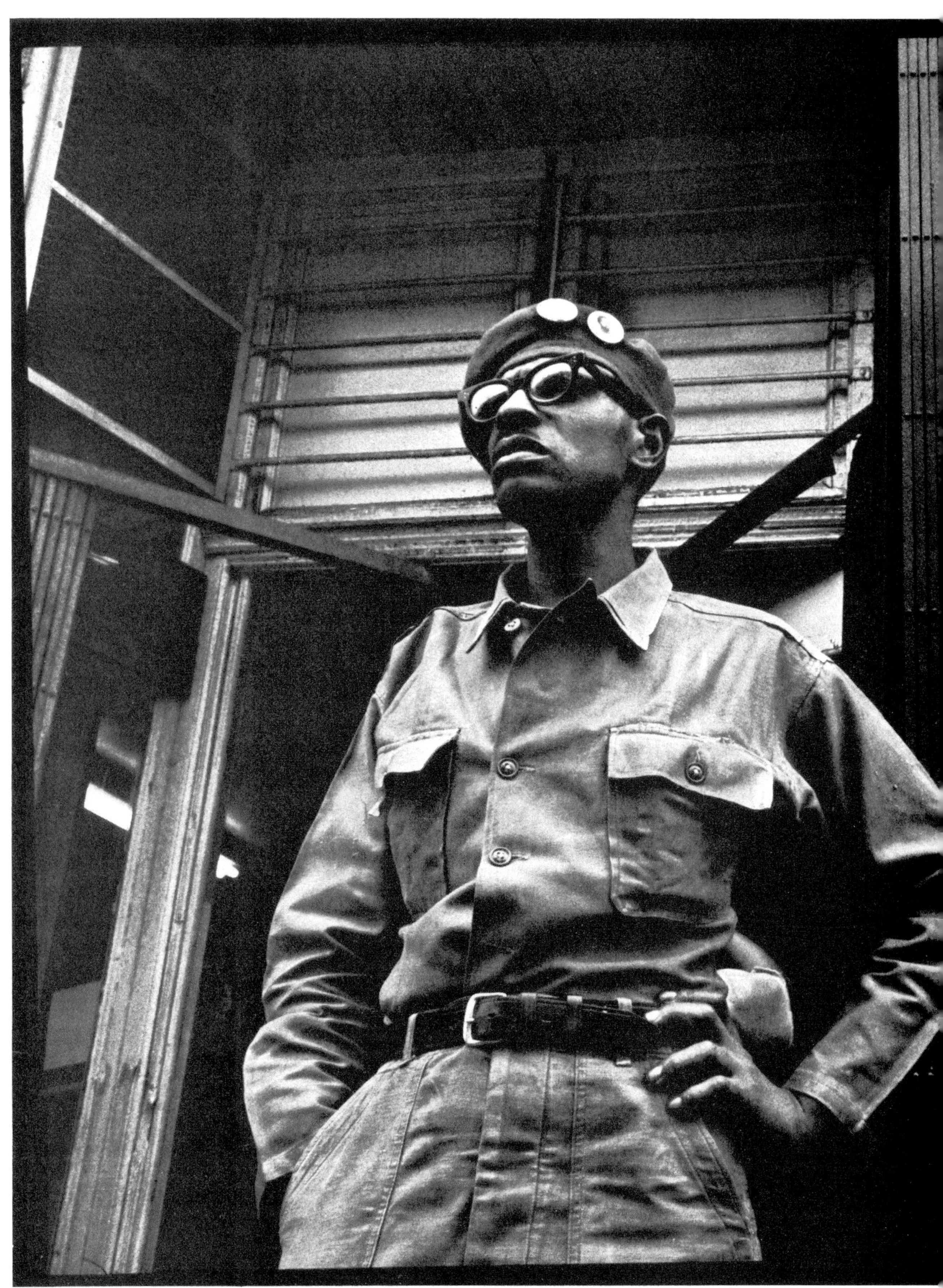

CHE JA-JA, BRONX OFFICE, MAY, 1970

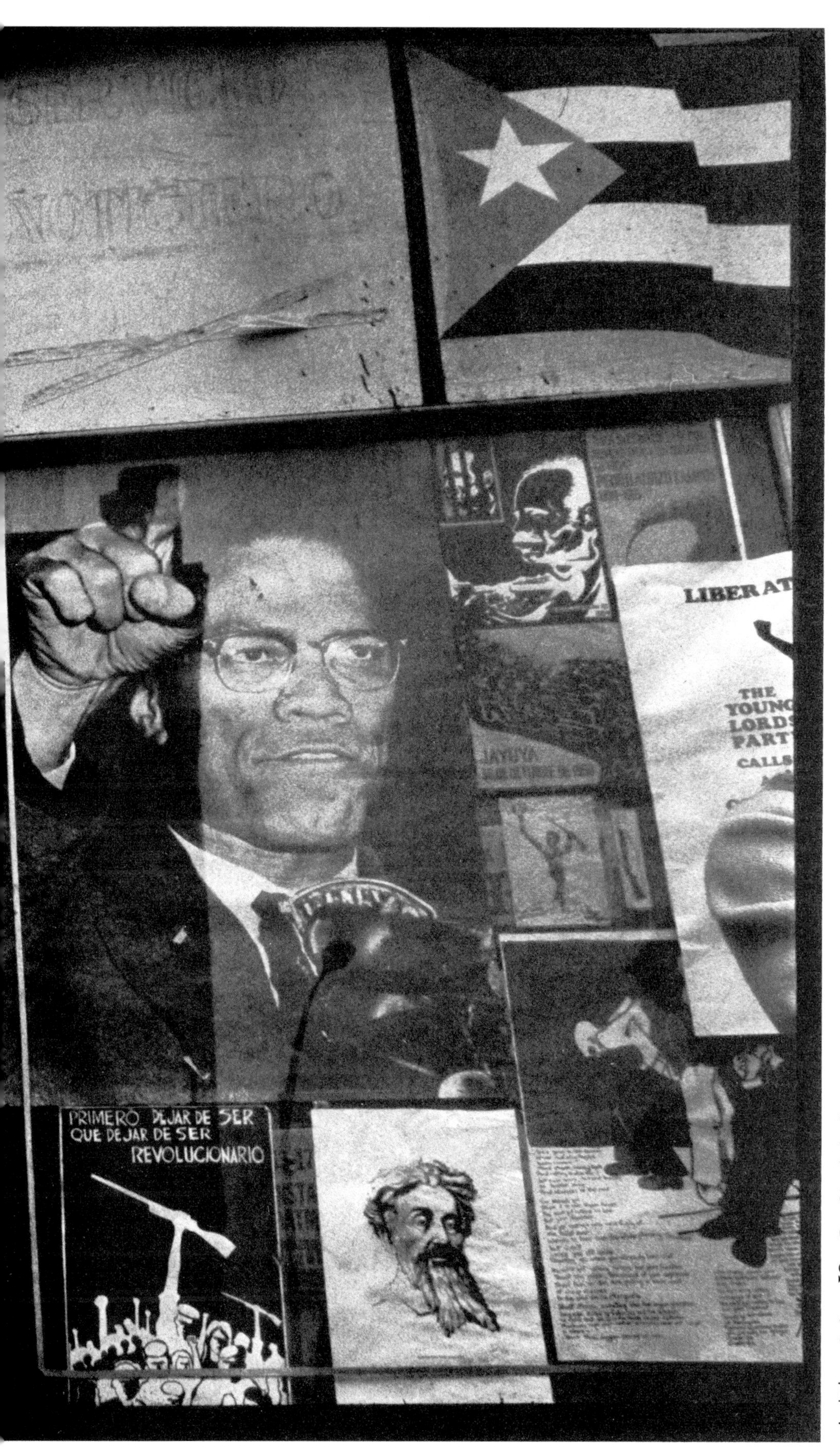

"We're talking about creating individuals who are 'selfless'–or as close to being selfless as possible. ...So that we say, 'First there is my nation, and last there is myself.'"

BOBBY LEMUS, RALLY FOR JUAN "FI" ORTIZ, EAST HARLEM, JUNE, 1970

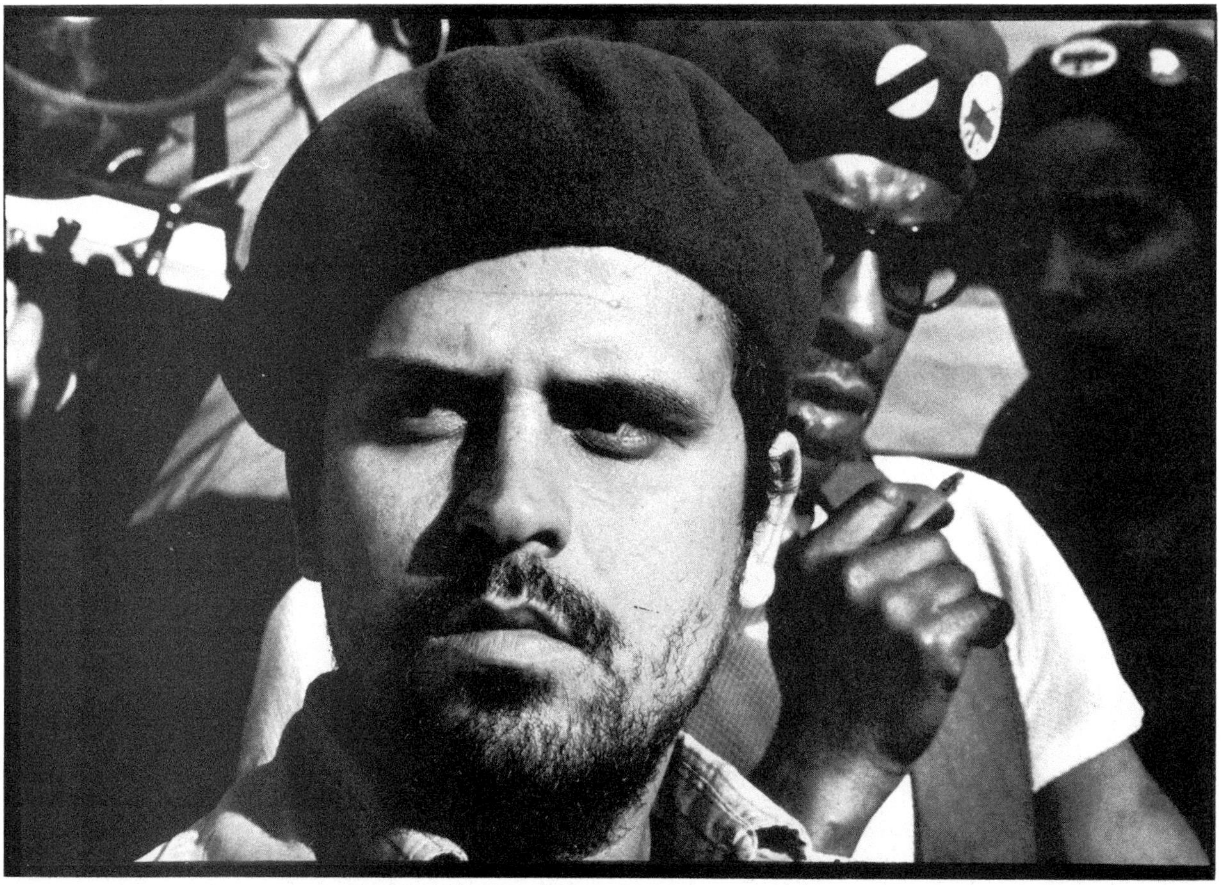

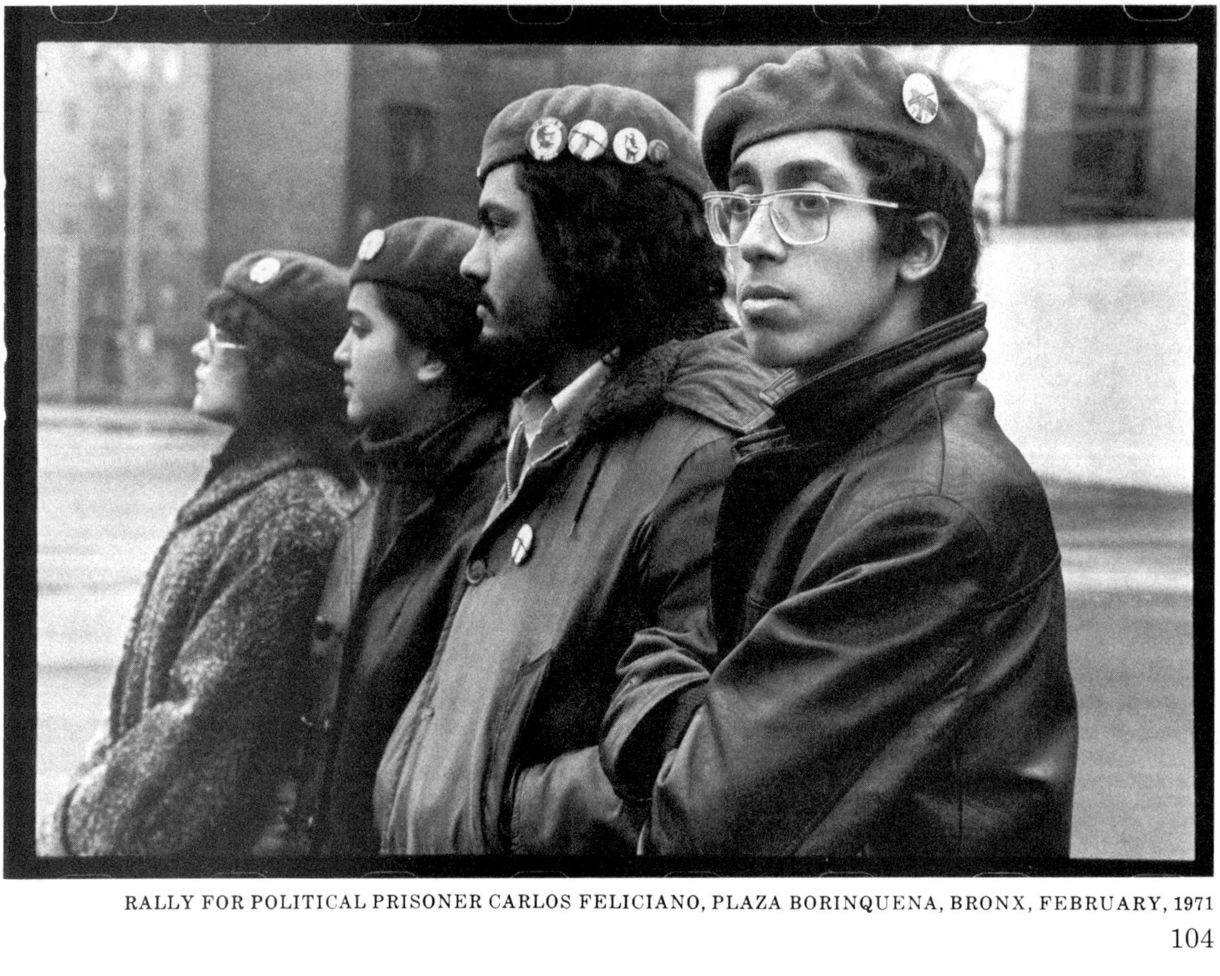

RALLY FOR POLITICAL PRISONER CARLOS FELICIANO, PLAZA BORINQUENA, BRONX, FEBRUARY, 1971

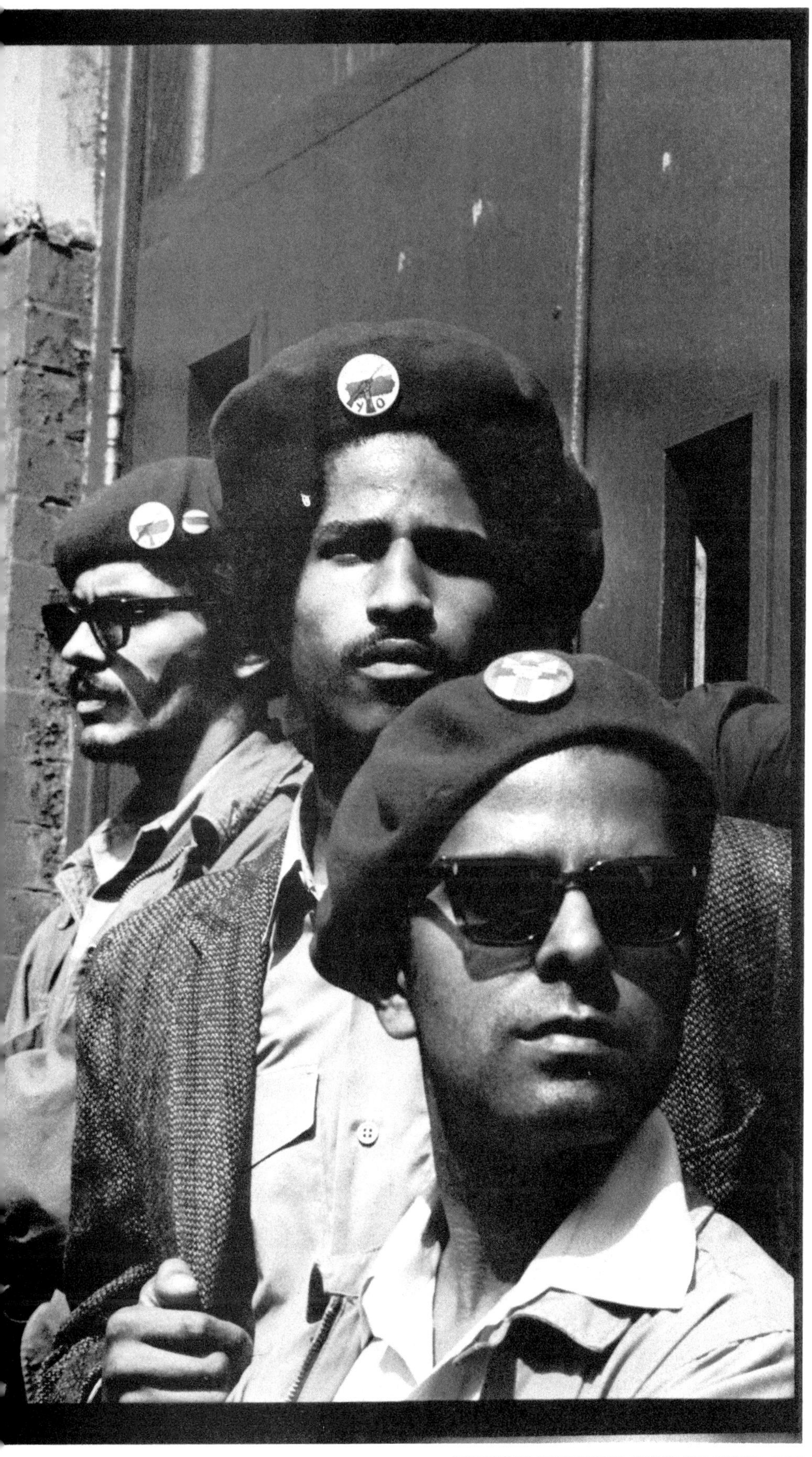

OUTSIDE PEOPLE'S CHURCH, JUNE, 1970

"Revolution is the most serious of jobs. It is not an ego trip or a party. When the people join in revolutionary war, they do so because they have been convinced by both actual conditions and political education that there is no other way out, that their lives and those of their families are threatened."

"People cheered the revolutionary contingent not because we were new, but because we truly represented them. We represented every Puerto Rican standing on the sidewalks. We marched for our people chanting, 'Despierta boricua, defiende lo tuyo. Jibaro sí, yanqui no! A Vietnam yo no voy, porque yanqui yo no soy.'"

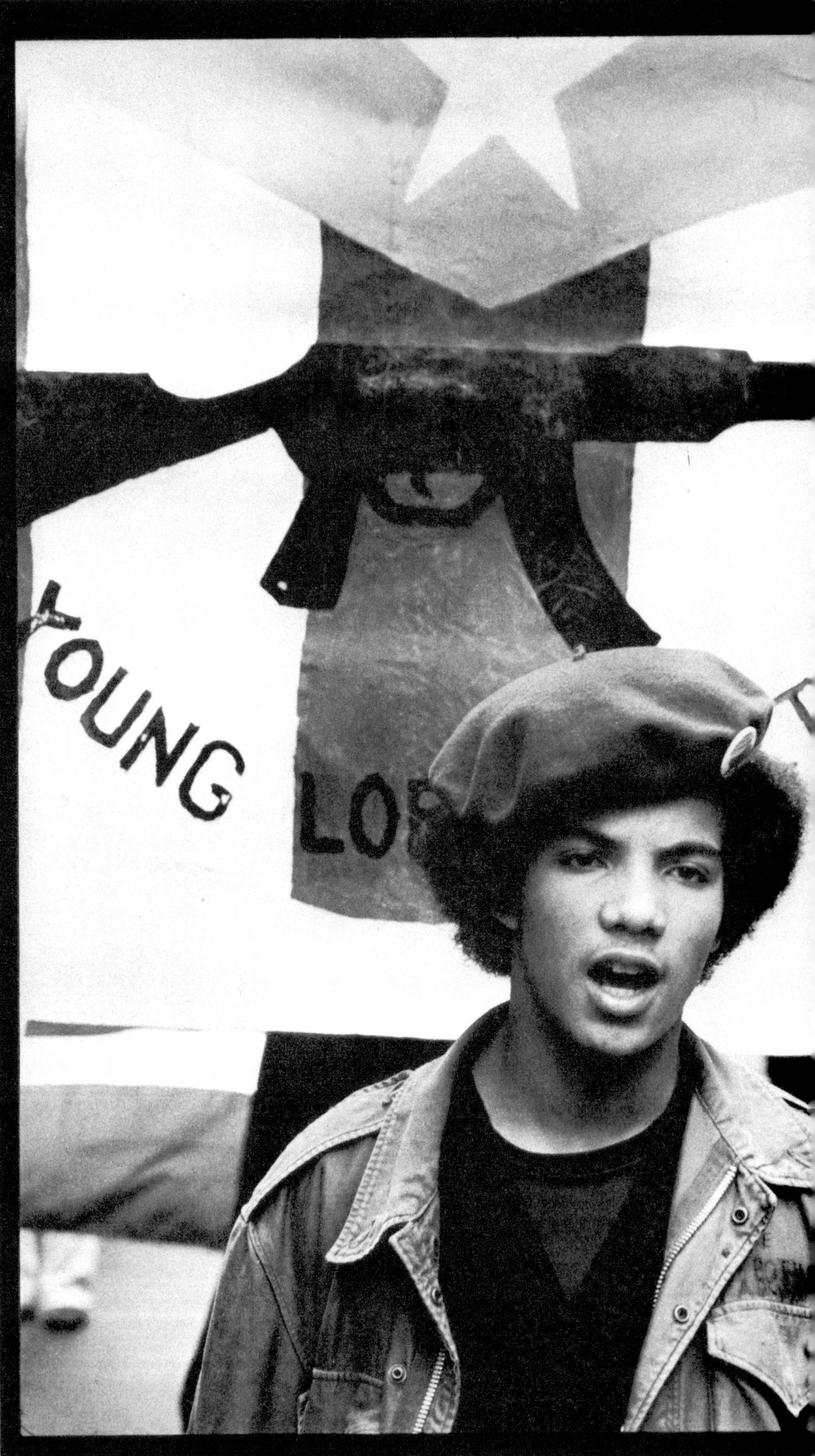

PUERTO RICAN DAY PARADE, JUNE, 1970

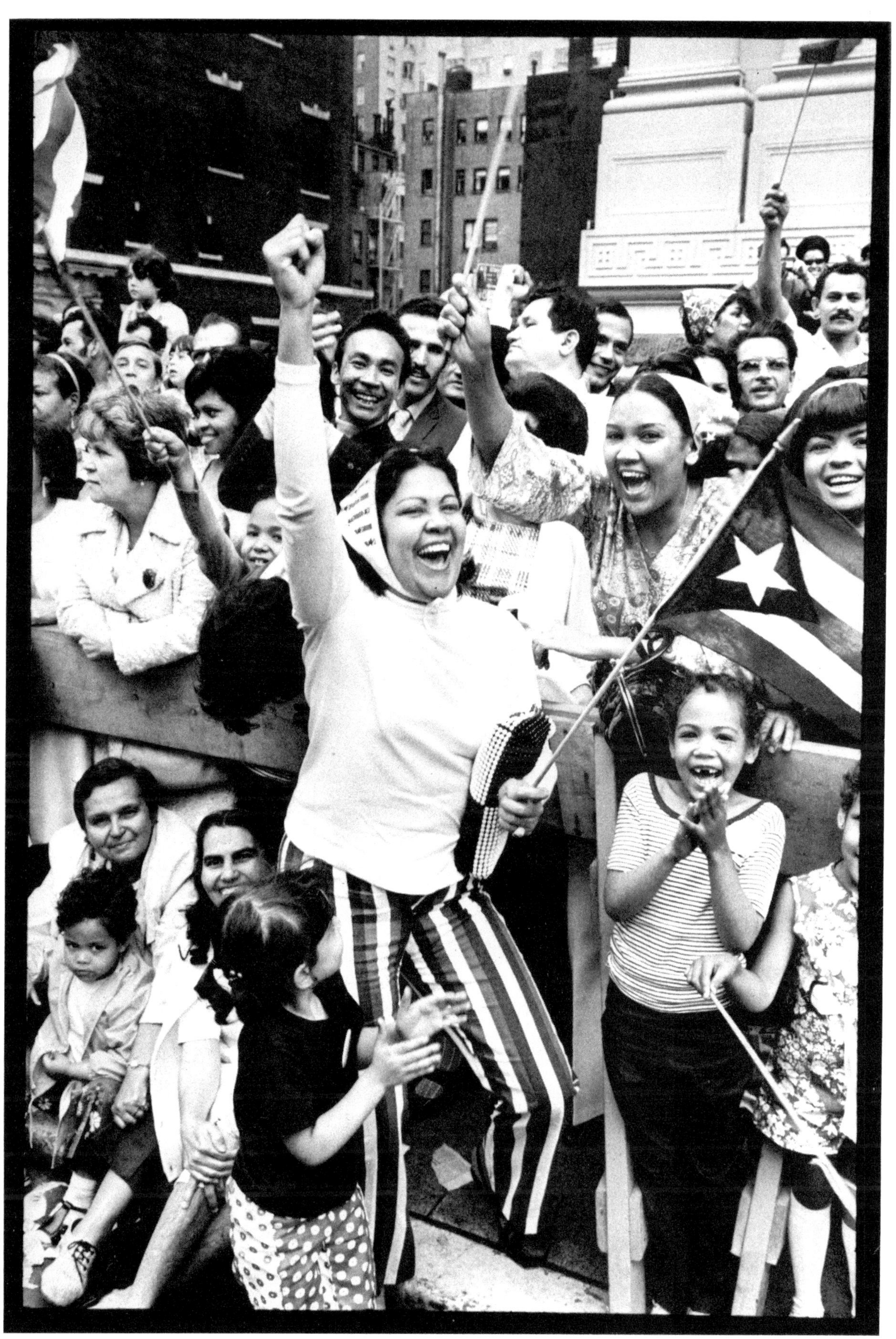

PUERTO RICAN DAY PARADE, PEOPLE CHEER YOUNG LORDS, JUNE, 1970

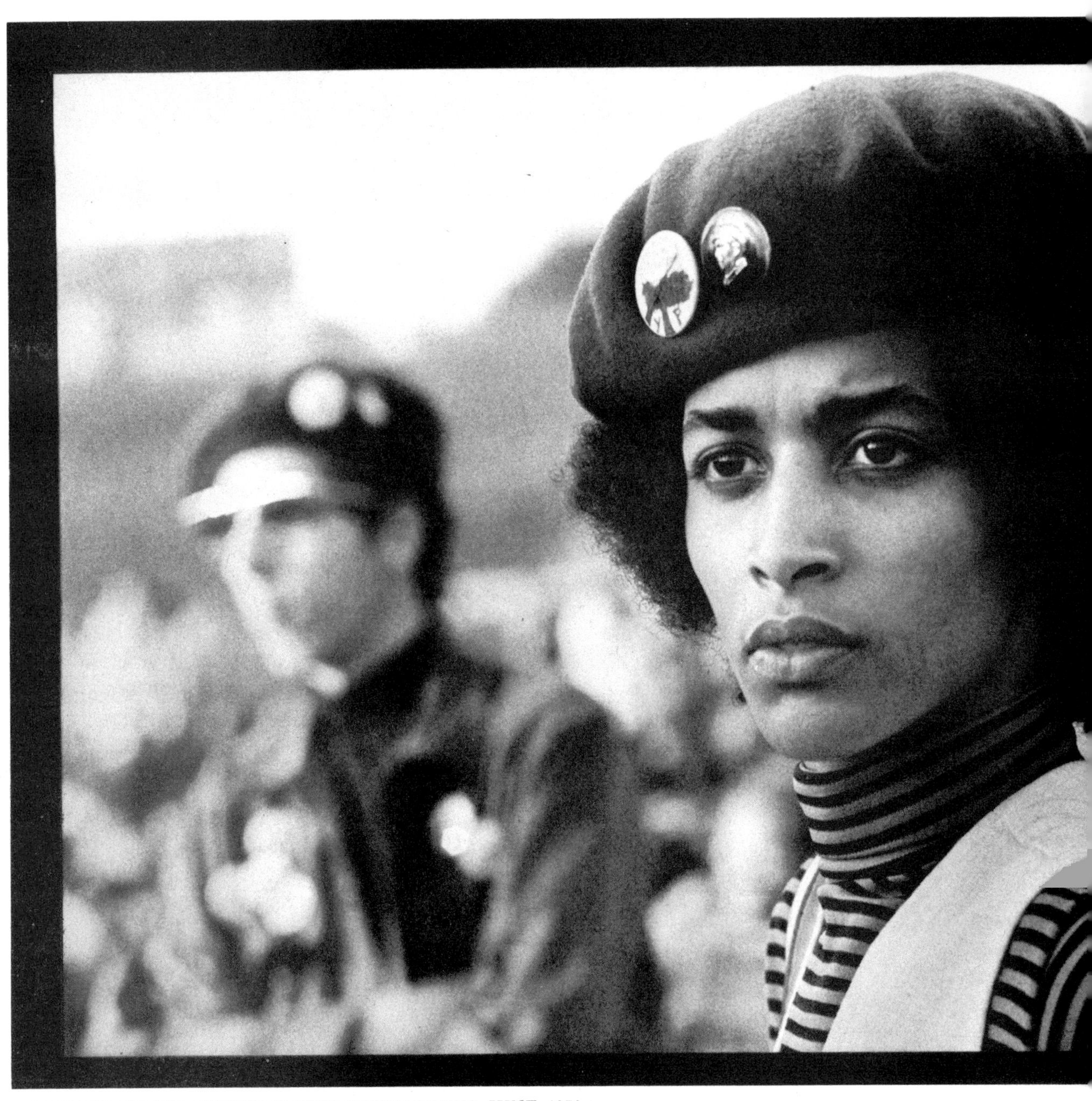

RICHIE RODRIGUEZ, DENISE OLIVER, BOBBY LEMUS, JUNE, 1970

MARCH FOR POLITICAL PRISONER CARLOS FELICIANO, BRONX, FEBRUARY, 1971

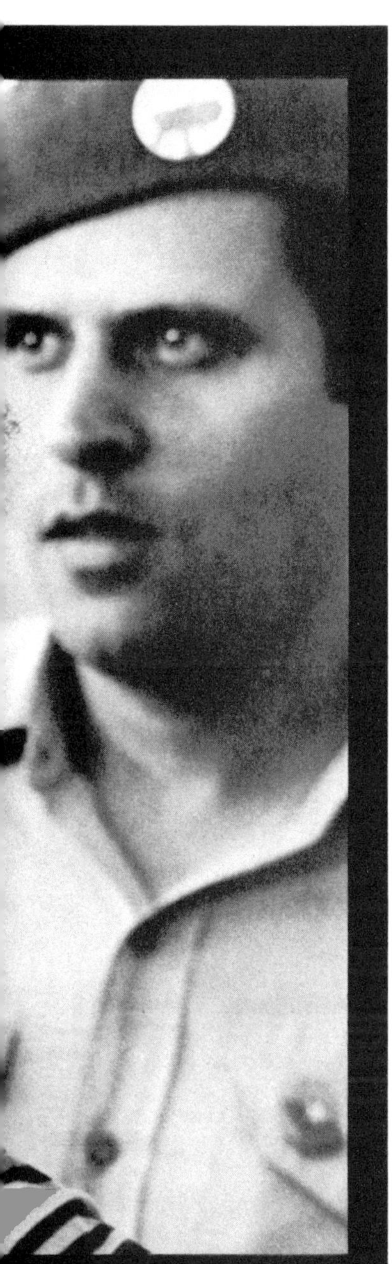

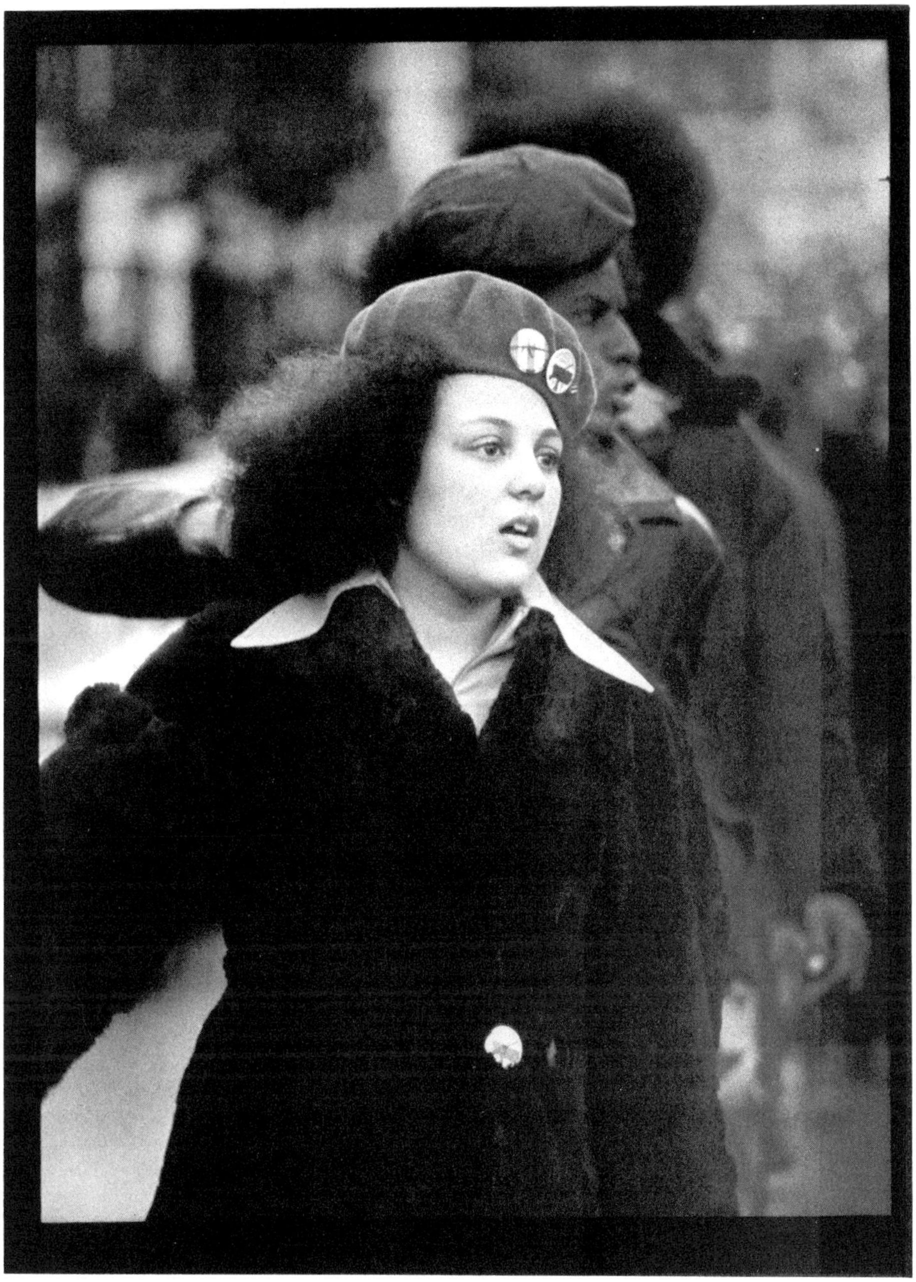

"We believe that a man's and a woman's
most precious possession is life.
We should therefore live our lives
so that we are not consumed by the anguish of
long years of purposeless existence,
or the shame of a trivial and cowardly past,
so that we may say when we die:
We give our energies to the most noble
cause in the world–the struggle
for the liberation of the human race!"

PEOPLE'S CHURCH—AFTER PUERTO RICAN DAY PARADE, JUNE, 1970

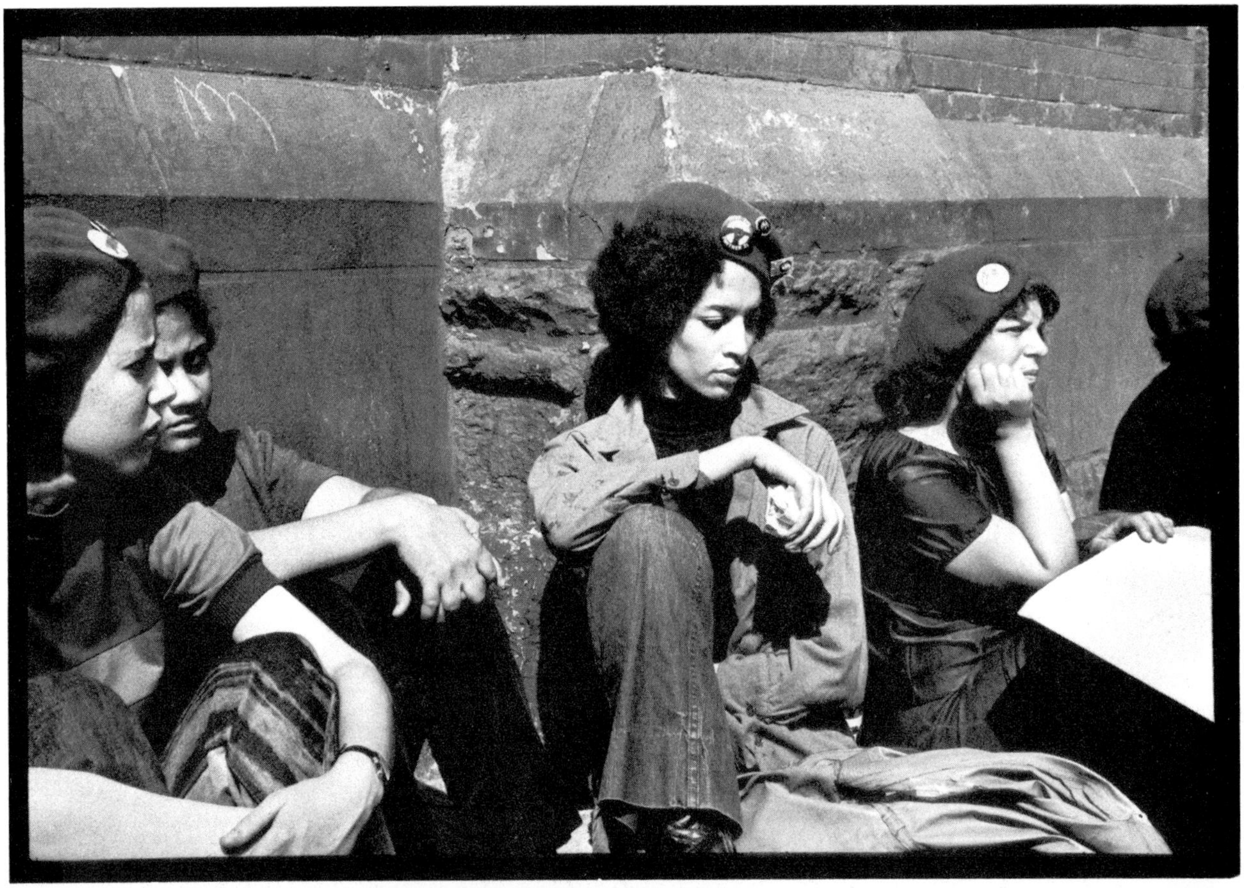

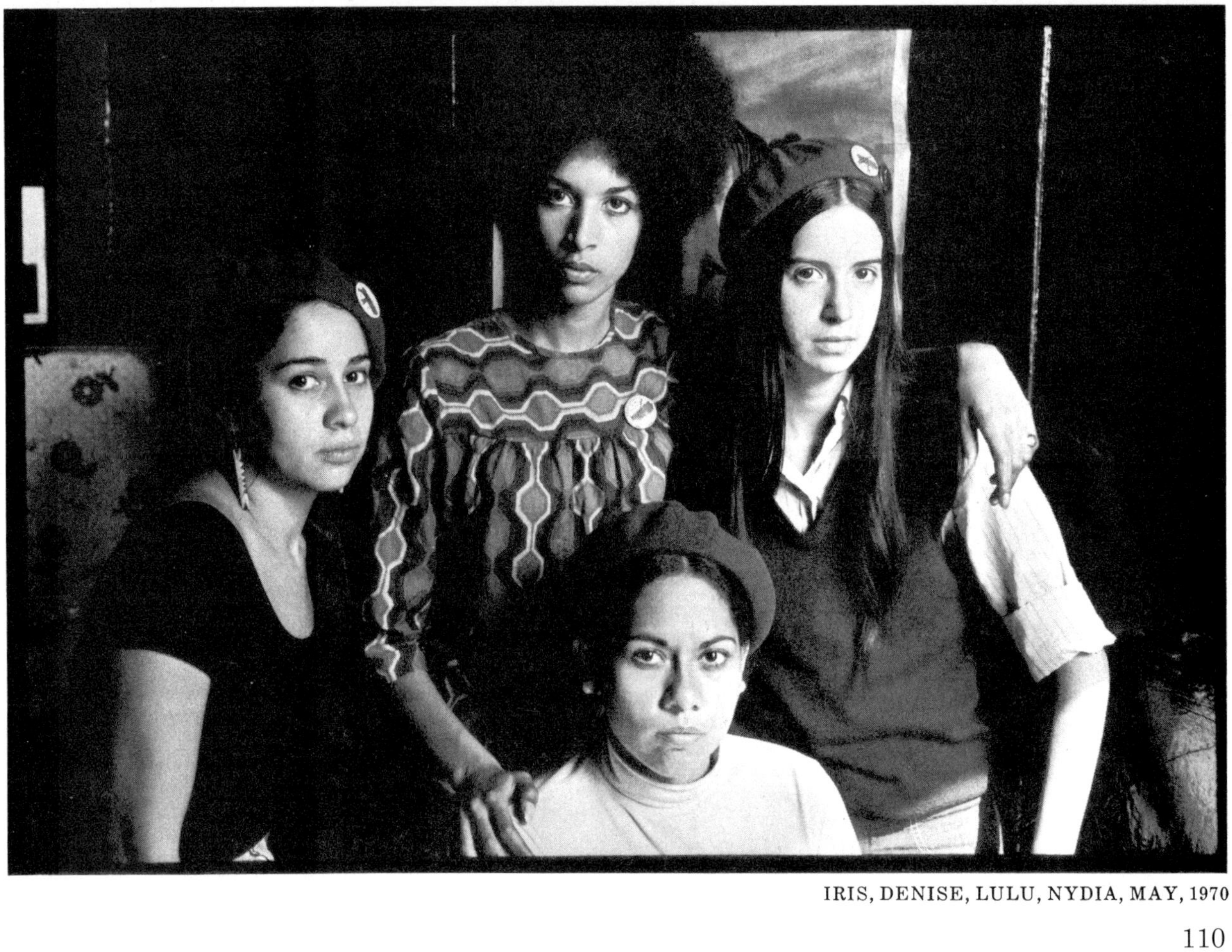

IRIS, DENISE, LULU, NYDIA, MAY, 1970

"Third World women have an integral role to play in the liberation of all oppressed people. In the struggle for national liberation they must press for the equality of women. The woman's struggle is the revolution within the revolution. Puerto Rican women will be neither behind nor in front of their brothers but always alongside them in mutual respect and love."

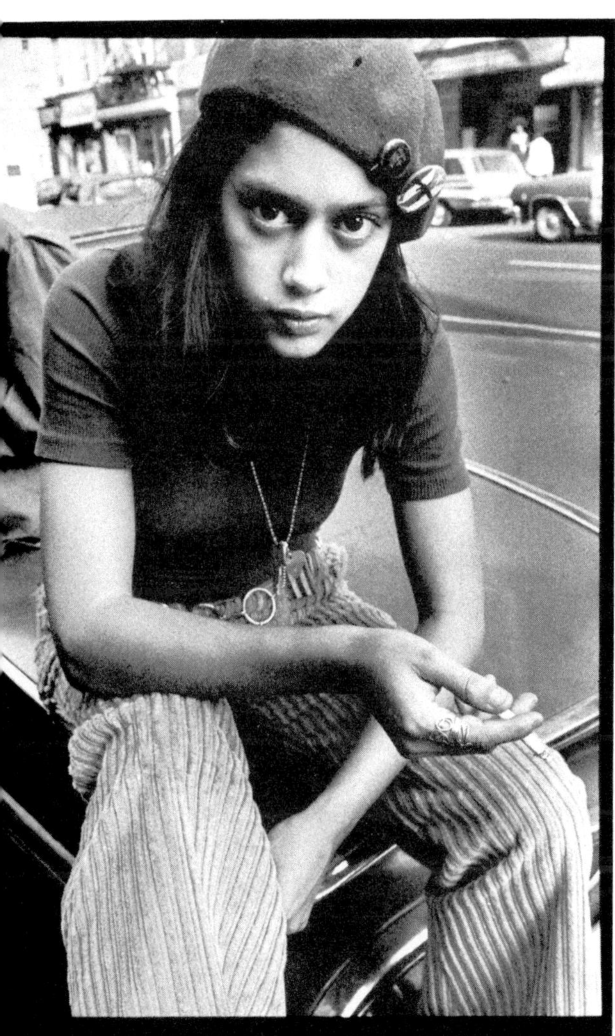

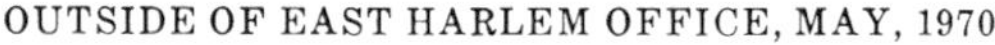

OUTSIDE OF EAST HARLEM OFFICE, MAY, 1970

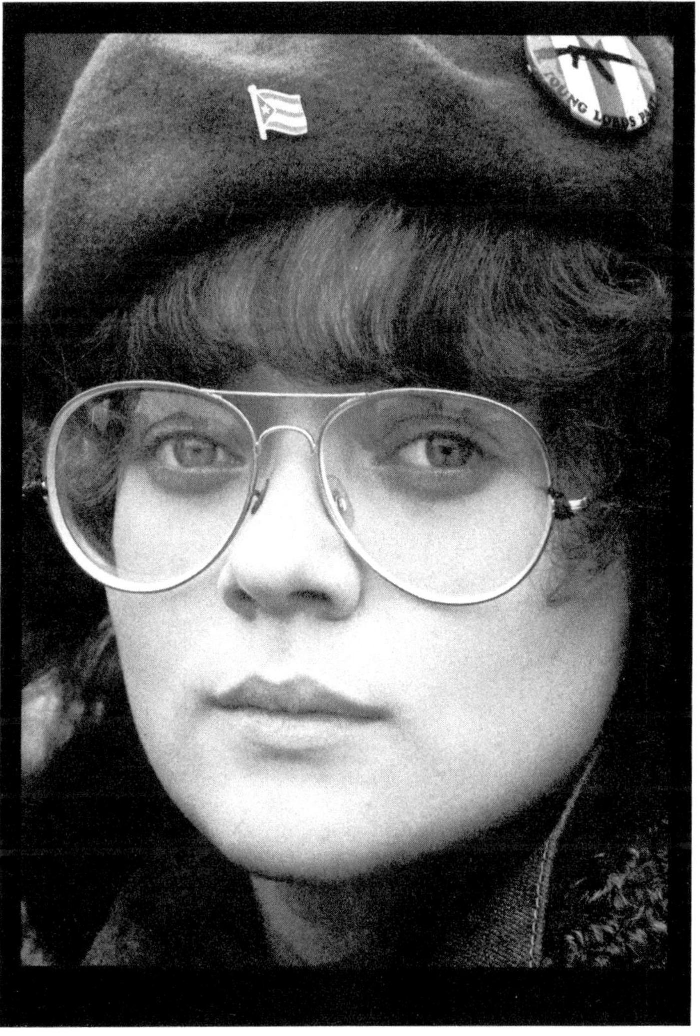

OLGIE ROBLES, FEBRUARY, 1971

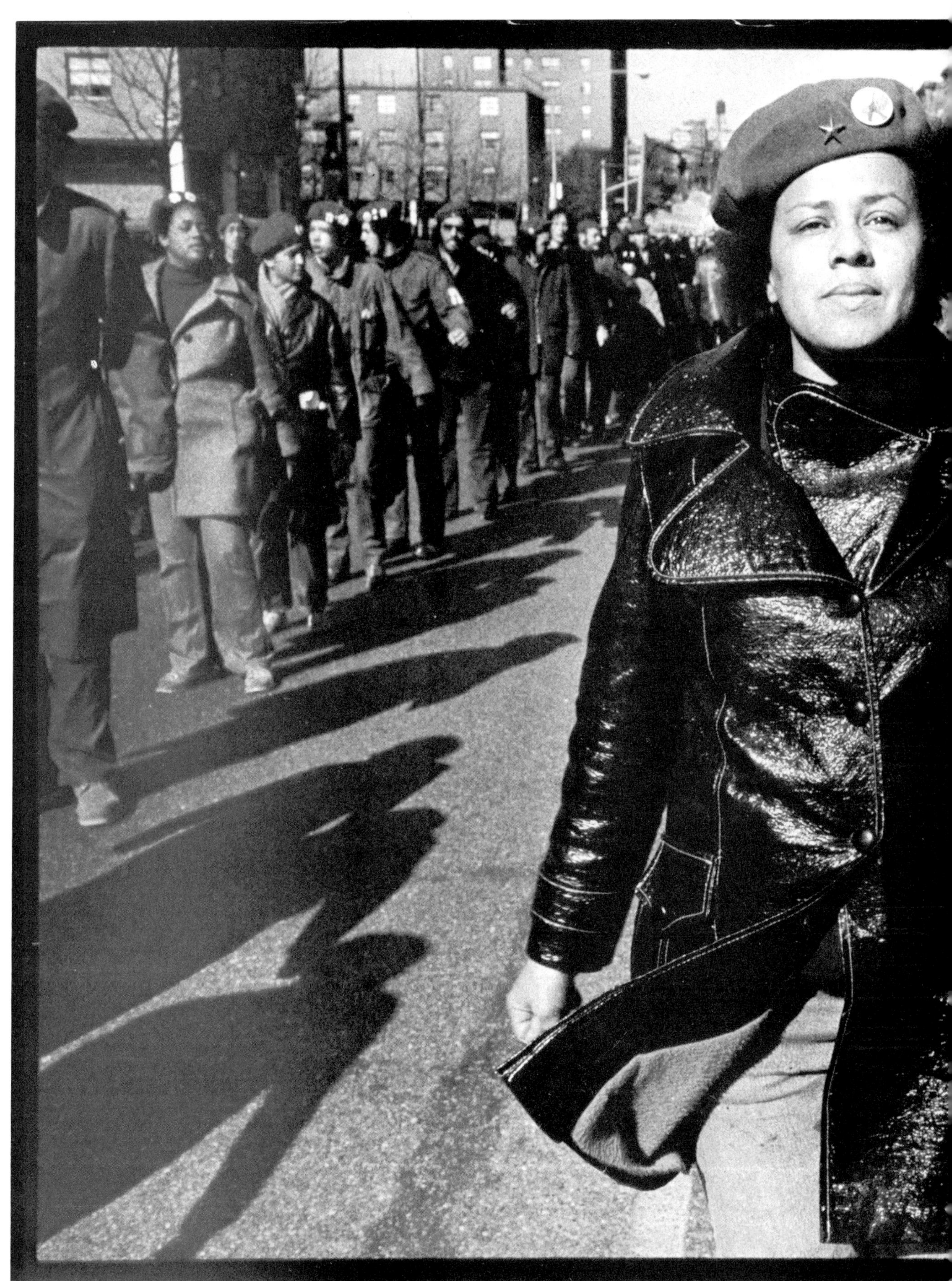

MARCH FOR POLITICAL PRISONER CARLOS FELICIANO, BRONX, MARCH, 1971

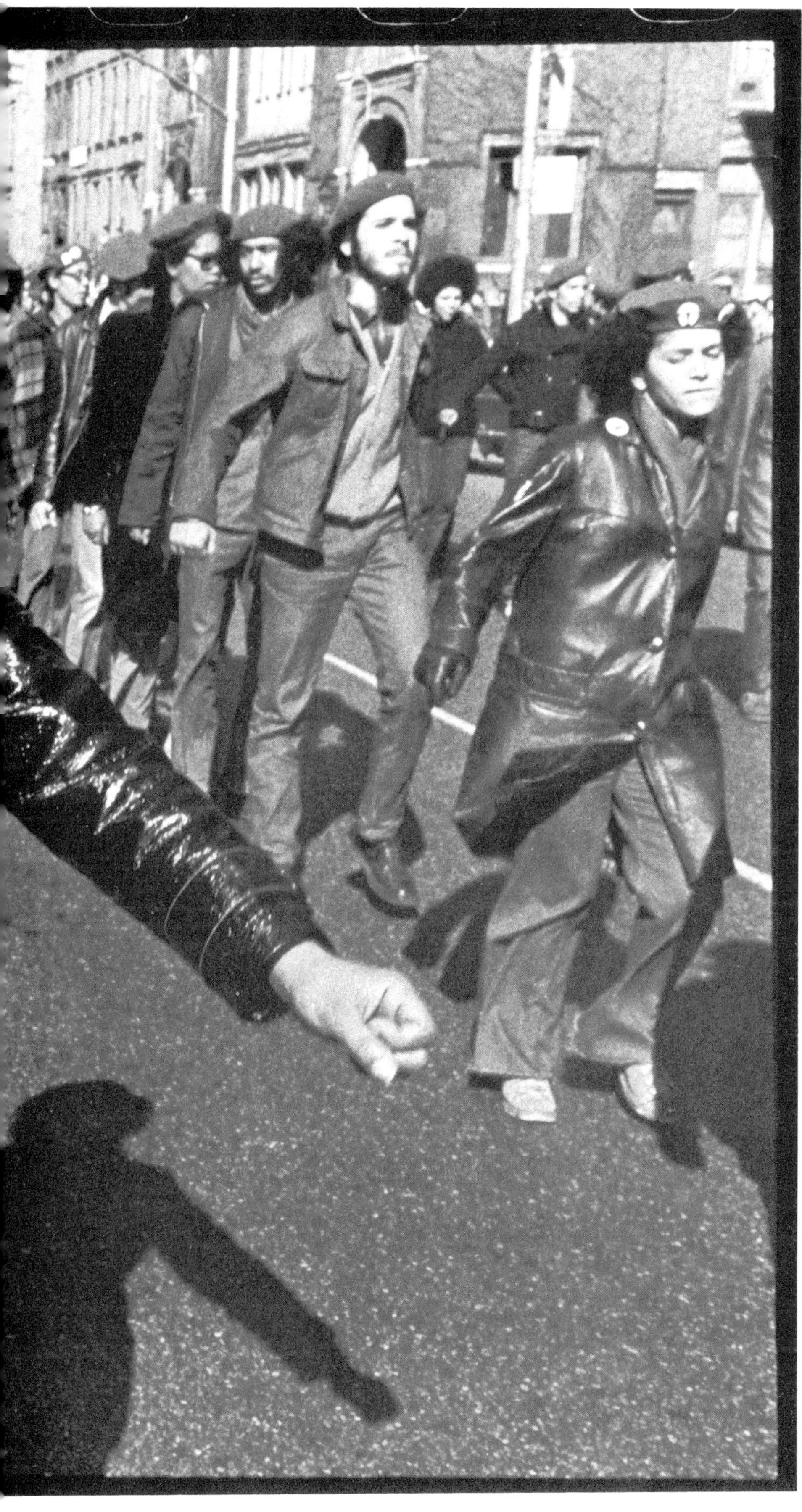

"Carlos Feliciano was accused of being a member of MIRA and was held on $100,000 bail. He was thrown into jail without any way of getting out. So the bail then becomes not bail, but ransom instead."

EAST HARLEM PROTESTS ARREST OF JUAN "FI" ORTIZ, JUNE, 1970

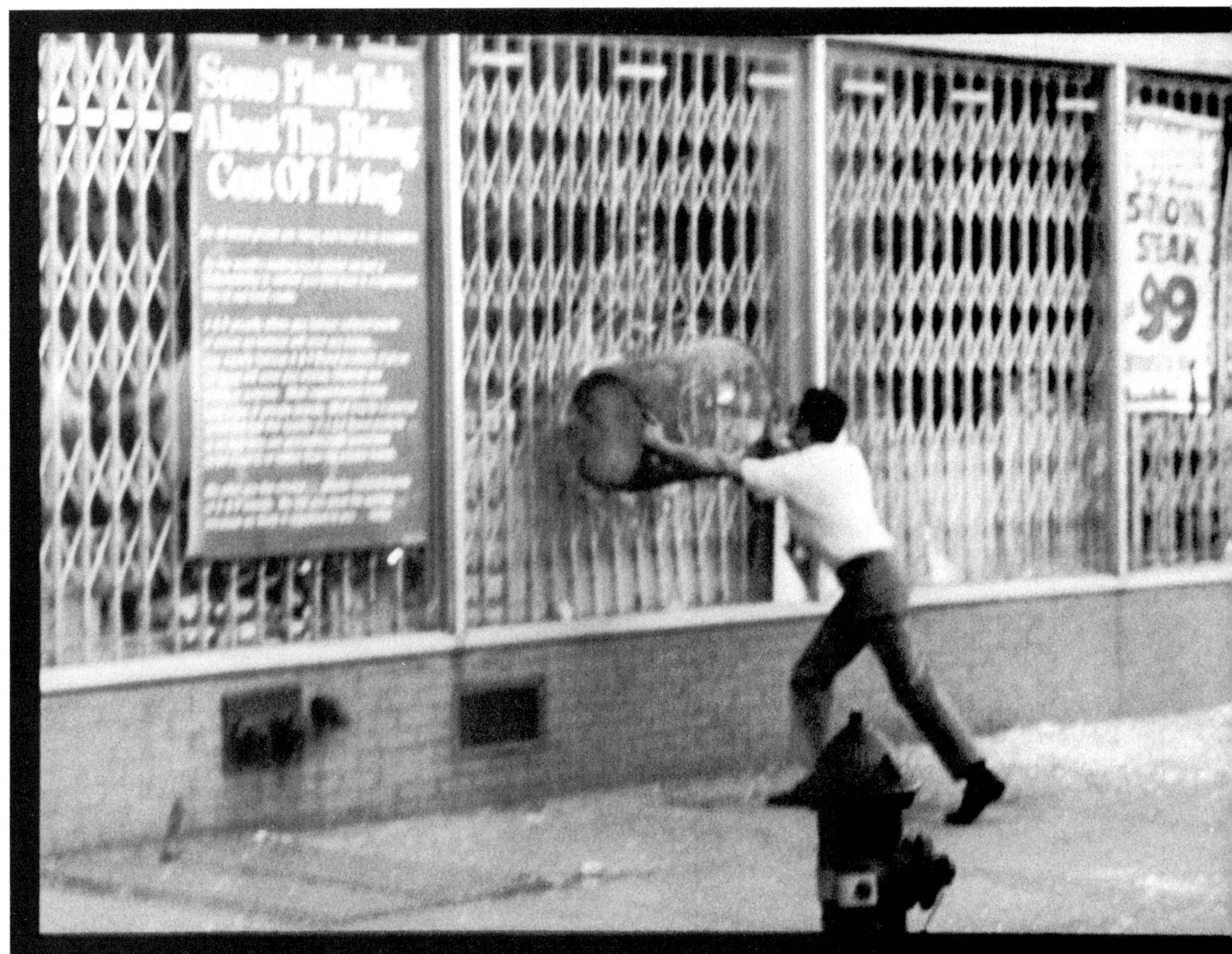

"The people were especially pissed when Fi was busted. As Minister of Finance, he bailed out many brothers and sisters and helped out many families. Behind the bullshit charges of kidnapping, armed robbery, and assault was an obvious attempt to destroy the revolutionary vanguard of the Puerto Rican Movement.... The people understood all this, and on Sunday night their rage exploded."

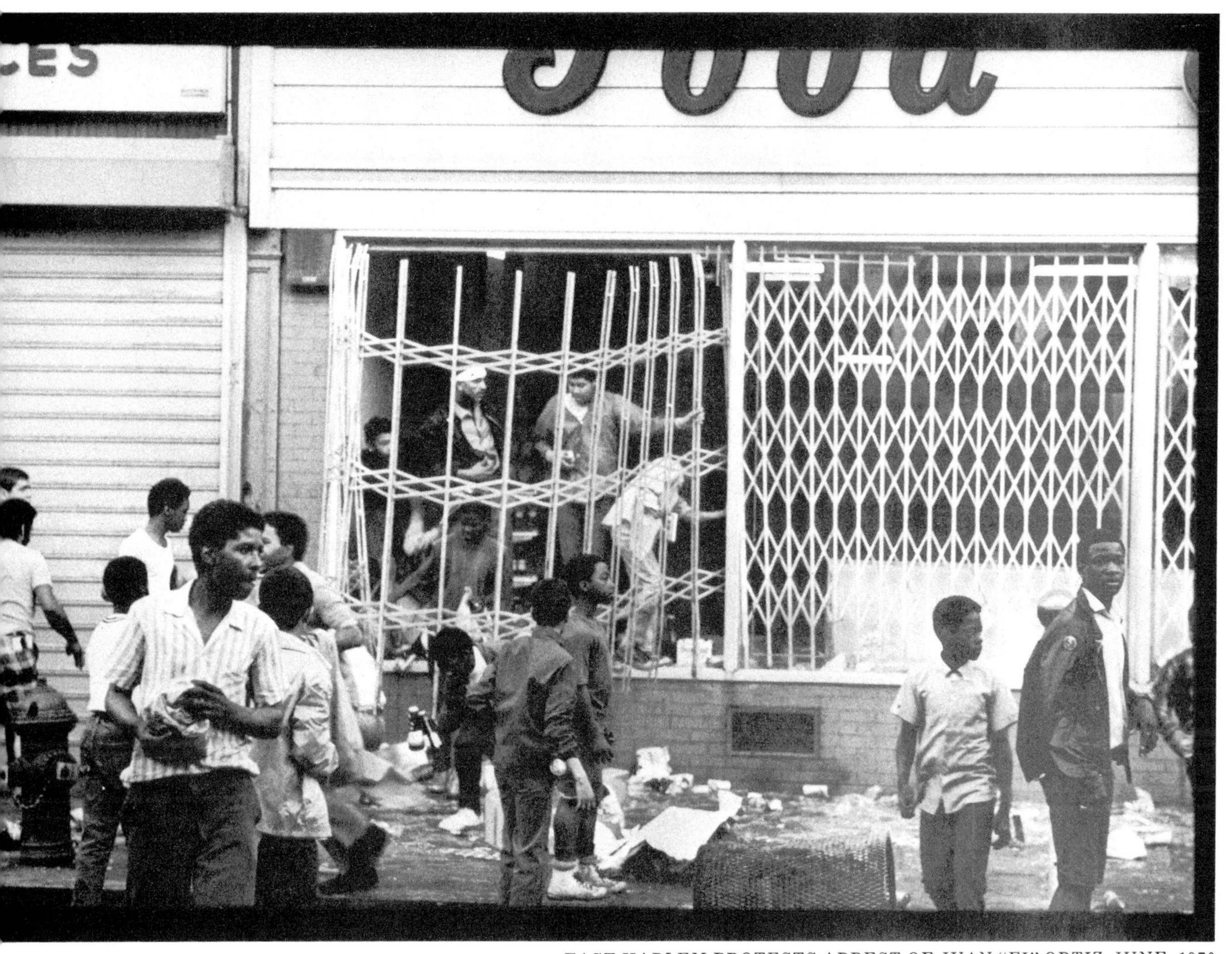

EAST HARLEM PROTESTS ARREST OF JUAN "FI" ORTIZ, JUNE, 1970

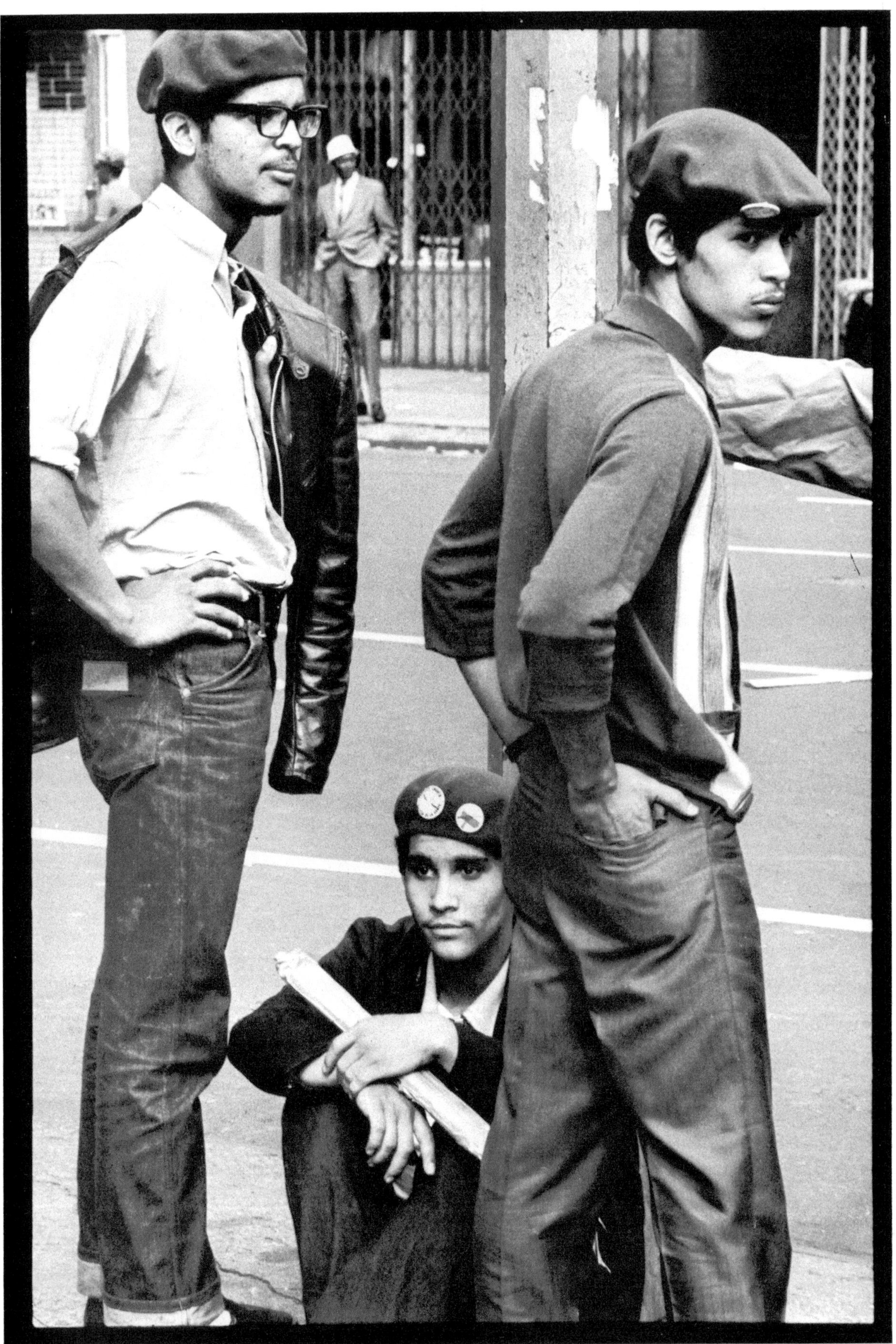

EAST HARLEM, JUNE, 1970

JUAN GONZALEZ SPEAKING ON THE STEPS OF SECOND PEOPLE'S CHURCH, OCTOBER, 1970

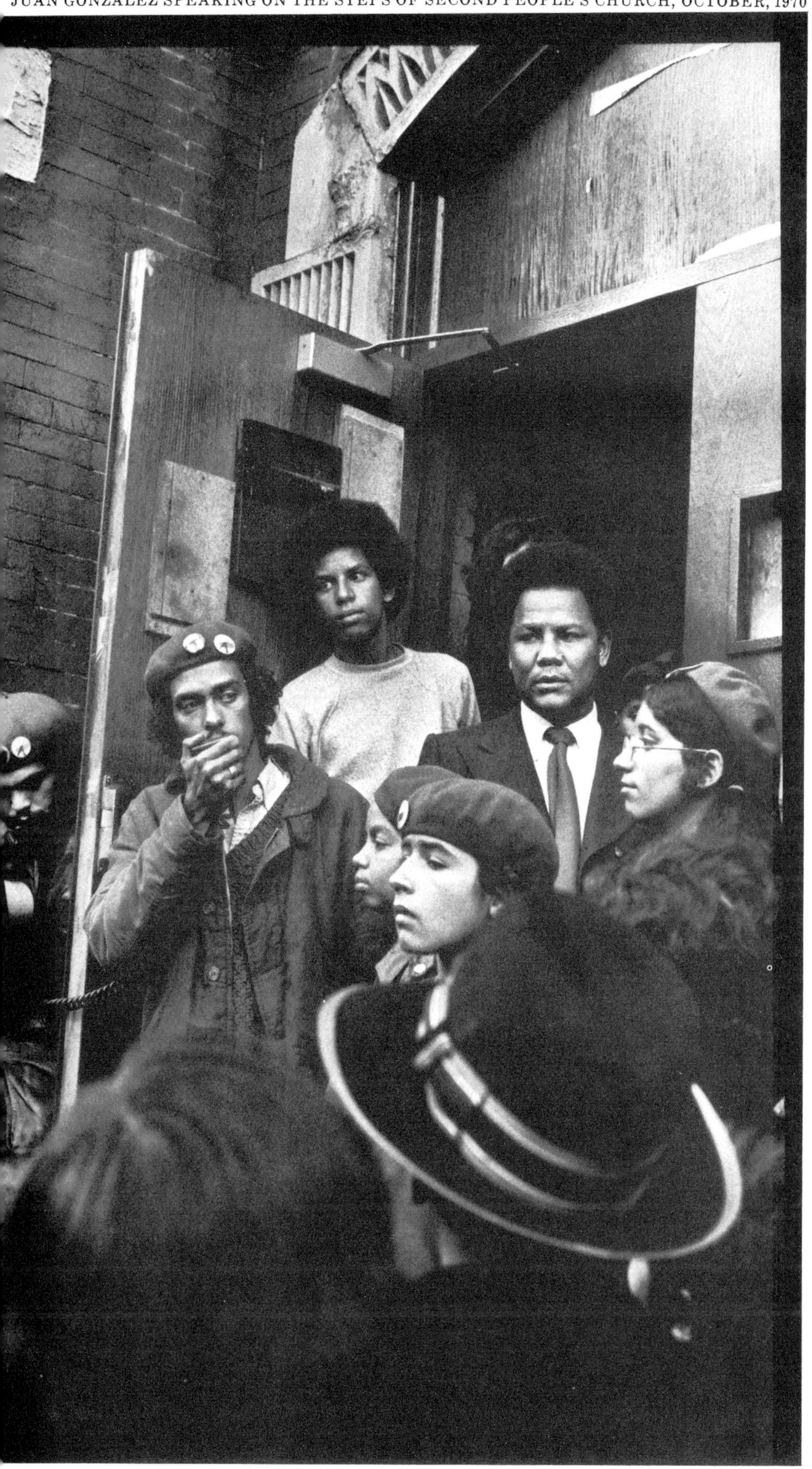

"Our motto is 'We Serve and Protect.' Only through organized change will we end addiction, eliminate landlords, build new cooperative housing, provide jobs for all, assure decent health for everyone, end all wars, and achieve independence for Puerto Rico."

POLICE BREAK UP HEALTH RALLY, 138TH STREET, BRONX, NEW YORK, JULY, 1970

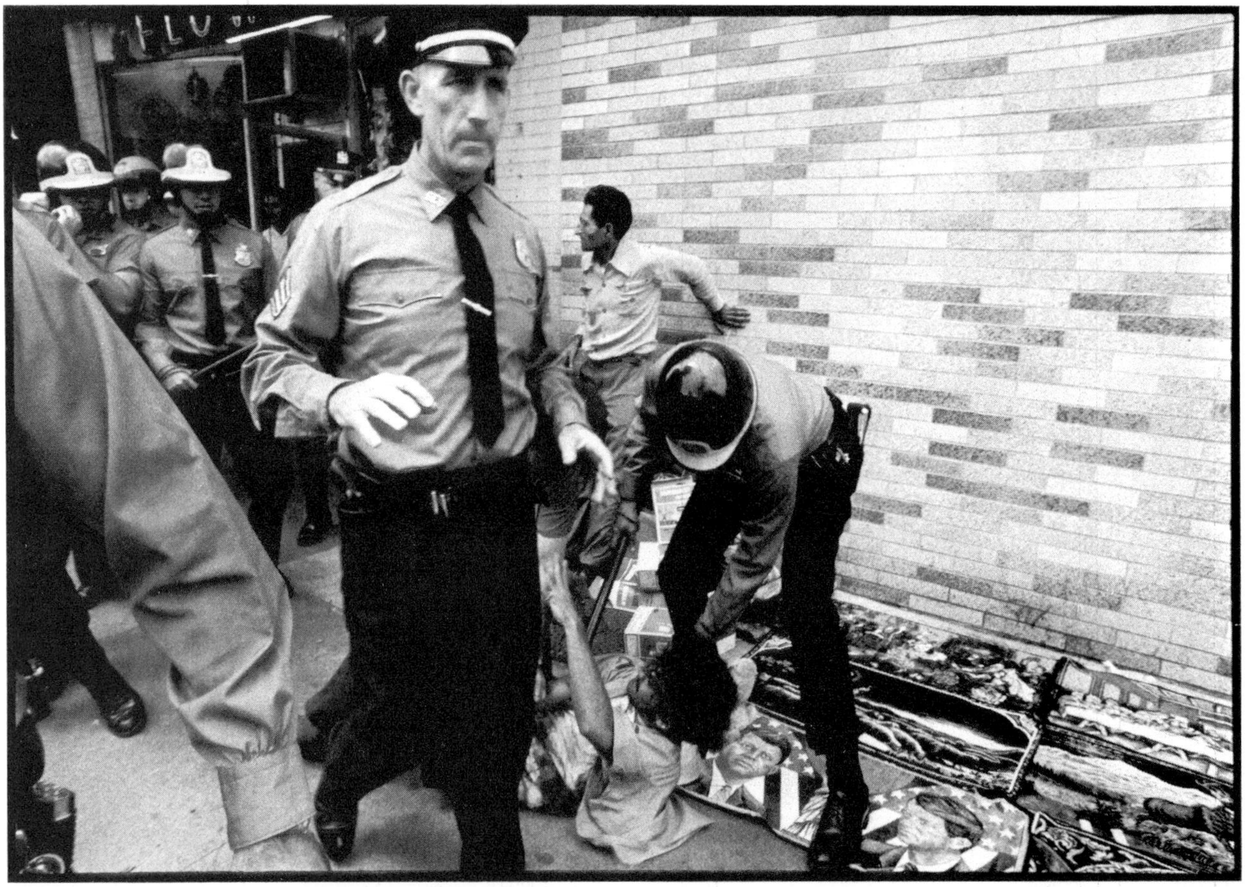

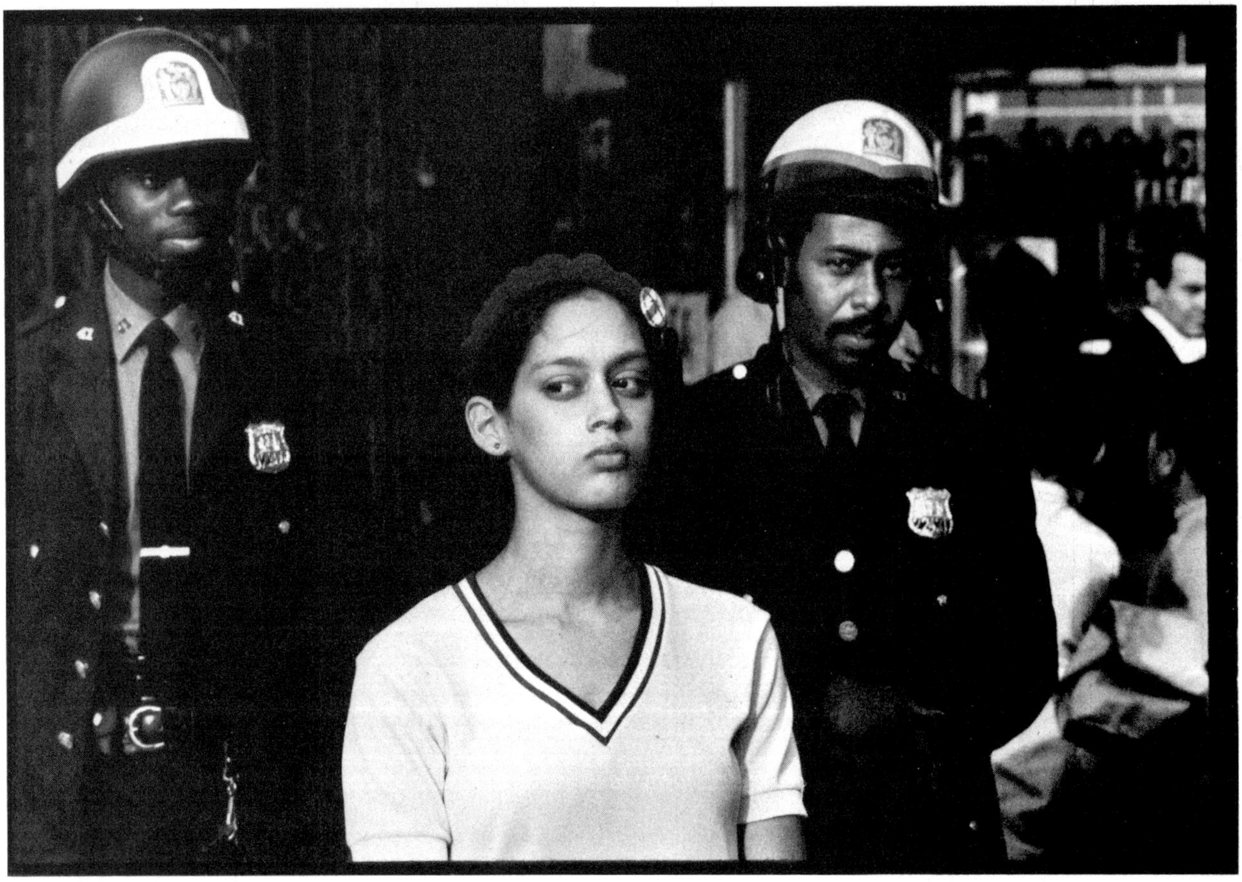

RALLY IN SUPPORT OF PRISON REBELLIONS, SEPTEMBER, 1970

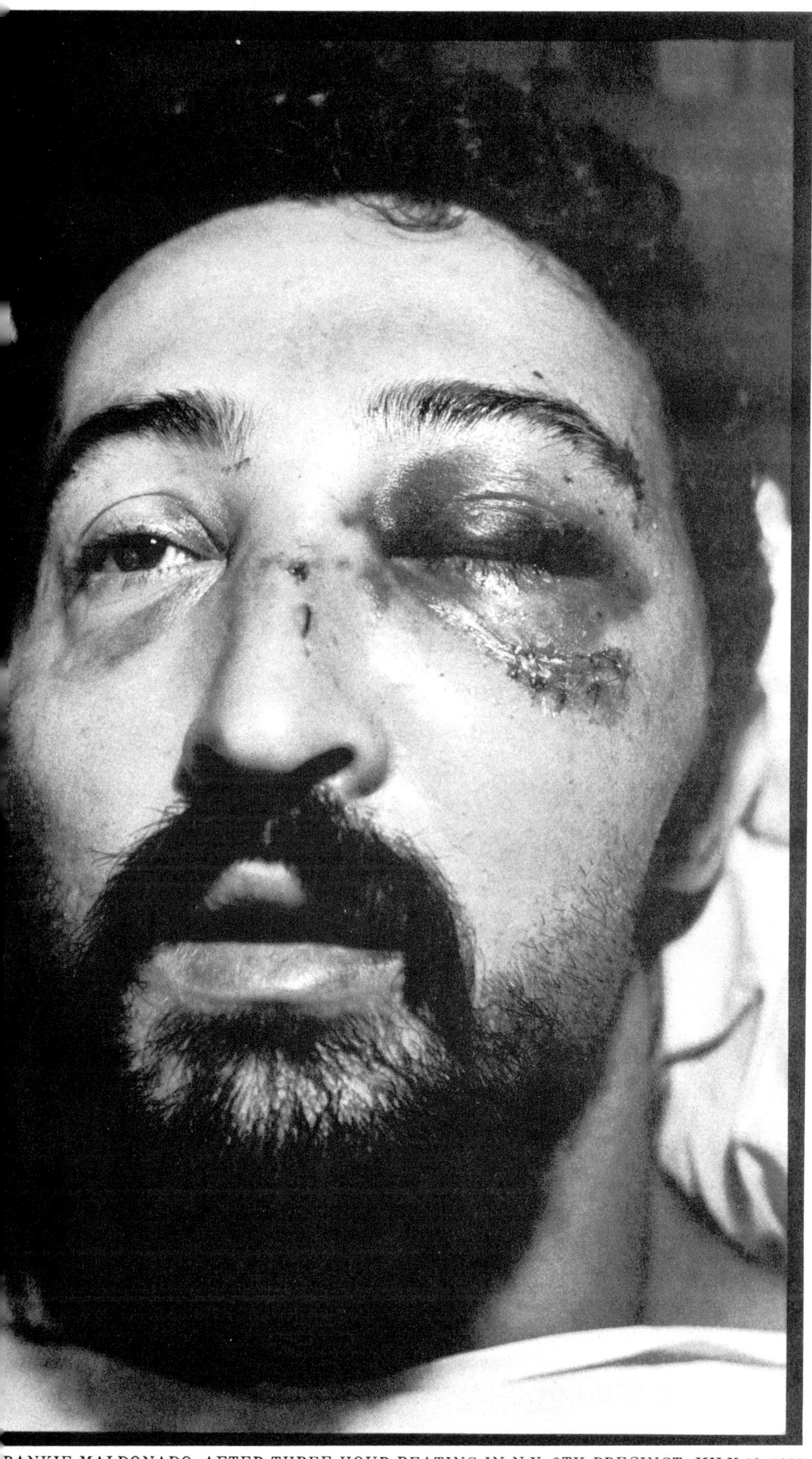

RANKIE MALDONADO, AFTER THREE-HOUR BEATING IN N.Y. 9TH PRECINCT, JULY 23, 1970

"The Lords saw some pigs harassing some brothers and went over to investigate.... At the sty, Frankie Maldonado was beaten by the entire pig population. When Bobby Lemus called our office we heard Frankie's screams coming over the phone. The next day a doctor saw the brother and reported twenty stitches to his face alone.... When he recovered consciousness it was hours before he recalled who he was."

MICKEY AGRAIT, EAST HARLEM OFFICE, OCTOBER, 1970

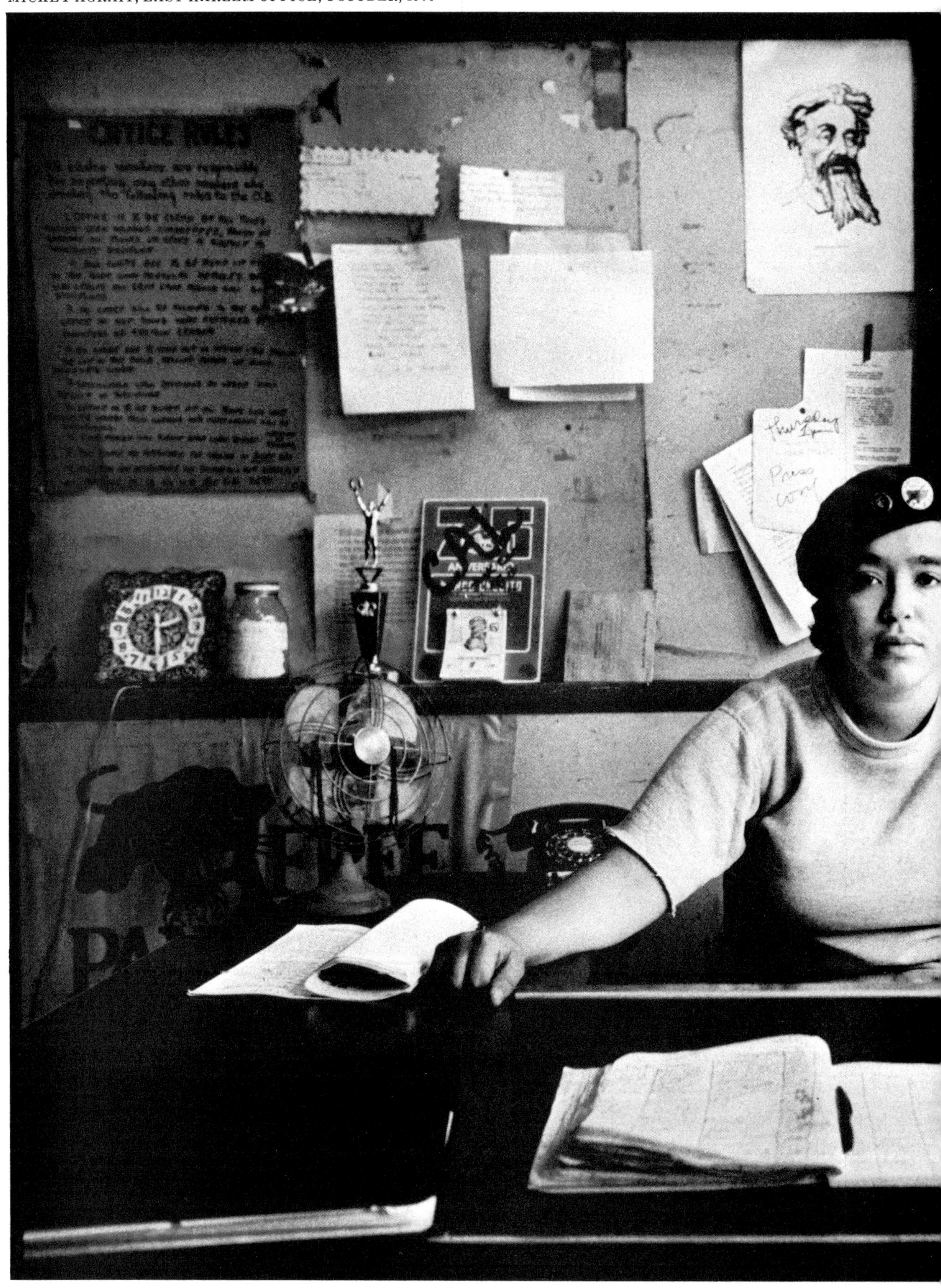

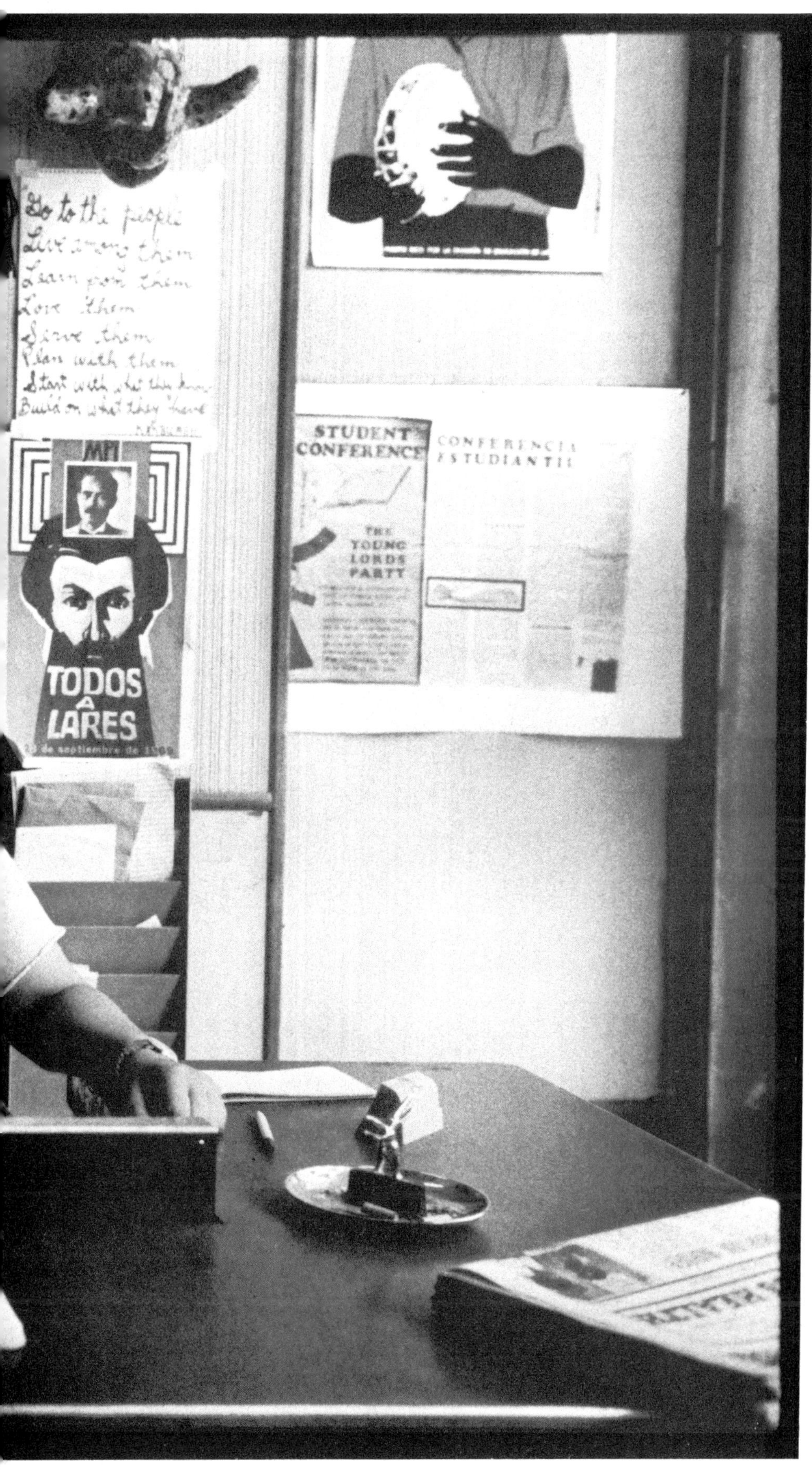

"If a pig ever kills me and I'm fighting for my people, I'll die happy because I'll know I gained something by dying. Now, if I'm not in the revolution and I just die of a heart attack, I'll probably die sad because I'll know I didn't do shit for nobody."

CENTRAL COMMITTEE MEETING: YORUBA, DENISE, FI, DAVID, JUAN, GLORIA, FEBRUARY, 1971

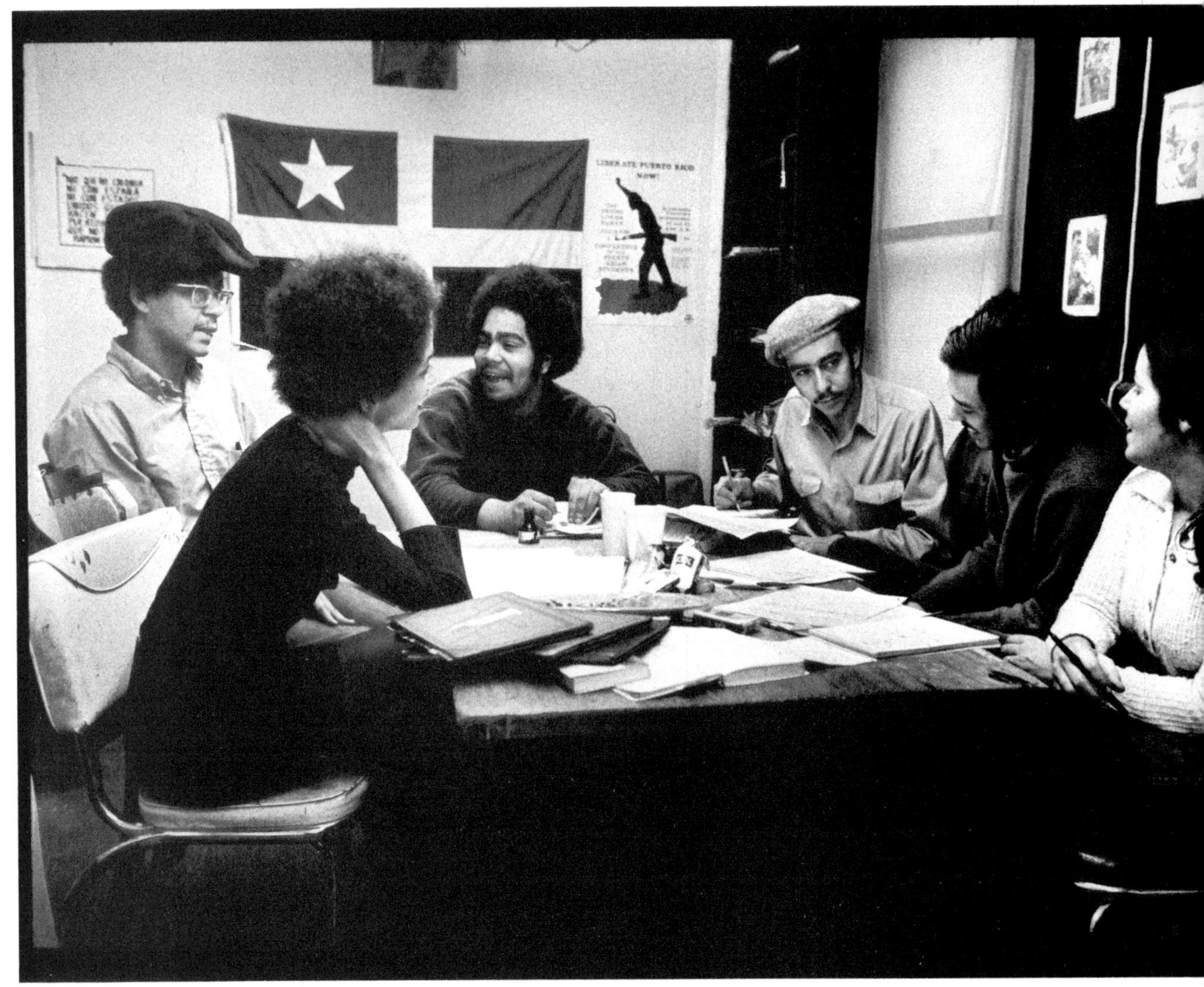

"We're here because we are trying
as best we can to take the power
of the state and put that back
in the hands of the people who for
so long have been denied everything.
It is a very deep, emotional thing
for people who've been told
so long that they're niggers,
spics, and they ain't worth shit,
to be doing this."

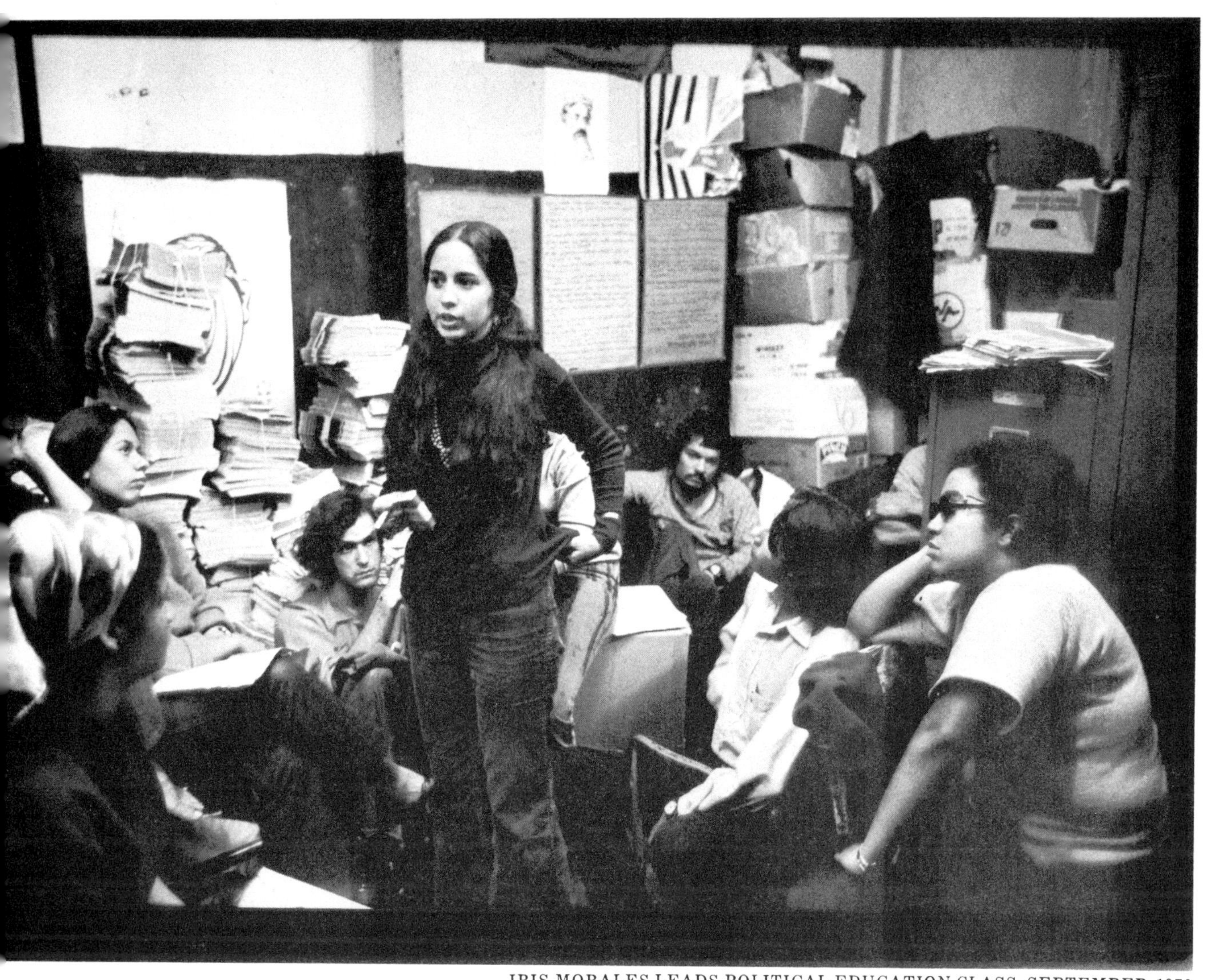

IRIS MORALES LEADS POLITICAL EDUCATION CLASS, SEPTEMBER, 1970

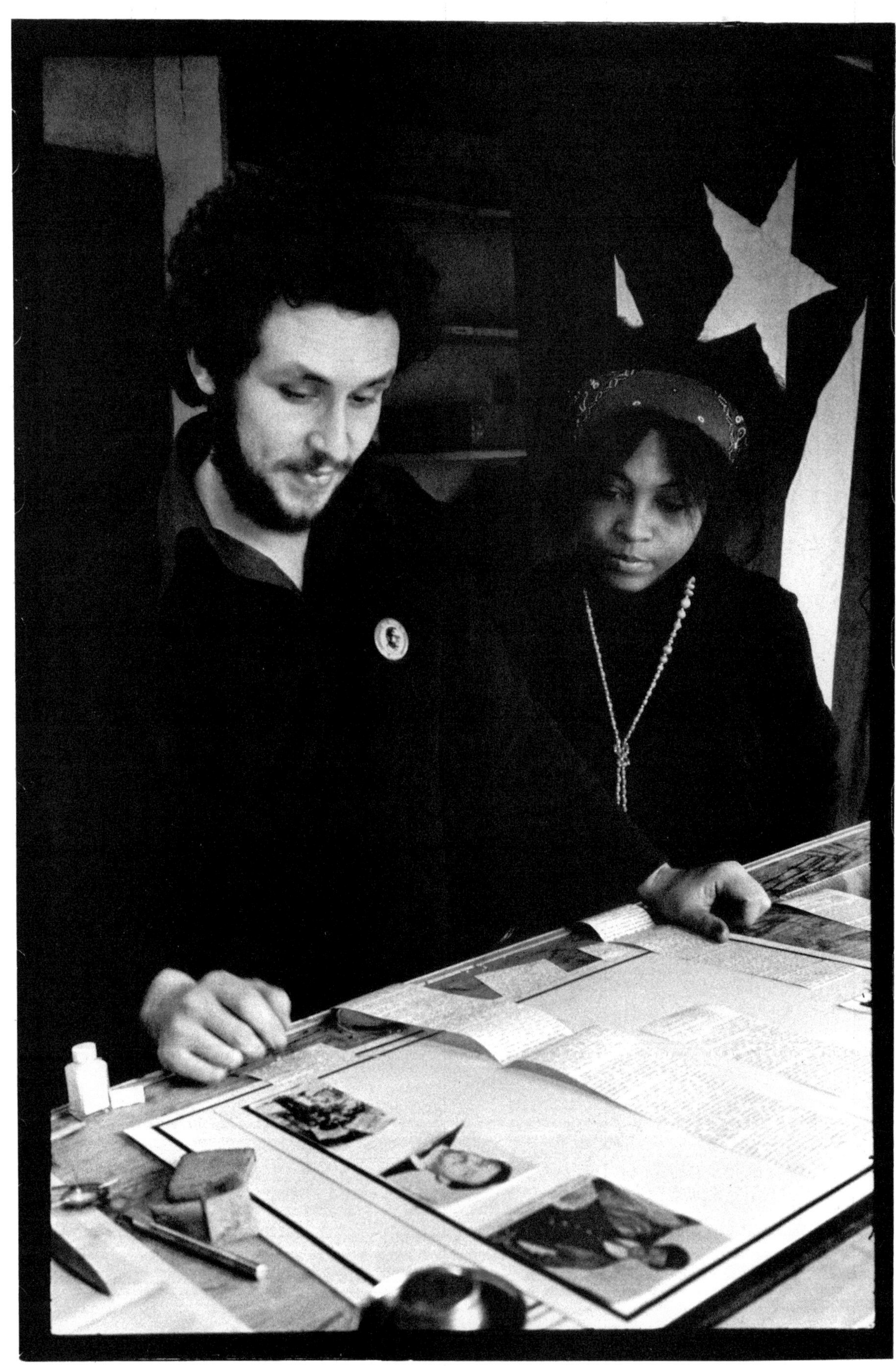

RICHIE PEREZ AND MECCA ADAI LAY OUT "PALANTE," JANUARY, 1971

GLORIA GONZALEZ, EAST HARLEM OFFICE, SEPTEMBER, 1970

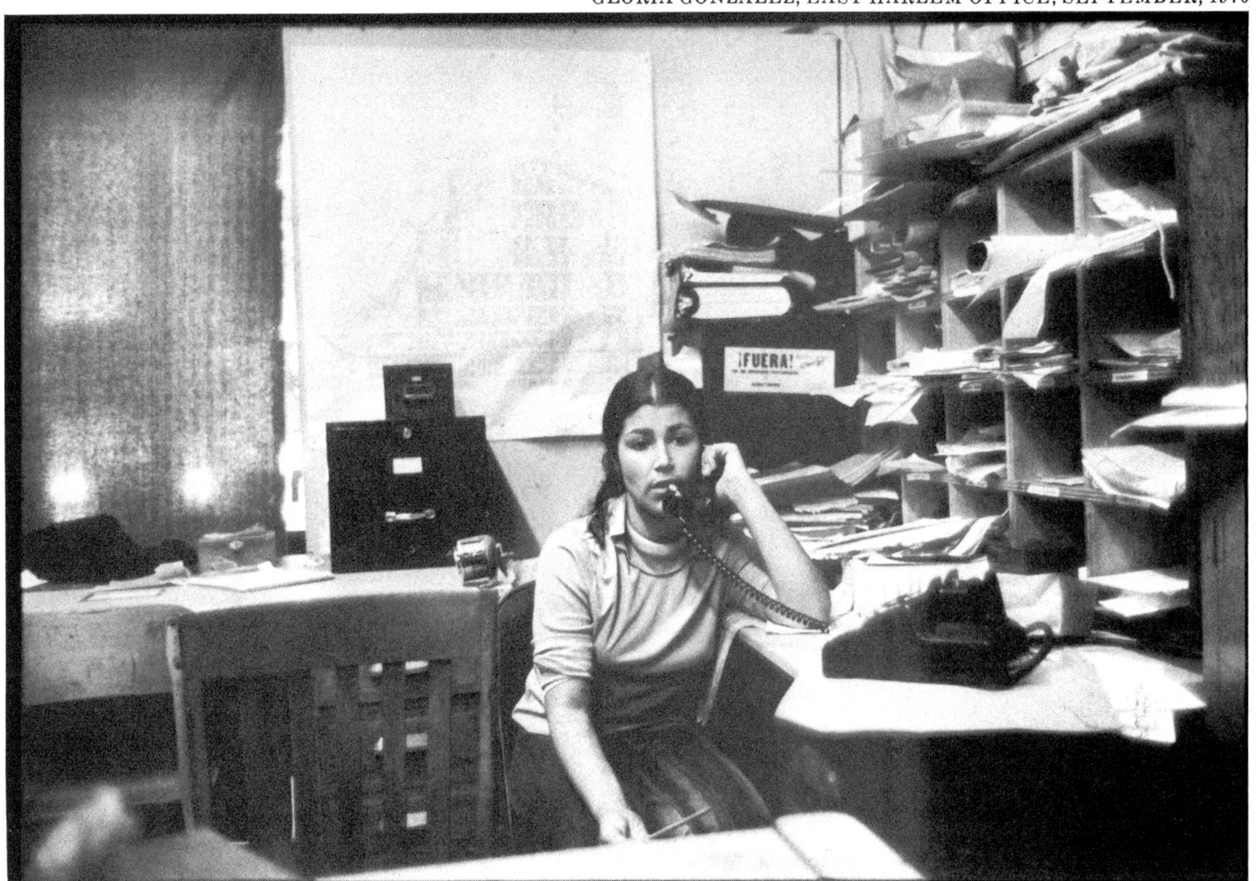

"We have successfully planted the seeds of freedom given to us by Nat Turner, Antonio Maceo, and John Brown, and made things a bit easier for our children than they were for us."

"There's a tendency to say 'the people' and put the people at arm's length. When we say 'people,' we're talking about ourselves. We're from these blocks, and we're from these schools, products of this whole thing."

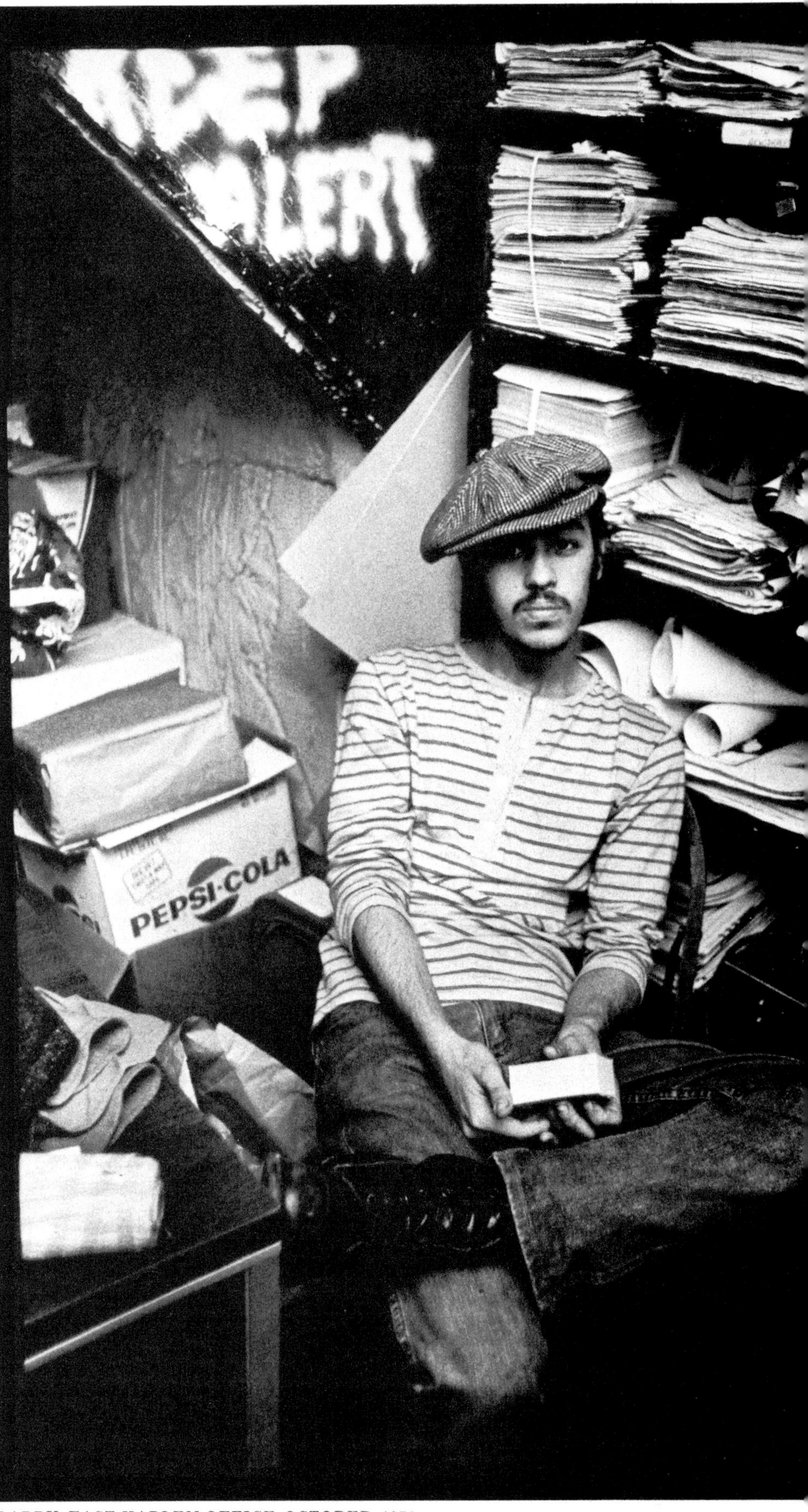

LARRY, EAST HARLEM OFFICE, OCTOBER, 1970

ALFREDO, BRONX OFFICE, NOVEMBER, 1970

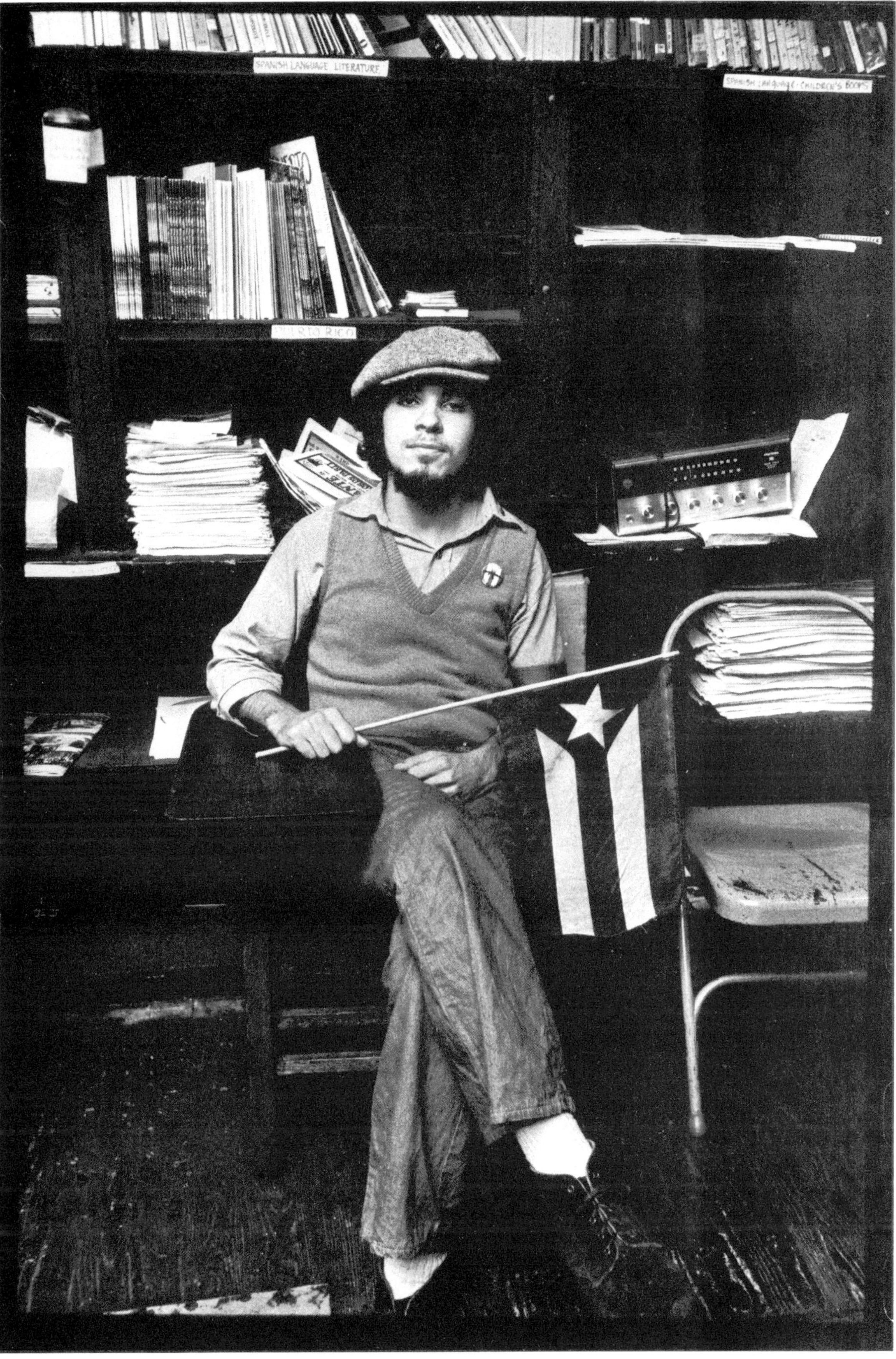

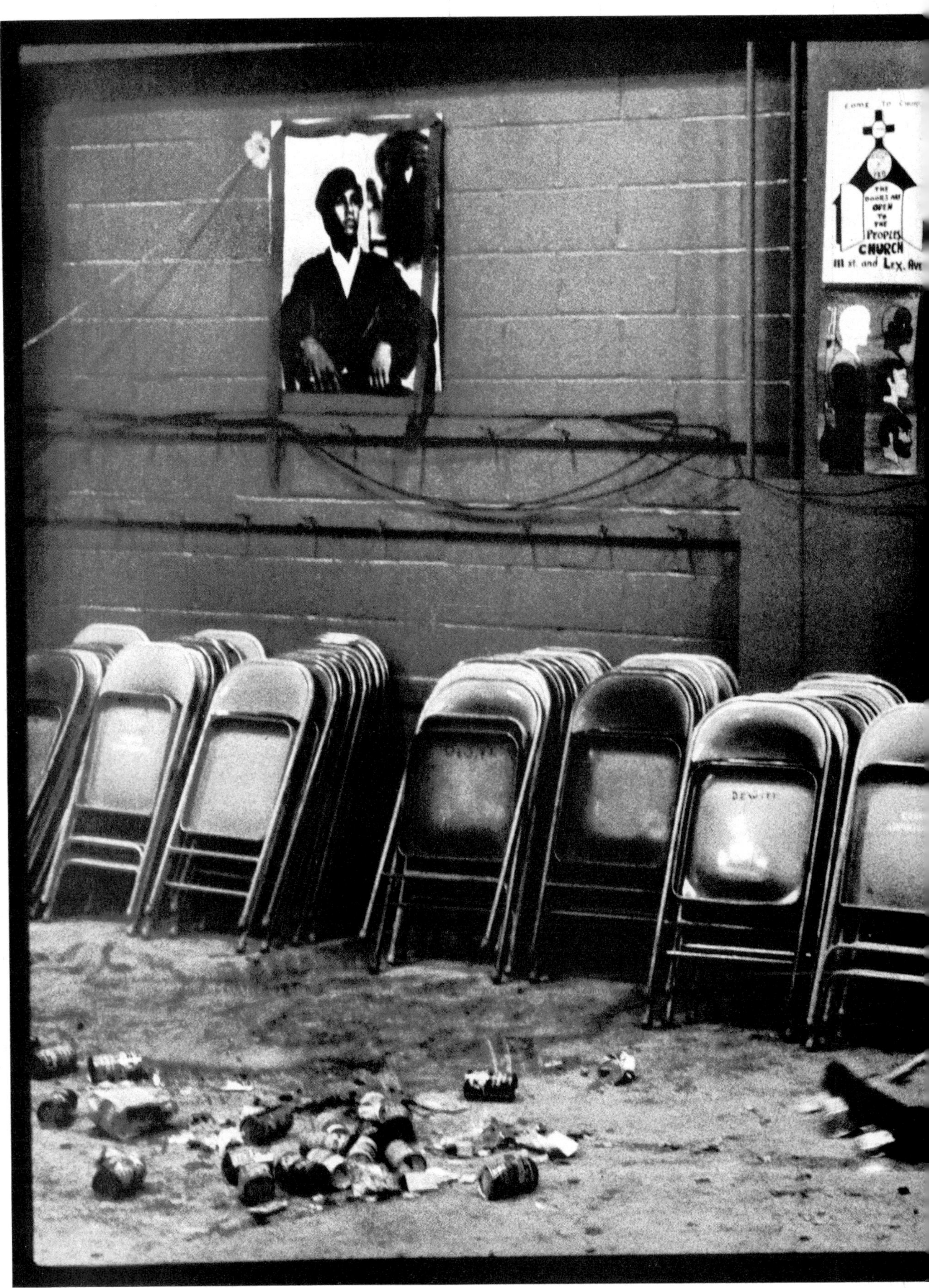

CLEANING UP AFTER BENEFIT DANCE, FEBRUARY, 1970

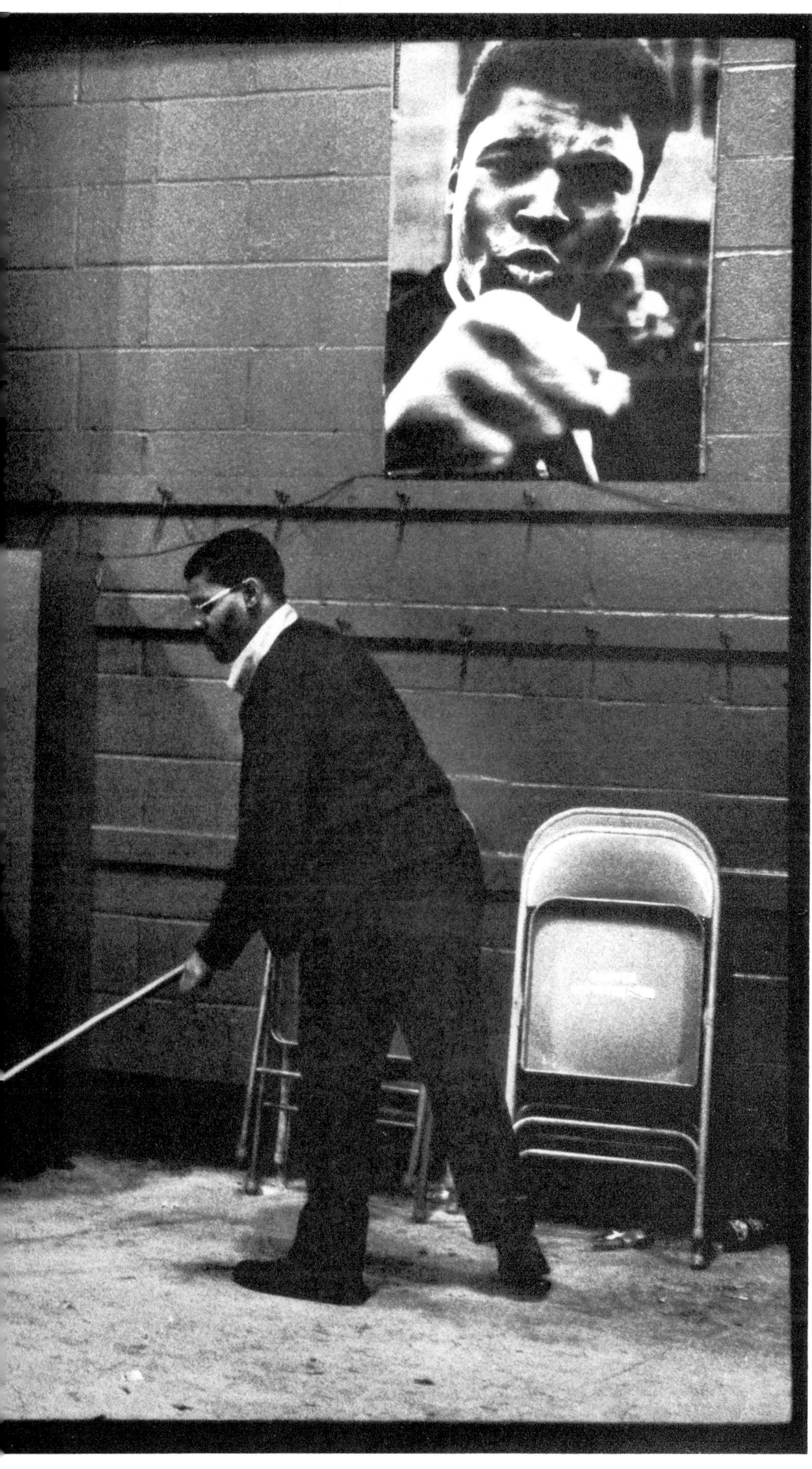

"It's not easy to construct a party. It's not easy to create the sort of discipline where an individual says, 'I will do what the Party tells me. I will do what my people want. If that means I can't do my own thing, that's part of the sacrifice of serving the people.'"

"We decided to begin a free clothing program when the Department of Welfare cut the checks to 66 cents a day in New York City and our younger brothers and sisters had to go to school with three-year-old clothing. Also the YLP is educating everyone to the fact that our people are the ones that make those clothes in the garment district and then have to pay for them, when they are rightfully ours!"

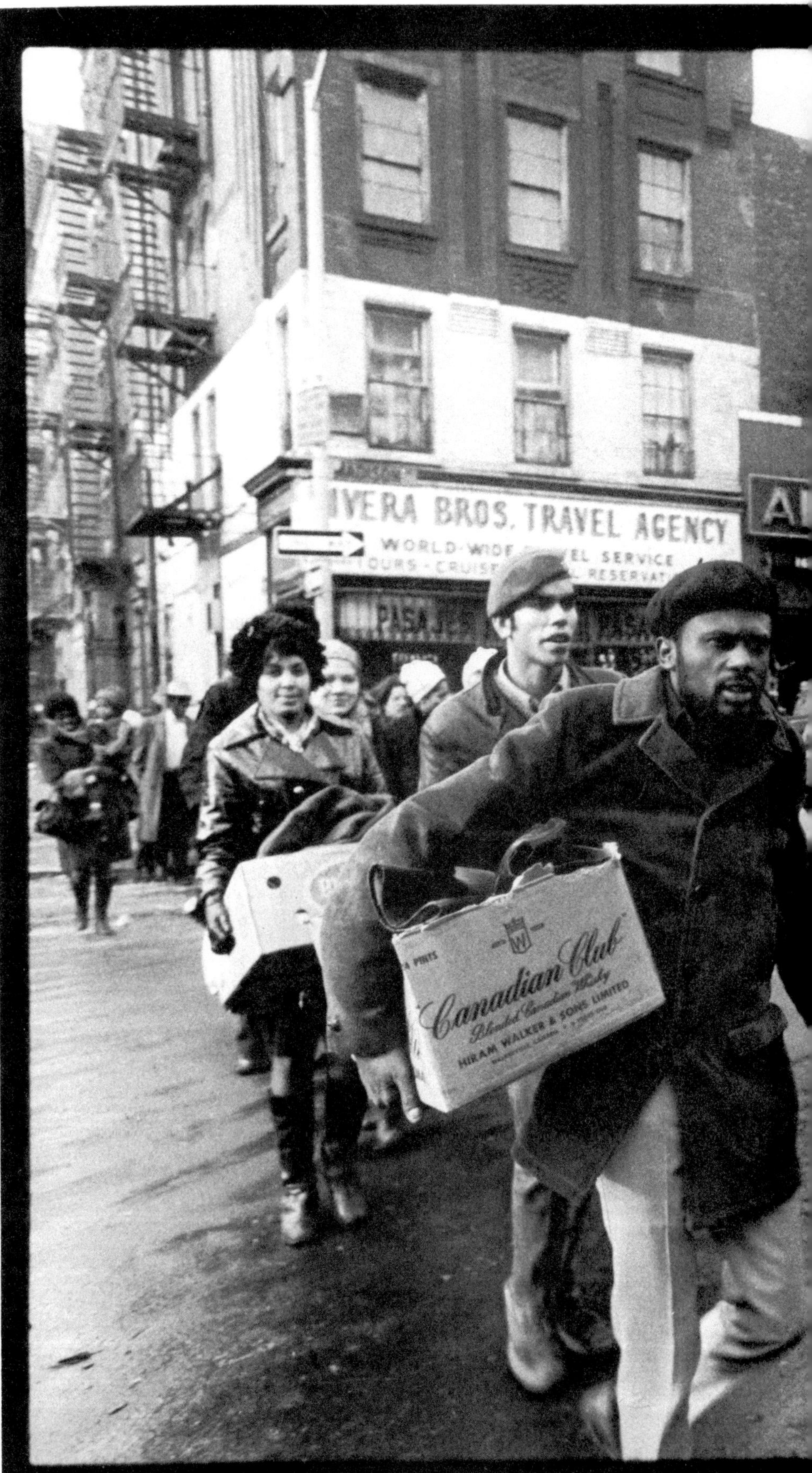

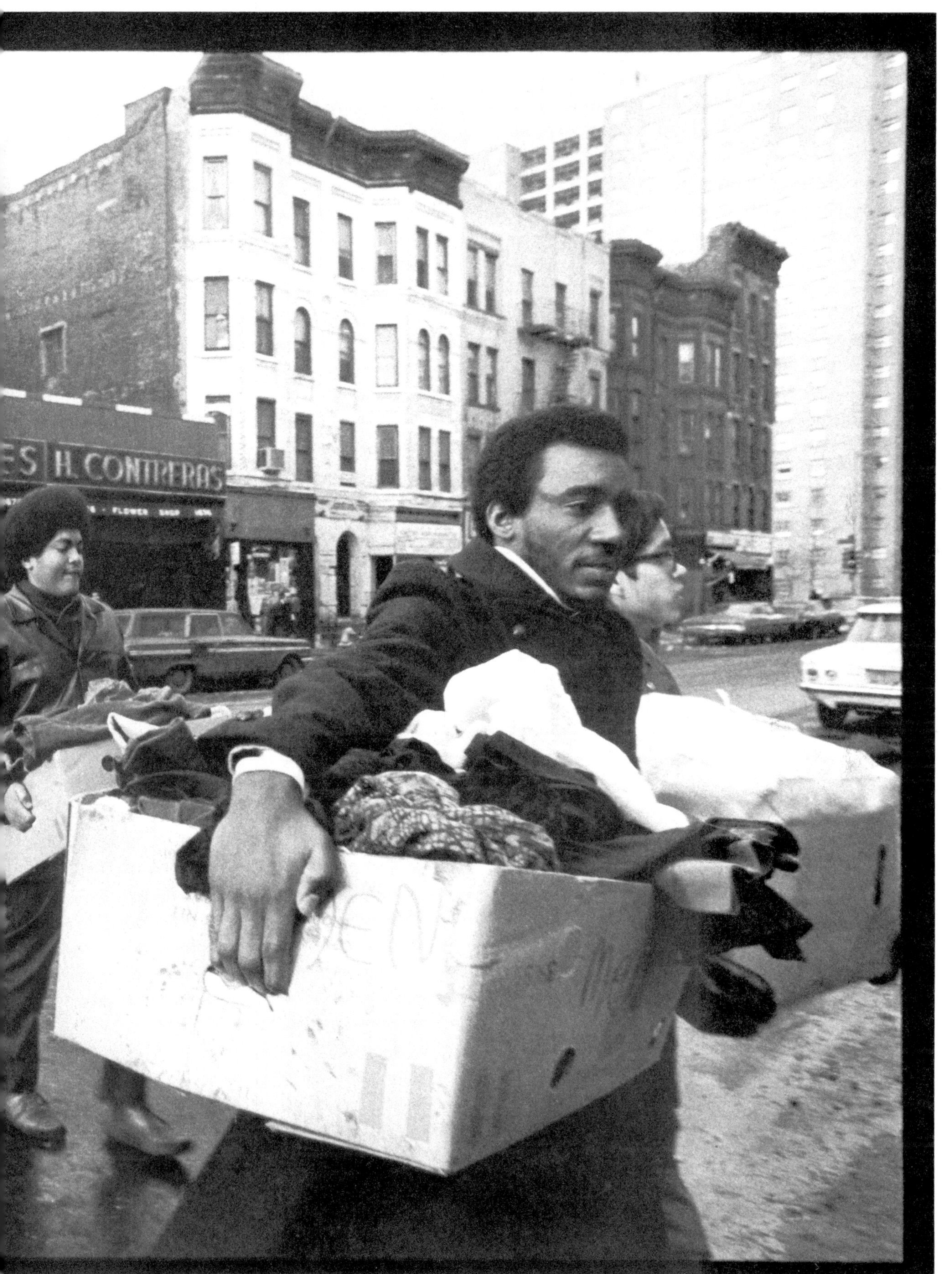

CARRYING CLOTHES TO THE FIRST PEOPLE'S CHURCH, JANUARY, 1970

"We know that Christmas
means a lot to young people.
We all went through this.
We want the same for the
poor children of our community
that children in other places enjoy.
We want these young years
to be as good as possible.
We know that as they grow up,
these children will begin
to see and understand
what is around them,
the conditions caused by
a system based on profit,
not people–and they will
move against this system."

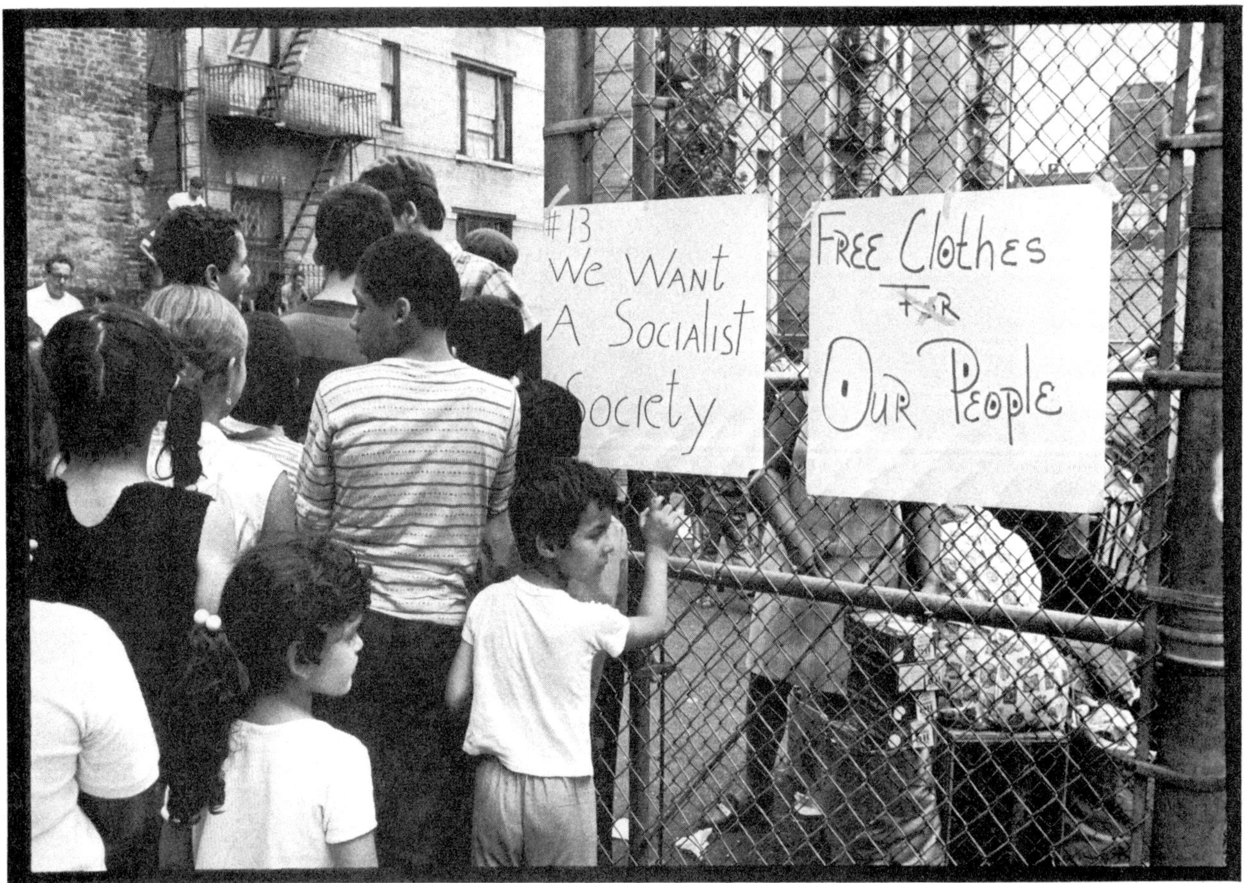

FREE CLOTHING DRIVE, BRONX, JULY, 1970

MARCHING TO FIRST PEOPLE'S CHURCH THROUGH STREETS OF EAST HARLEM, DECEMBER, 1969

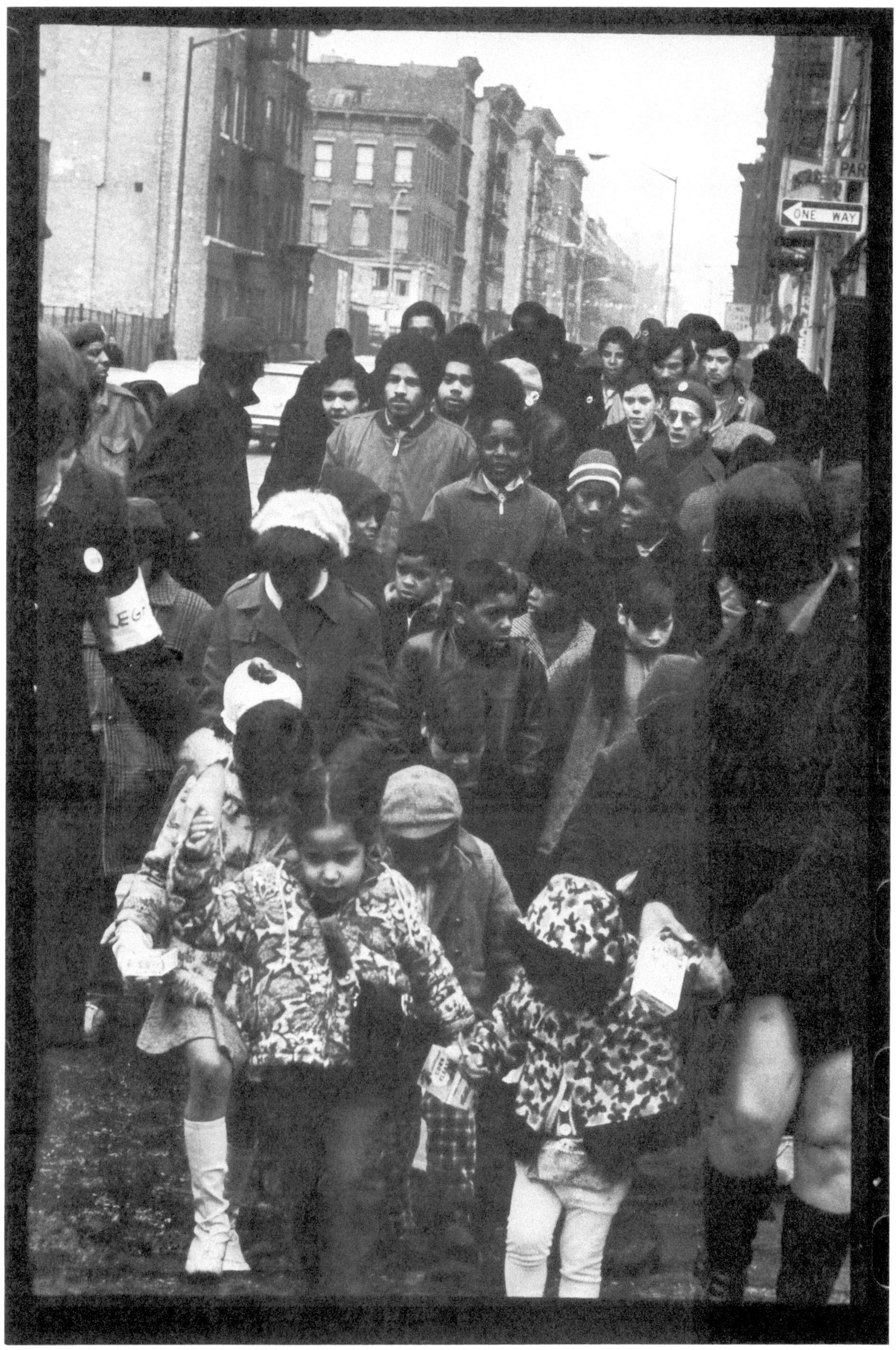

A CASE OF SEVERE BEDBUG BITES, FREE HEALTH CLINIC, FIRST PEOPLE'S CHURCH, DECEMBER, 1969

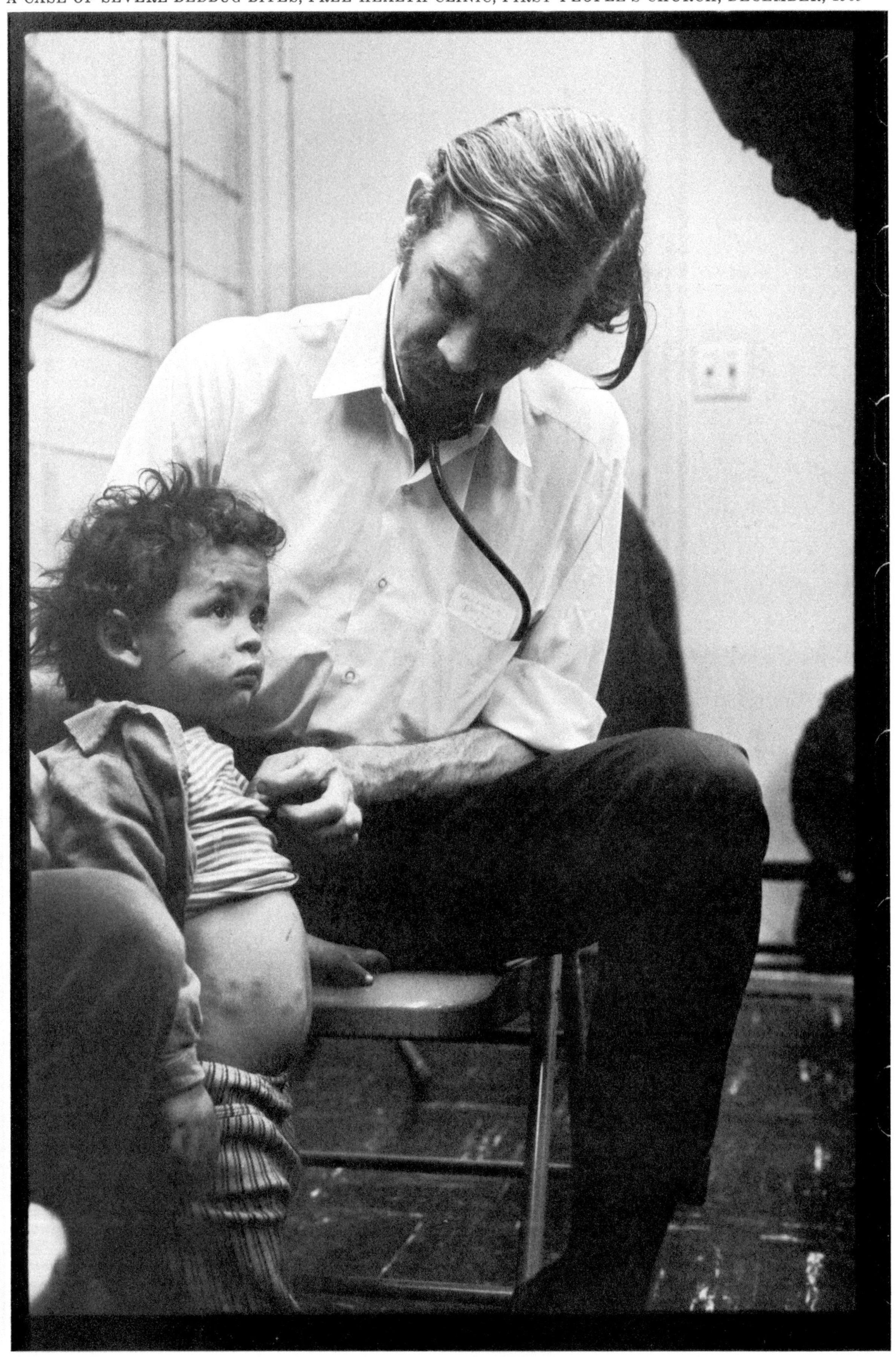

DOOR-TO-DOOR TB TESTING, LOWER EAST SIDE, DECEMBER, 1970

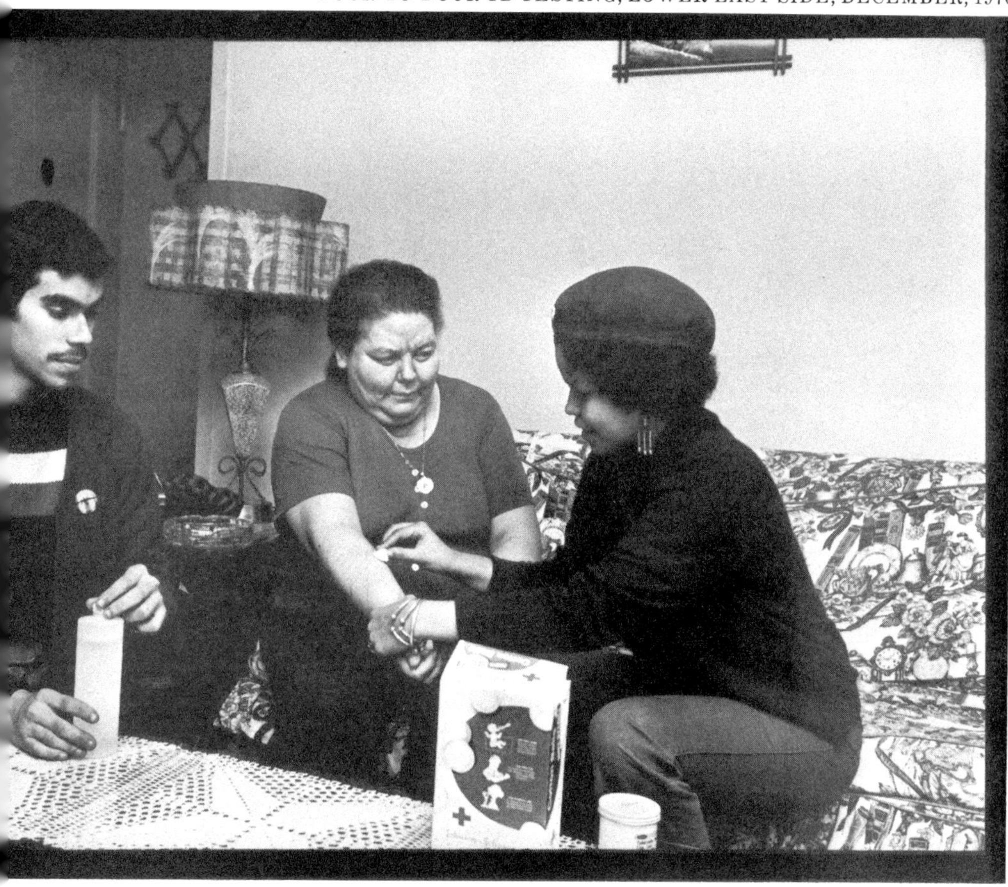

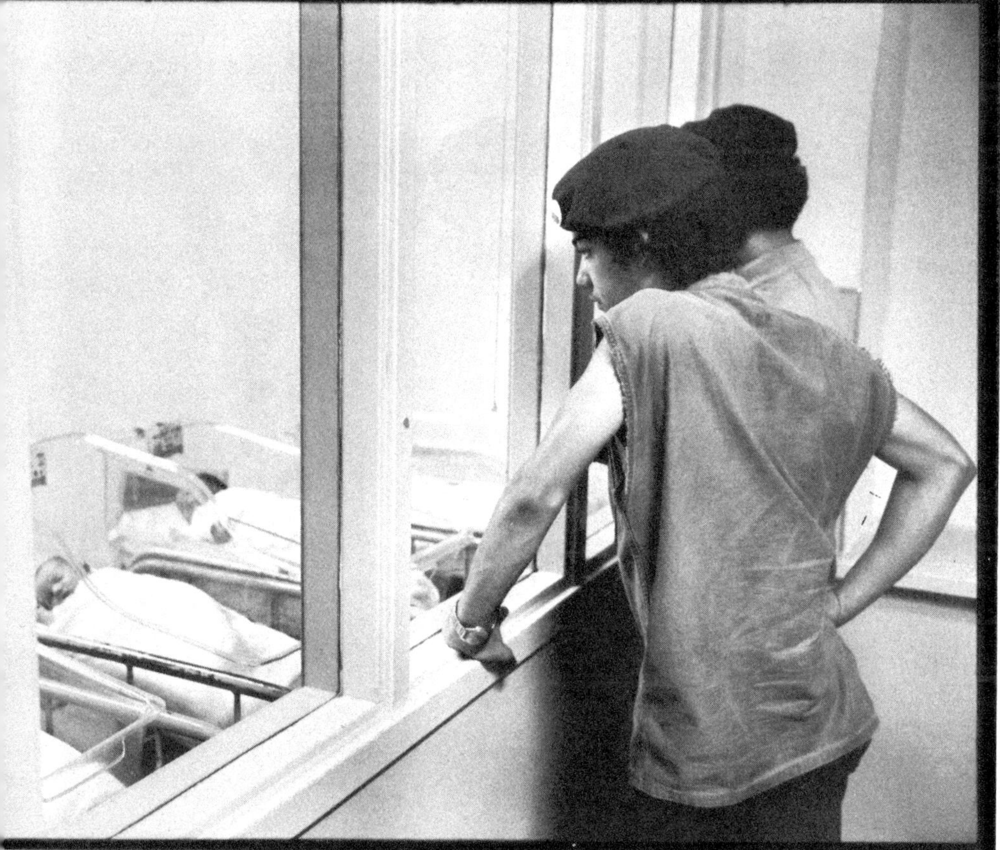

A BABY IS BORN TO THE REVOLUTION, AUGUST, 1970

"When we began testing the children of El Barrio for lead poisoning, we did it out of necessity. Before any of us were Young Lords, we experienced what our children are going through today: getting bit by rats, sleeping with bedbugs, but most of all eating lead paint. Many of our children die every year of lead poisoning, while the landlord is only concerned if we pay the rent for the rathole that is killing our children."

FREE BREAKFAST PROGRAM, SECOND PEOPLE'S CHURCH, OCTOBER, 1970

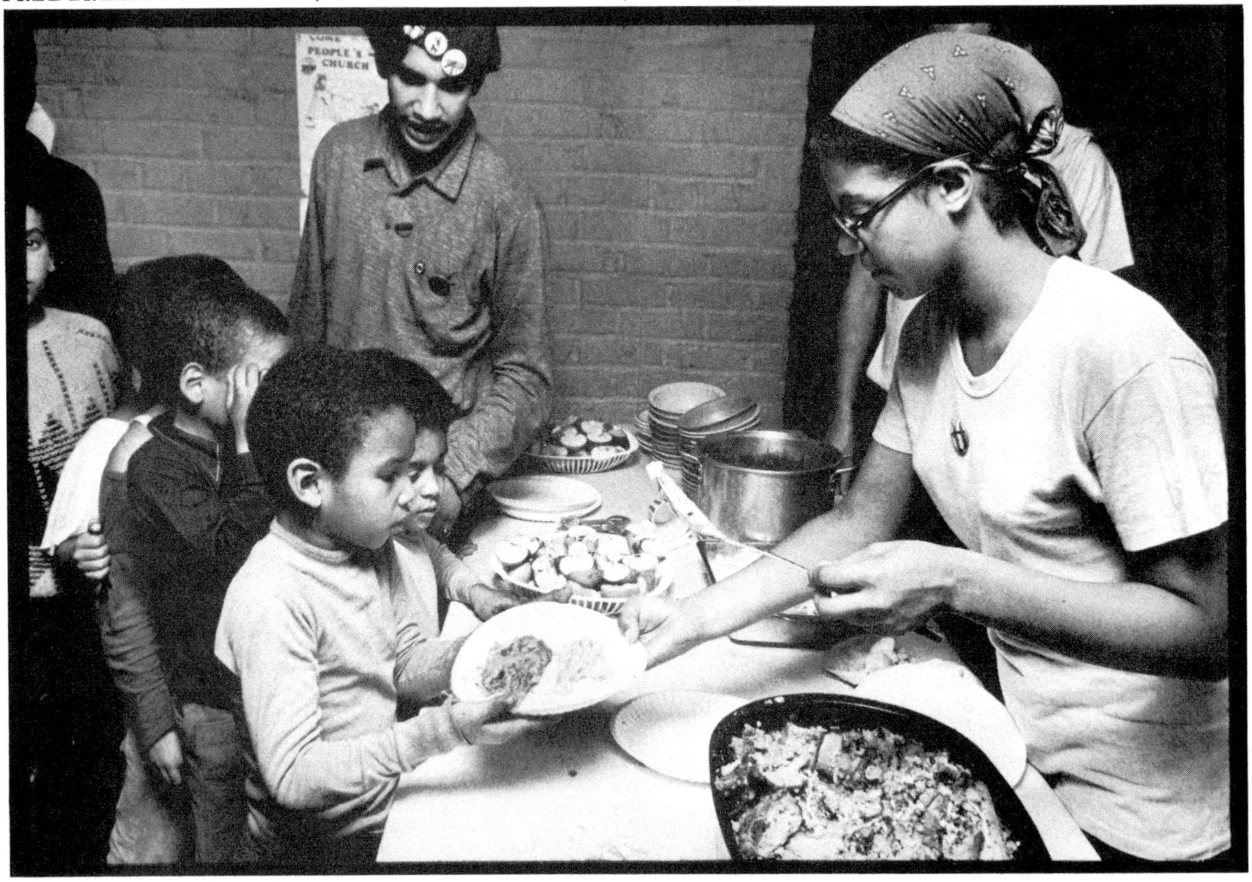

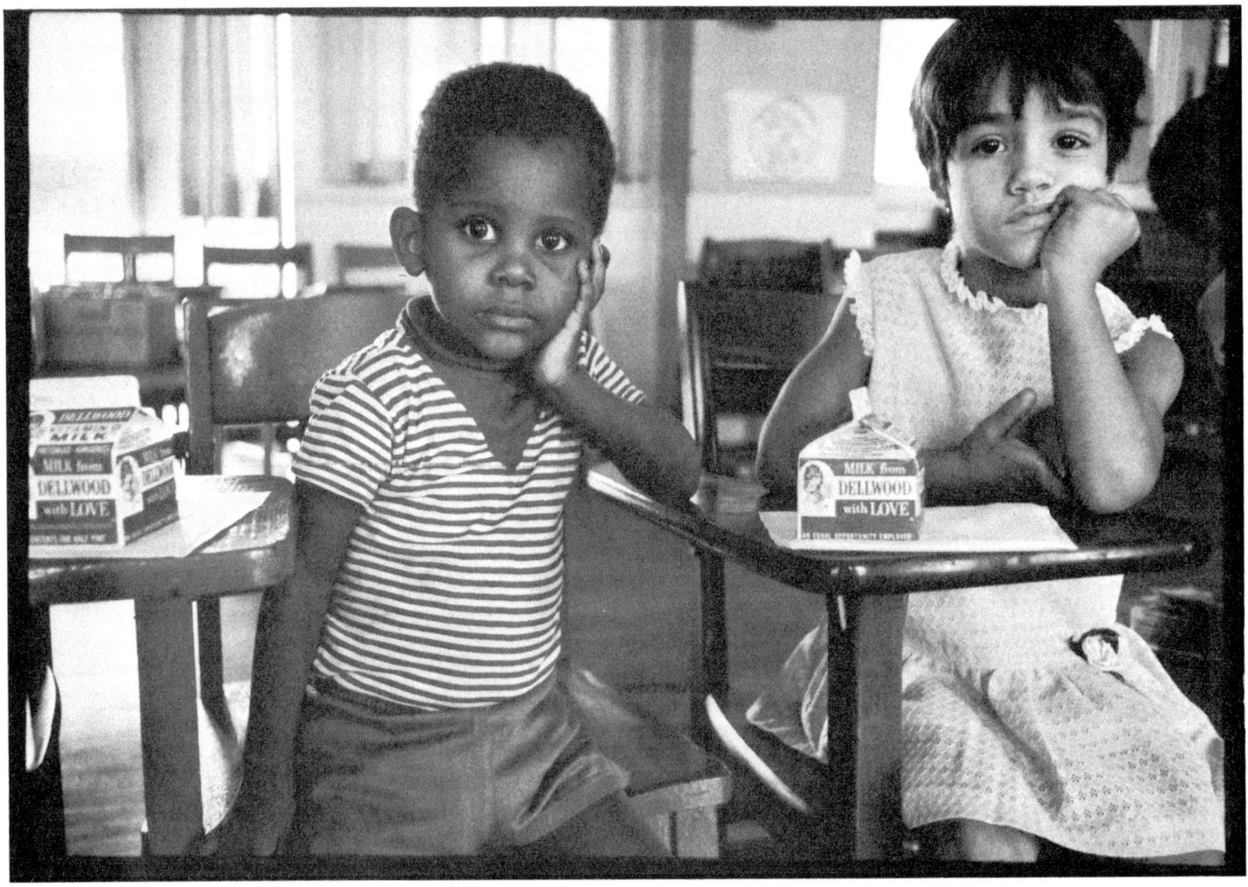

YOUNG LORDS DAY CARE CENTER, LINCOLN HOSPITAL, JULY, 1970

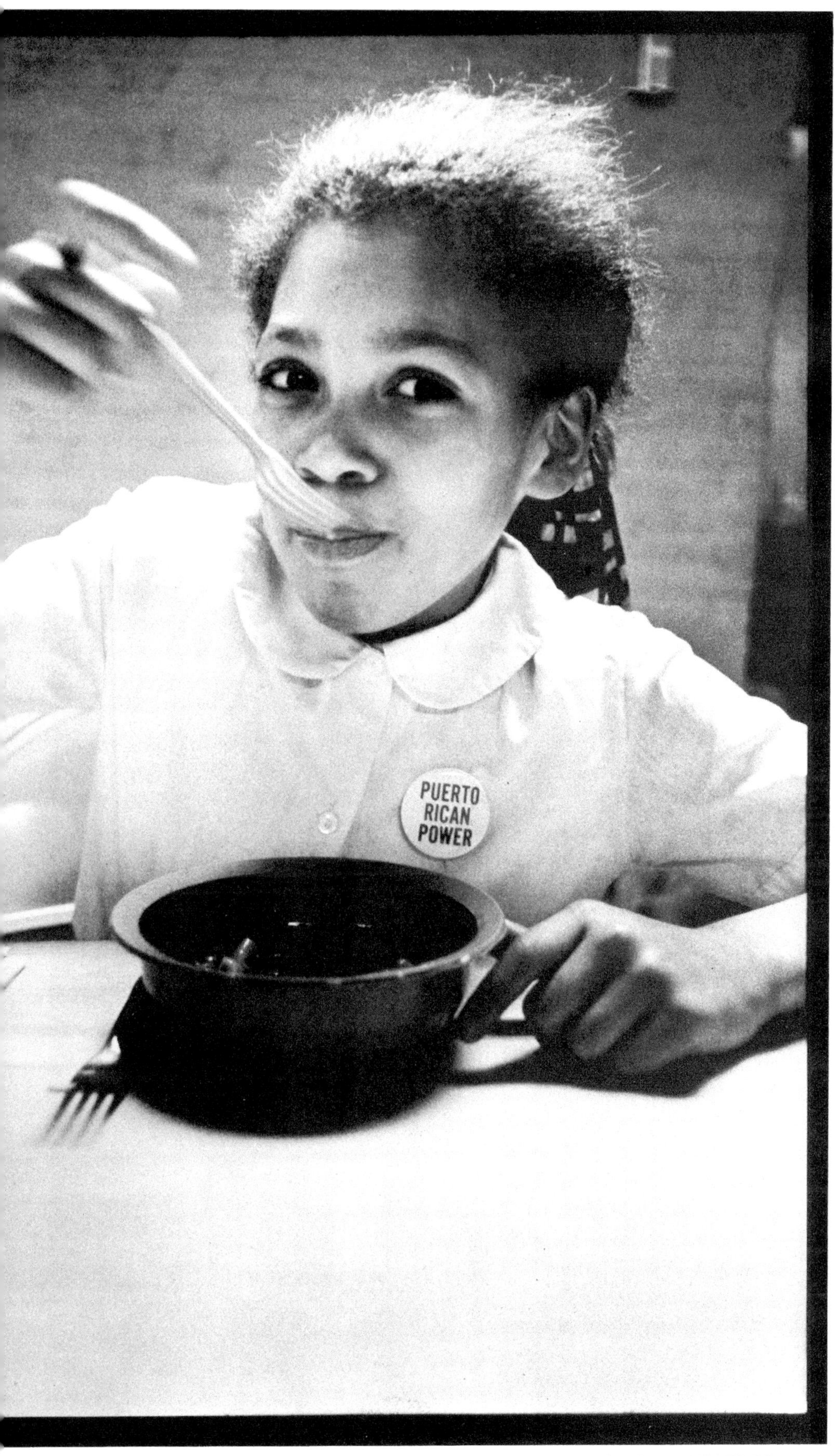

FREE BREAKFAST PROGRAM, FIRST PEOPLE'S CHURCH, DECEMBER, 1969

"Free breakfast programs deal with the immediate physical needs of our people. We feed the children a full meal that will help them function throughout the school day. The meals include eggs, bacon, sausages, french toast, pancakes, hot and cold cereals, and fruits."

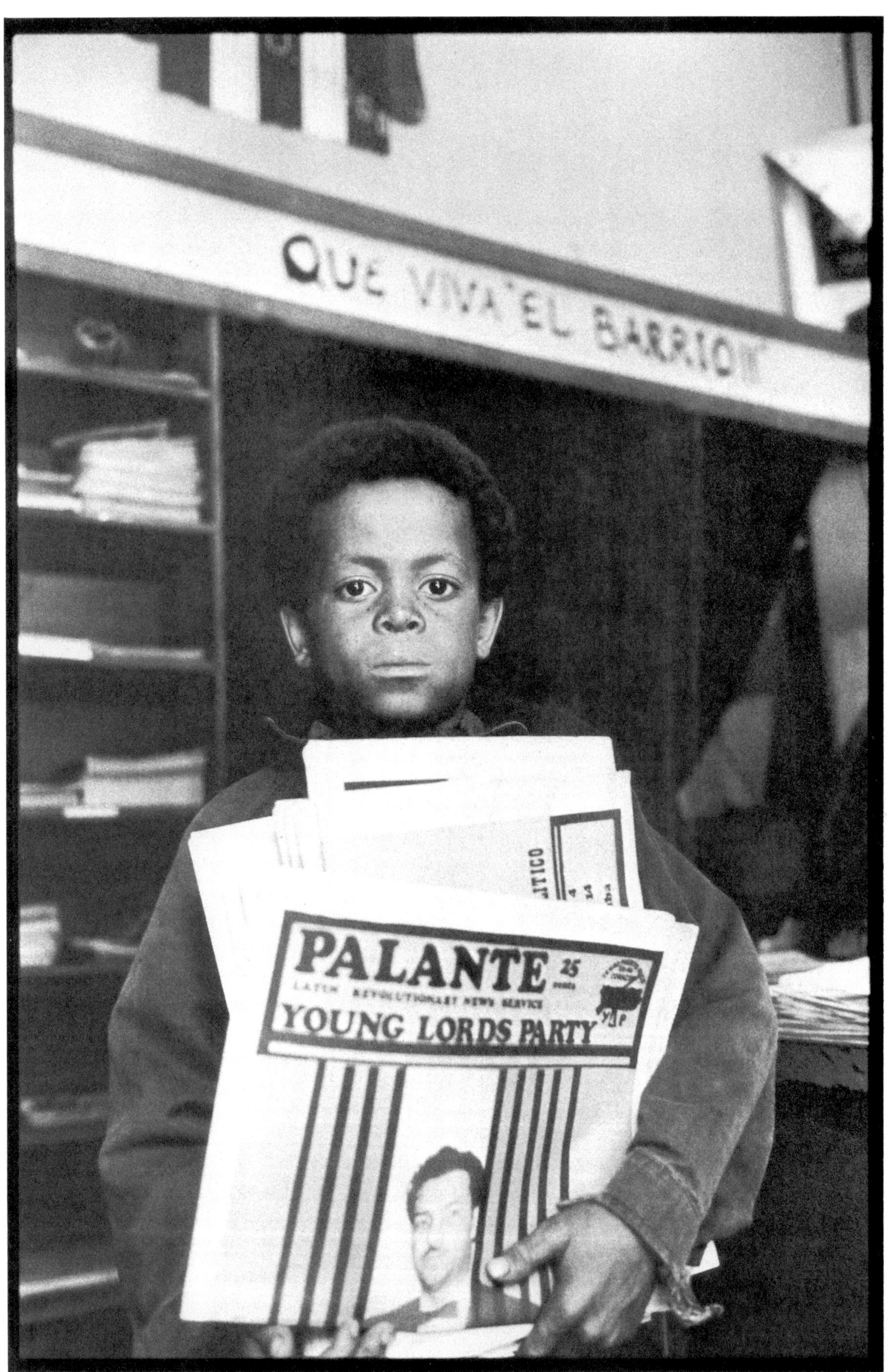

EAST HARLEM OFFICE, MAY, 1970

AUGIE SELLING "PALANTE," RANDALL'S ISLAND, JULY, 1970

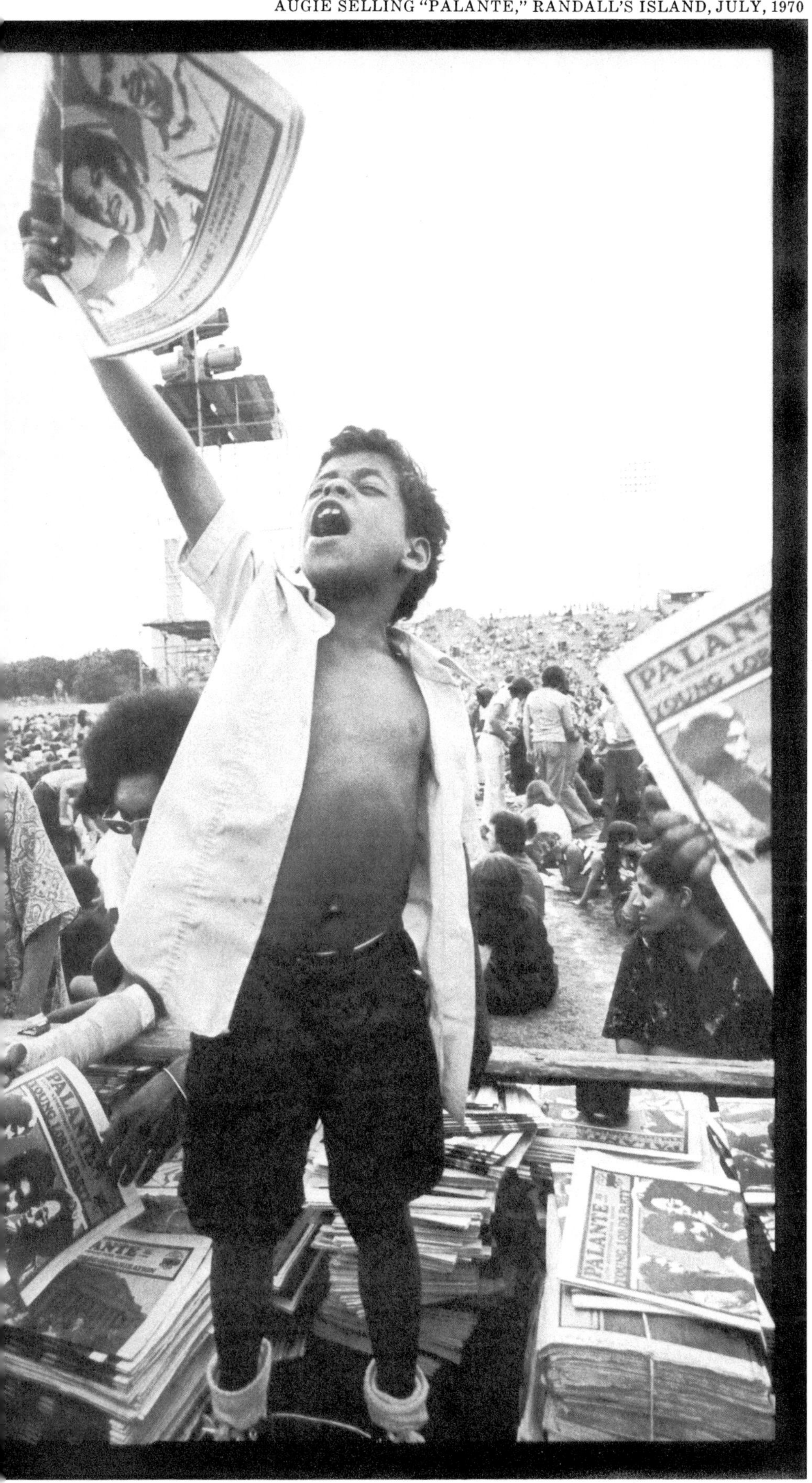

"Language is one of the ways that people are able to communicate and to build a way of fighting back against the enemy–to maintain those ties of identity and therefore strengthen themselves to fight."

GEORGIE SELLING "PALANTE," RANDALL'S ISLAND, JULY, 1970

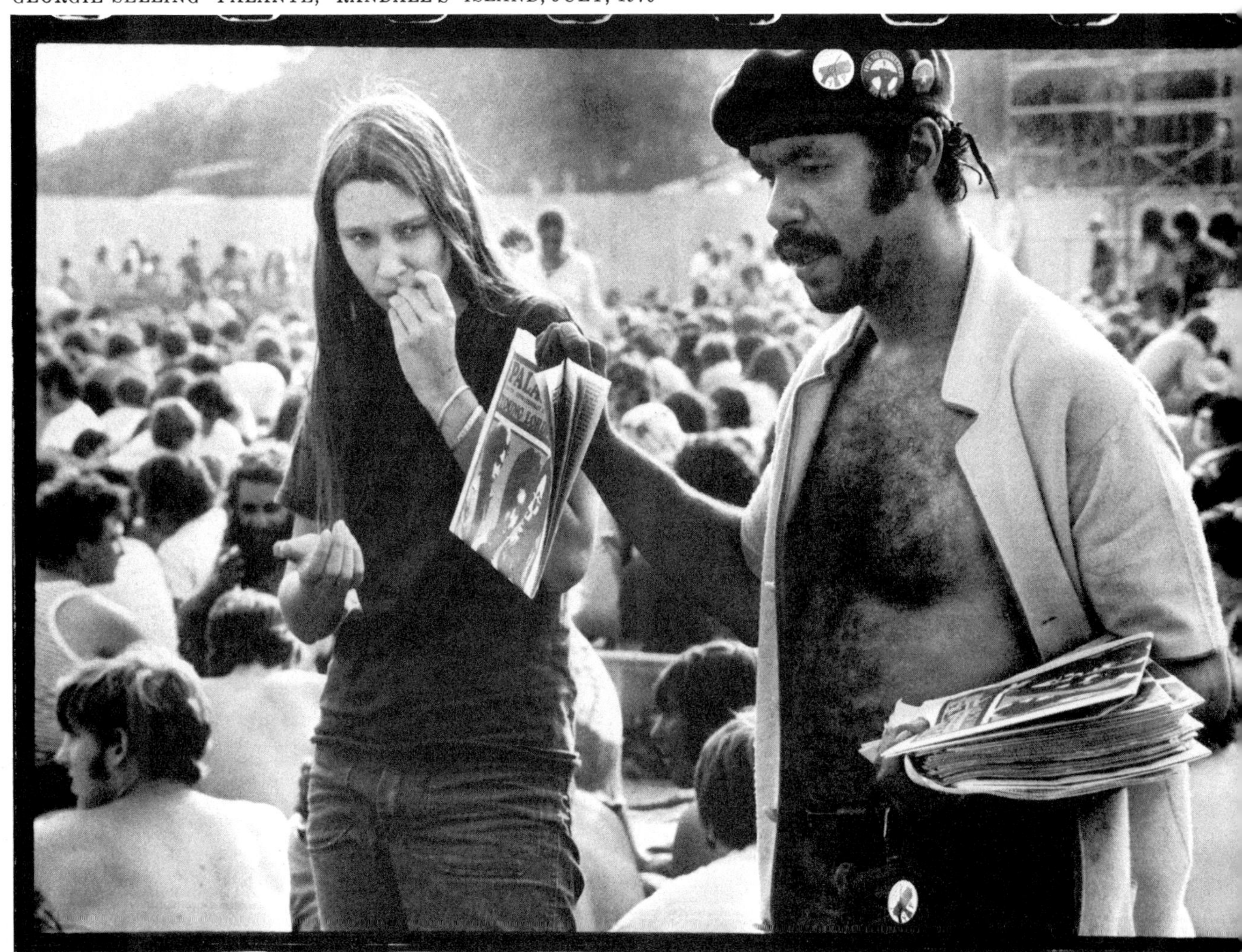

"The reason why you study history
is 'cause you're gonna make history.
The reason you study the past
is 'cause you're concerned about
making a new life, not making
the same mistakes that our people
did before us."

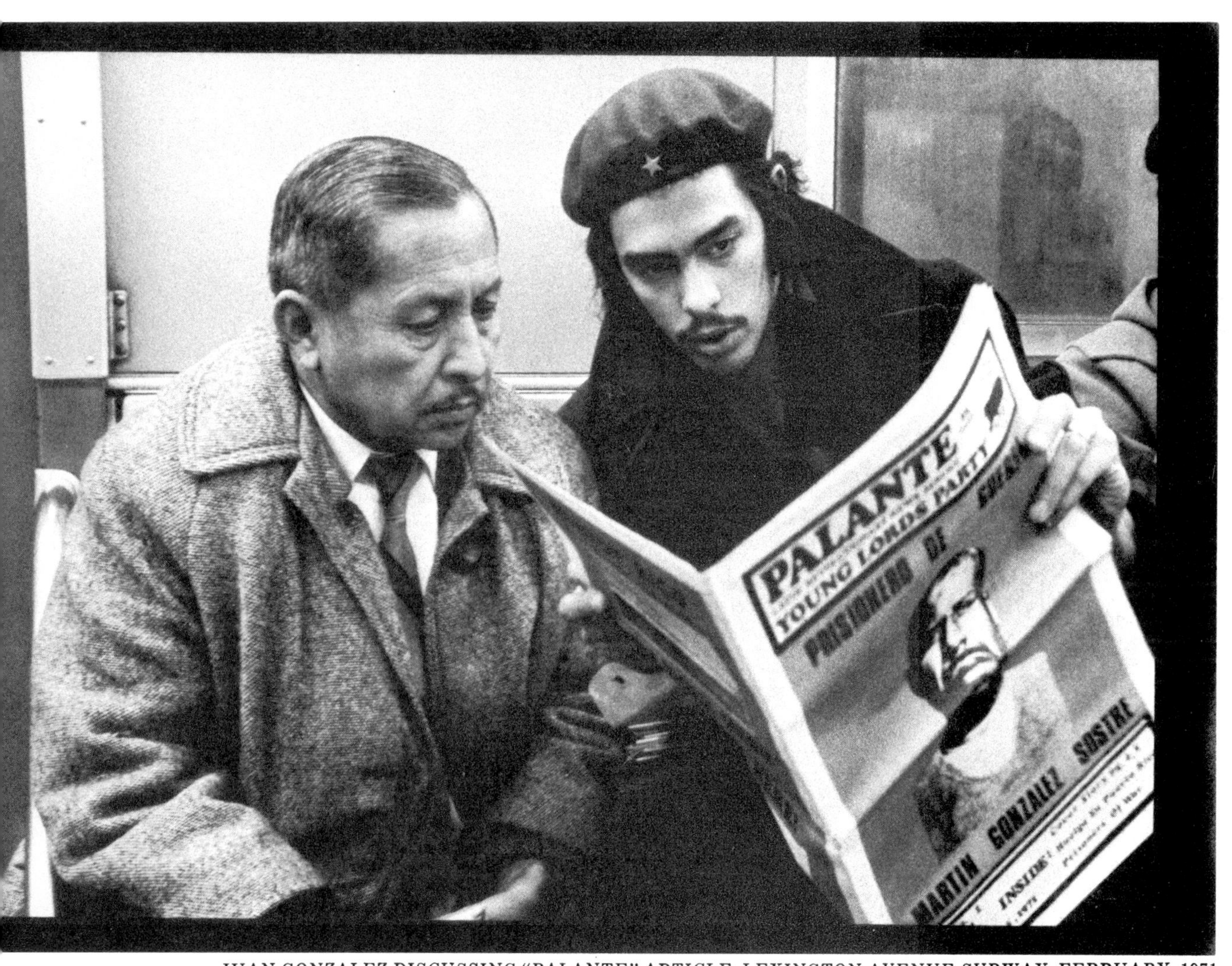

JUAN GONZALEZ DISCUSSING "PALANTE" ARTICLE, LEXINGTON AVENUE SUBWAY, FEBRUARY, 1971

BENJIE ON 111TH STREET

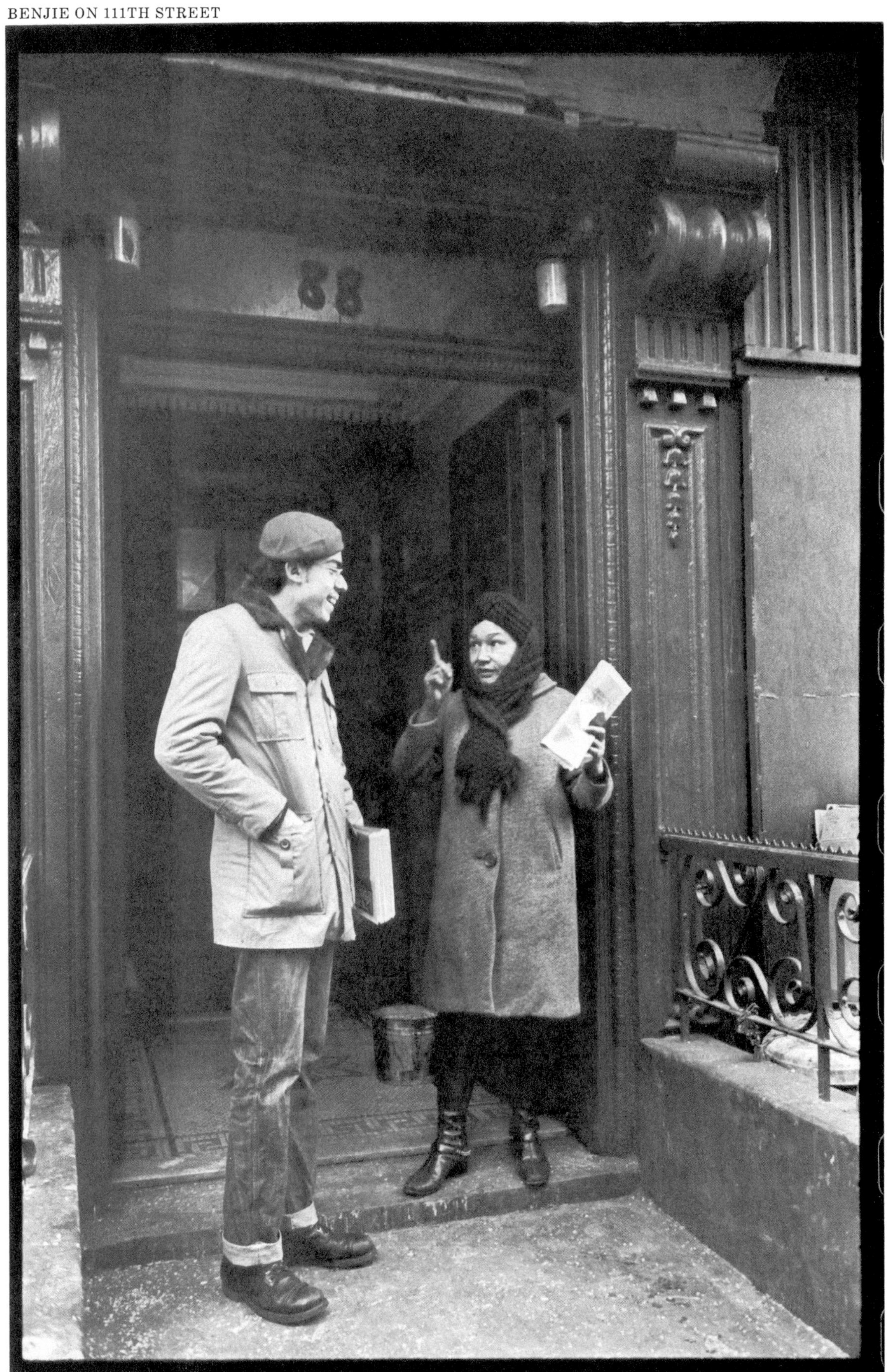

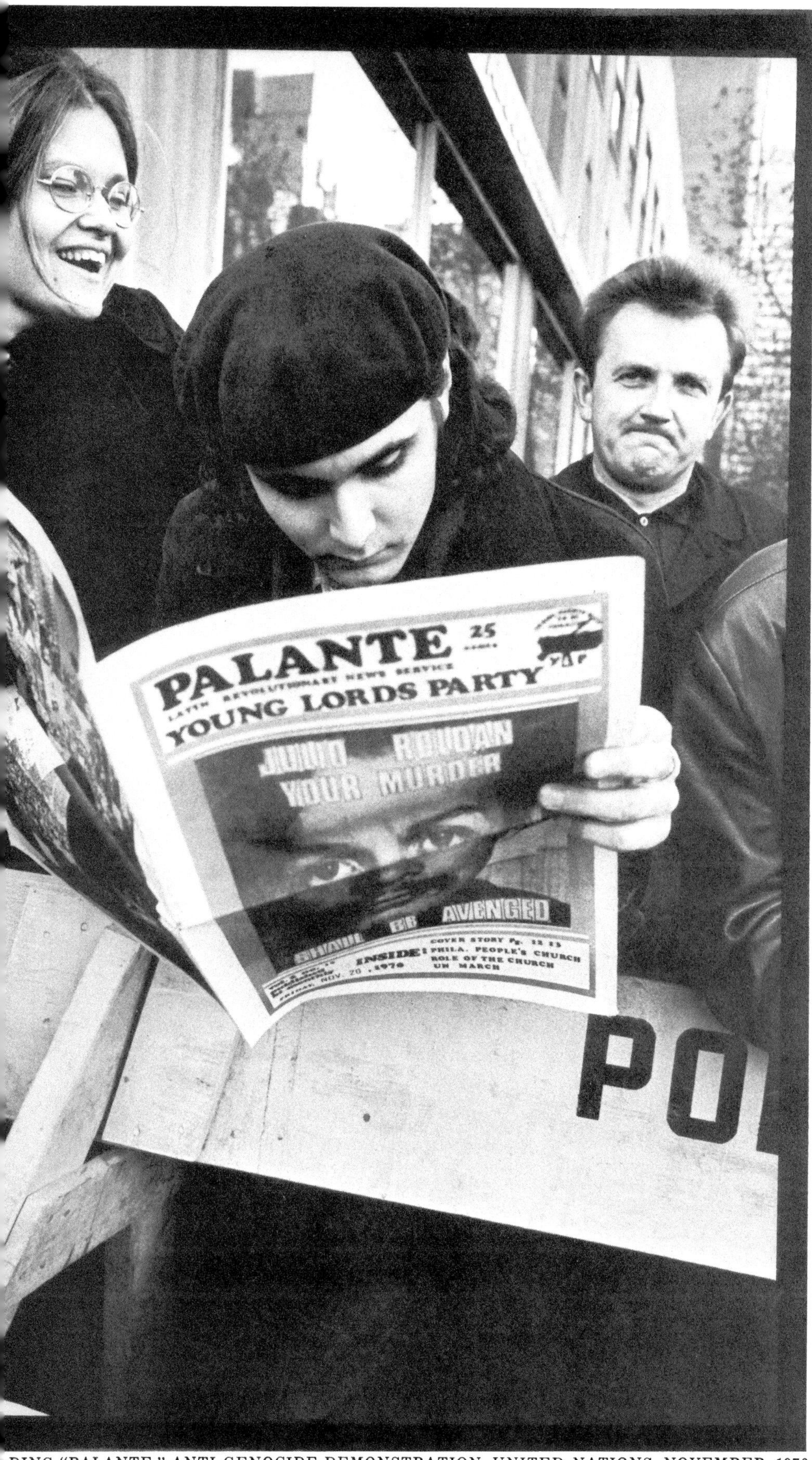

“We are showing people an alternative to the tenement, to the street, to the workplace, to the ‘fanguito’…. The main thing is, they can take any Young Lord now, because now they’ve got to kill an idea.”

DING “PALANTE,” ANTI-GENOCIDE DEMONSTRATION, UNITED NATIONS, NOVEMBER, 1970

YOUNG LORDS PARTY

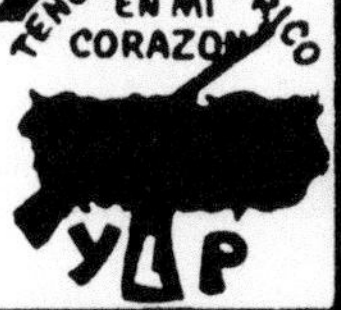

13 POINT PROGRAM AND PLATFORM

THE YOUNG LORDS PARTY IS A REVOLUTIONARY POLITICAL PARTY FIGHTING FOR THE LIBERATION OF ALL OPPRESSED PEOPLE

1. WE WANT SELF-DETERMINATION FOR PUERTO RICANS, LIBERATION ON THE ISLAND AND INSIDE THE UNITED STATES.

For 500 years, first spain and then the united states have colonized our country. Billions of dollars in profits leave our country for the united states every year. In every way we are slaves of the gringo. We want liberation and the Power in the hands of the People, not Puerto Rican exploiters. QUE VIVA PUERTO RICO LIBRE!

2. WE WANT SELF-DETERMINATION FOR ALL LATINOS.

Our Latin Brothers and Sisters, inside and outside the united states, are oppressed by amerikkkan business. The Chicano people built the Southwest, and we support their right to control their lives and their land. The people of Santo Domingo continue to fight against gringo domination and its puppet generals. The armed liberation struggles in Latin America are part of the war of Latinos against imperialism. QUE VIVA LA RAZA!

3. WE WANT LIBERATION OF ALL THIRD WORLD PEOPLE.

Just as Latins first slaved under spain and the yanquis, Black people, Indians, and Asians slaved to build the wealth of this country. For 400 years they have fought for freedom and dignity against racist Babylon. Third World people have led the fight for freedom. All the colored and oppressed peoples of the world are one nation under oppression. NO PUERTO RICAN IS FREE UNTIL ALL PEOPLE ARE FREE!

4. WE ARE REVOLUTIONARY NATIONALISTS AND OPPOSE RACISM.

The Latin, Black, Indian and Asian people inside the u.s. are colonies fighting for liberation. We know that washington, wall street, and city hall will try to make our nationalism into racism; but Puerto Ricans are of all colors and we resist racism. Millions of poor white people are rising up to demand freedom and we support them. These are the ones in the u.s. that are stepped on by the rulers and the government. We each organize our people, but our fights are the same against oppression and we will defeat it together. POWER TO ALL OPPRESSED PEOPLE!

5. WE WANT EQUALITY FOR WOMEN. DOWN WITH MACHISMO AND MALE CHAUVANISM.

Under capitalism, women have been oppressed by both society and our men. The doctrine of machismo has been used by men to take out their frustrations on wives, sisters, mothers, and children. Men must fight along with sisters in the struggle for economic and social equality and must recognize that sisters make up over half of the revolutionary army: sisters and brothers are equals fighting for our people. FORWARD SISTERS IN THE STRUGGLE!

6. WE WANT COMMUNITY CONTROL OF OUR INSTITUTIONS AND LAND.

We want control of our communities by our people and programs to guarantee that all institutions serve the needs of our people. People's control of police, health services, churches, schools, housing, transportation and welfare are needed. We want an end to attacks on our land by urban renewal, highway destruction, and university corporations. LAND BELONGS TO ALL THE PEOPLE!

7. WE WANT A TRUE EDUCATION OF OUR AFRO-INDIO CULTURE AND SPANISH LANGUAGE.

We must learn our long history of fighting against cultural, as well as economic genocide by the spaniards and now the yanquis. Revolutionary culture, culture of our people, is the only true teaching. JIBARO SI, YANQUI NO!

8. WE OPPOSE CAPITALISTS AND ALLIANCES WITH TRAITORS.

Puerto Rican rulers, or puppets of the oppressor, do not help our people. They are paid by the system to lead our people down blind alleys, just like the thousands of poverty pimps who keep our communities peaceful for business, or the street workers who keep gangs divided and blowing each other away. We want a society where the people socialistically control their labor. VENCEREMOS!

9. WE OPPOSE THE AMERIKKKAN MILITARY.

We demand immediate withdrawal of all u.s. military forces and bases from Puerto Rico, VietNam, and all oppressed communities inside and outside the u.s.. No Puerto Rican should serve in the u.s. army against his Brothers and Sisters, for the only true army of oppressed people is the People's Liberation Army to fight all rulers. U.S. OUT OF VIETNAM, FREE PUERTO RICO NOW!

10. WE WANT FREEDOM FOR ALL POLITICAL PRISONERS AND PRISONERS OF WAR.

No Puerto Rican should be in jail or prison, first because we are a nation, and amerikkka has no claims on us; second, because we have not been tried by our own people (peers). We also want all freedom fighters out of jail, since they are prisoners of the war for liberation. FREE ALL POLITICAL PRISONERS AND PRISONERS OF WAR!

11. WE ARE INTERNATIONALISTS.

Our people are brainwashed by television, radio, newspapers, schools and books to oppose people in other countries fighting for their freedom. No longer will we believe these lies, because we have learned who the real enemy is and who our real friends are. We will defend our sisters and brothers around the world who fight for justice and are against the rulers of this country. QUE VIVA CHE GUEVARA!

12. WE BELIEVE ARMED SELF-DEFENSE AND ARMED STRUGGLE ARE THE ONLY MEANS TO LIBERATION

We are oppose to violence - the violence of hungry children, illiterate adults, diseased old people, and the violence of poverty and profit. We have asked, petitioned, gone to courts, demonstrated peacefully, and voted for politicians full of empty promises. But we still ain't free. The time has come to defend the lives of our people against repression and for revolutionary war against the businessmen, politicians, and police. When a government oppresses the people, we have the right to abolish it and create a new one. ARM OURSELVES TO DEFEND OURSELVES!

13. WE WANT A SOCIALIST SOCIETY.

We want liberation, clothing, free food, education, health care, transportation, full employment and peace. We want a society where the needs of the people come first, and where we give solidarity and aid to the people of the world, not oppression and racism. HASTA LA VICTORIA SIEMPRE!

PARTIDO DE LOS YOUNG LORDS

PROGRAMA Y PLATAFORMA DE 13 PUNTOS

EL PARTIDO DE LOS YOUNG LORDS ES UN PARTIDO POLITICO REVOLUCIONARIO QUE LUCHA POR LA LIBERACION DE TODOS LOS PUEBLOS OPRIMIDOS.

1. QUEREMOS AUTODETERMINACION PARA TODOS LOS PUERTORRIQUENOS --- LIBERACION EN LA ISLA Y DENTRO DE LOS ESTADOS UNIDOS.

Hace 500 anos que nuestra isla ha estado colonizada: primero por espana y luego por los estados unidos. Billones de dolares en ganancias salen todos los anos de nuestra isla hacia los estados unidos. En todo sentido somos esclavos de los yanquis. Nosotros queremos la liberacion y el poder en las manos del pueblo, no en las de explotadores puertorriquenos. ¡QUE VIVA PUERTO RICO LIBRE!

2. QUEREMOS AUTODETERMINACION PARA TODOS LOS LATINOS.

Nuestras hermanas y hermanos latinos, dentro y fuera de los e.e. u.u., son oprimidos por las empresas norteamerikkkanas. El pueblo Chicano construyo el sur-oeste de este pais, y nosotros apoyamos su derecho a controlar sus vidas y su tierra. El pueblo Dominicano continua su lucha contra la dominacion yanqui y sus generales titeres. La lucha armada en Latinoamerica forma parte de la guerra de todos los Latinos contra el imperialismo. ¡QUE VIVA LA RAZA!

3. QUEREMOS LIBERACION PARA TODOS LOS PUEBLOS DEL TERCER MUNDO.

Tal como los Latinos trabajaron como esclavos, primero bajo espana y luego bajo los e.e. u.u., los pueblos Negros, Indios, y Asiaticos han laborado como esclavos para crear la riqueza de este pais. Por 400 años estos han luchado contra la injusticia y la indigidad impuesta sobre ellos por esta babilonia racista. El Tercer Mundo ha dirigido la lucha por la liberacion. Todos los pueblos oprimidos y de color forman una nacion bajo la opresion. ¡NINGUN PUERTORRIQUENO SERA LIBRE HASTA QUE TODOS LOS PUEBLOS NO SEAN LIBRES!

4. SOMOS NACIONALISTAS REVOLUCIONARIOS Y NOS OPONEMOS AL RACISMO.

Los pueblos Latinos, Negros, Indios, y Asiaticos dentro de los e.e. u.u. son colonias en lucha por la liberacion. Reconocemos que washington, wall street, y city hall trataran de convertir nuestro nacionalismo en racismo, pero los puertorriquenos somos de todos los colores y resistimos el racismo. Millones de personas pobres blancas se estan levantando a exigir su libertad, y a estas tambien nosotros las apoyamos. Son estas las que son pisoteadas por el gobierno y los dirigentes de los e.e. u.u. Cada cual organiza su pueblo, pero la lucha contra la opresion es una y unidos venceremos. ¡PODER A TODOS LOS PUEBLOS OPRIMIDOS!

5. QUEREMOS IGUALDAD PARA LAS MUJERES. ABAJO CON EL MACHISMO Y CON EL CHAUVINISMO MASCULINO.

Bajo el capitalismo, la mujer es oprimida por ambos elementos, la sociedad y el hombre. La doctrina del machismo es usada por el hombre para desenvolver sus frustraciones en las esposas, hermanas, madres, y en los hijos. El hombre debe pelear a lado de sus hermanas en la lucha por la igualdad economica y social y debe reconocer que la mitad del ejercito revolucionario se va a componer de hermanas: las hermanas y los hermanos somos iguales, luchando jumtos por nuestro pueblo. ¡ADELANTE HERMANAS EN LA LUCHA!

6. QUEREMOS CONTROL COMUNAL DE TODAS NUESTRAS INSTITUCIONES Y TIERRA.

Queremos que nuestras comunidades sean controladas por el pueblo, y exigimos programas que garanticen que todas las instituciones sirvan a las necesidades del pueblo. Queremos que el pueblo controle la policia, los servicios de salud, las iglesias, las escuelas, las viviendas, el transporte, y el bienestar publico. Queremos que se ponga fin a los asaltos que sobre nuestra tierra llevan a cabo la "eliminacion" urbana, la "destruccion" de carreteras y las universidades y corporaciones. ¡LA TIERRA PERTENECE A TODO EL PUEBLO!

7. QUEREMOS UNA EDUCACION VERDADERA DE NUESTRA CULTURA AFRO-TAINA Y EL USO DEL LENGUAJE ESPANOL.

Tenemos que aprender la historia de nuestra lucha contra el genocidio cultural y economico impuesto sobre nosotros por el yanqui. Cultura revolucionaria, la cultura de nuestro pueblo, es la unica ensenanza verdadera. ¡JIBARO SI, YANQUI NO!

8. NOS OPONEMOS A LOS CAPITALISTAS Y A LAS ALIANZAS CON LOS TRAIDORES.

Los gobernantes puertorriquenos, titeres del opresor, no ayudan al pueblo. Aquellos son pagados por el sistema para que dirijan a nuestro pueblo por callejones sin salida. De la misma manera miles de alcahuetes contra la pobreza son pagados para que apaciguen a nuestras comunidades para el beneficio de los negociantes. Del mismo modo los trabajadores sociales dividen a nuestras gangas y las mantienen peleandose entre si. Queremos una sociedad en la cual el pueblo controle su labor de un modo socialista. VENCEREMOS!

9. NOS OPONEMOS AL EJERCITO NORTEAMERIKKKANO.

Demandamos la retirada inmeidata de las fuerzas militares norteamerikkkanas de Puerto Rico, Vietnam, y de todas las comunidades oprimidas dentro y fuera de los e.e. u.u. Ningun puertorriqueno debera inscribirse en el ejercito norteamerikkkano para luchar contra sus hermanos y hermanas oprimidas. El verdadero ejercito de un pueblo oprimido es el ejercito popular, el cual combatira a todos los gobernantes. ESTADOS UNIDOS FUERA DE VIETNAM! QUE VIVA PUERTO RICO LIBRE!

10. QUEREMOS LA LIBERTAD DE TODOS LOS PRISIONEROS POLITICOS Y DE TODOS LOS PRISIONEROS DE GUERRA.

Ningun Puertorriqueno debe estar en la carcel, primero porque nosotros somos una nacion y amerikkka no tiene ninguna reclamacion con nosotros; segundo, porque nosotros no hemos sido tratados por nuestra propia gente (nuestros semejantes). Tambien queremos a todos los luchadores de la libertad fuera de la carcel, porque ellos son prisioneros de la guerra de la liberacion. LIBERTAD A TODOS LOS PRISIONEROS POLITICOS Y PRISIONEROS DE GUERRA!

11. NOSOTROS SOMOS INTERNACIONALISTAS.

Nuestro pueblo es enganado por la television, el radio, los periodicos, las escuelas, y los libros para oponer a nuestra gente en contra de otros pueblos que estan luchando por su liberacion. Muy pronto ya no creeremos estas mentiras que todos estos medios han impuesto en nosotros, porque habremos aprendido quien es el verdadero enemigo y quienes son nuestros verdaderos amigos. Defenderemos a nuestras hermanas y hermanos alrededor del mundo que luchan por la justicia y que estan en contra de los duenos de este pais. VIVA EL "CHE" GUEVARA!

12. CREEMOS QUE LA AUTO-DEFENSA Y LA LUCHA ARMADA SON LOS UNICOS MEDIOS PARA LOGRAR NUESTRA LIBERACION.

Nos oponemos a la violencia --- la violencia de ninos hambrientos, adultos analfabetos, viejos enfermos, y la violencia de la pobreza y las ganancias. Hemos pedido y peticionado; hemos ido a las cortes; hemos menifestado pacificamente y hemos votado por politicos llenos de promesas falsas. Y todavia no somos libres. Ha llegado el momento en que nos tenemos que defender contra la represion. Tenemos que iniciar una guerra revolucionaria contra el negociante, el politico y el policia. Cuando un gobierno oprime al pueblo, el tiene el derecho de abolirlo y crear un gobierno nuevo. ARMEMONOS PARA DEFENDERNOS!

13. QUEREMOS UNA SOCIEDAD SOCIALISTA!

Queremos liberacion, alimentos gratis, ropas, viviendas, educacion, atencion medica, transporte, servicios de gas, luz y otros servicios y empleos para todos. Queremos una sociedad en la cual las necesidades del pueblo se antepongan a todo; una sociedad que de a los pueblos del mundo solidaridad y apoyo, no opresion o racismo. HASTA LA VICTORIA SIEMPRE!

RAFAEL VIERA, LINCOLN HOSPITAL, JUNE, 1970

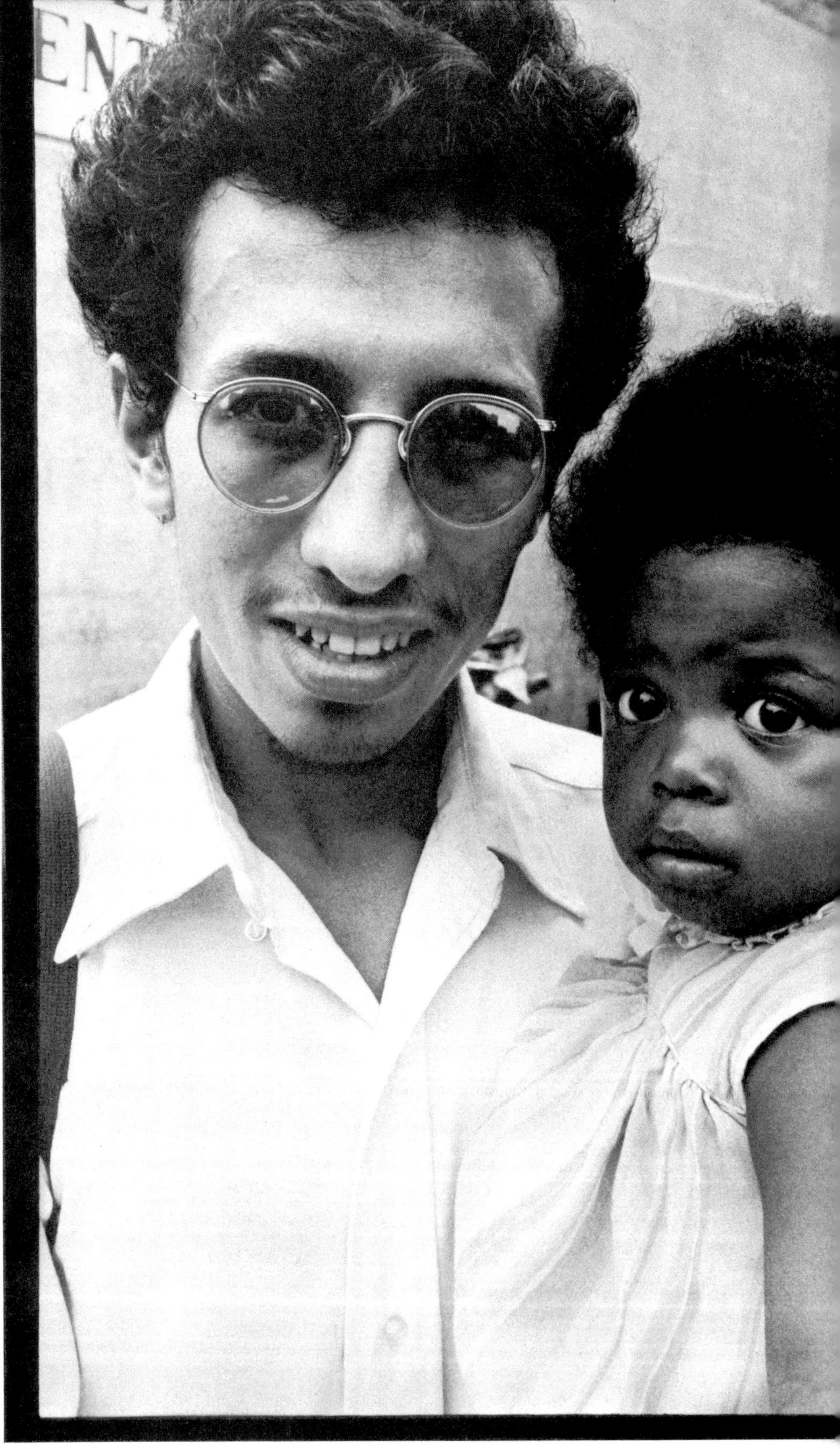

"When people start getting old minds, forget it–no matter how young they may be. An old mind is a mind that refuses to accept changes, right. If that should come down, the Party either has to get some new people with young minds, or we better find a new party."

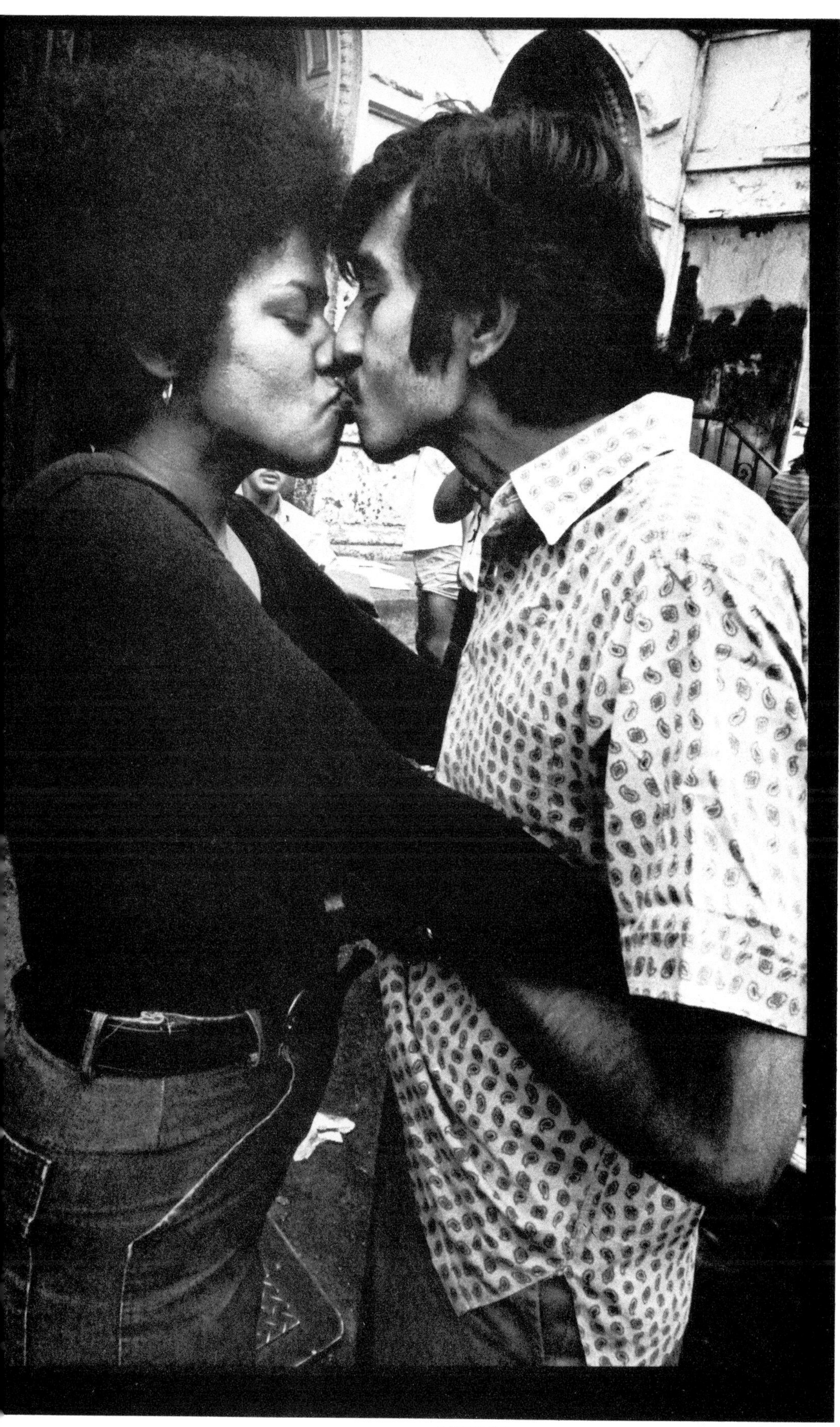

OUTSIDE EAST HARLEM OFFICE, AUGUST, 1970

SECOND PEOPLE'S CHURCH, DOLESA AND COOKIE, OCTOBER, 1970

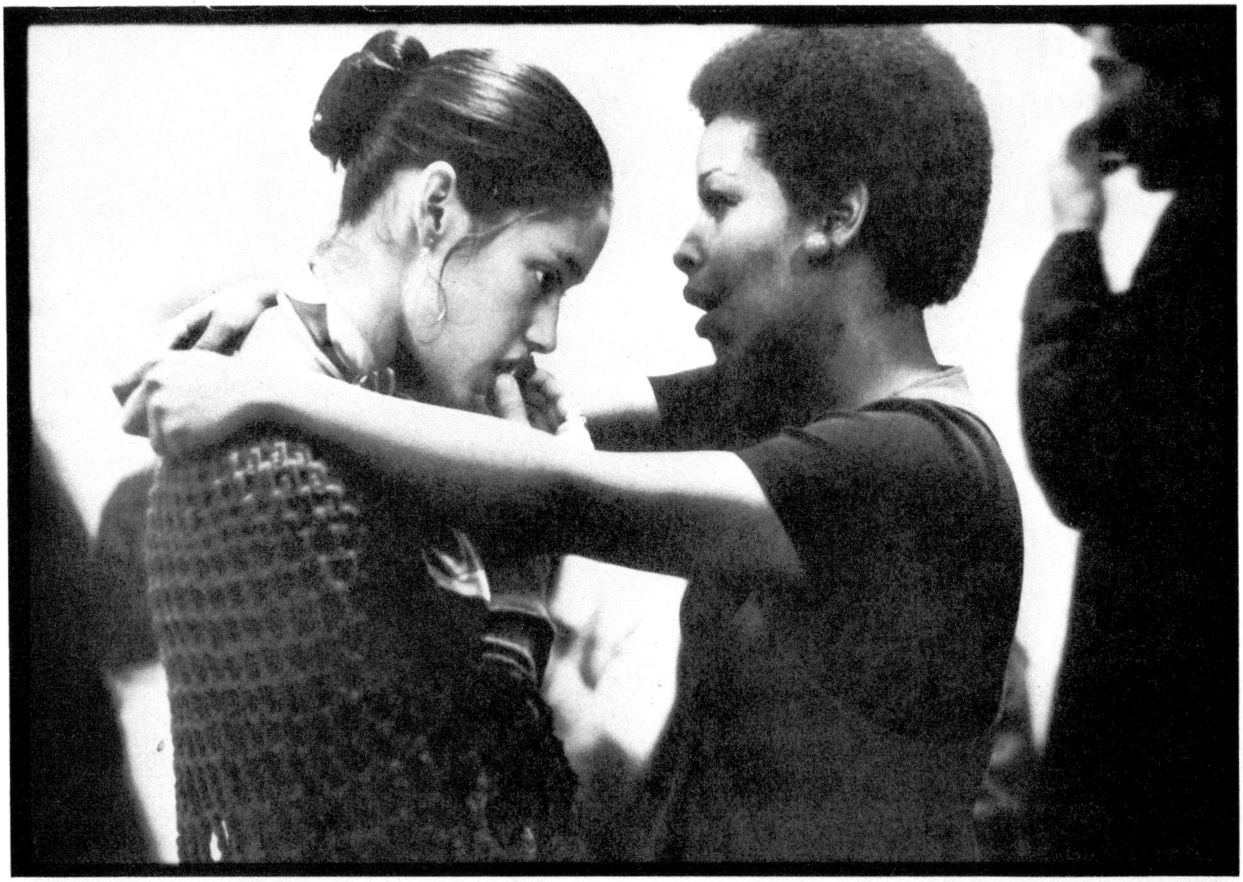

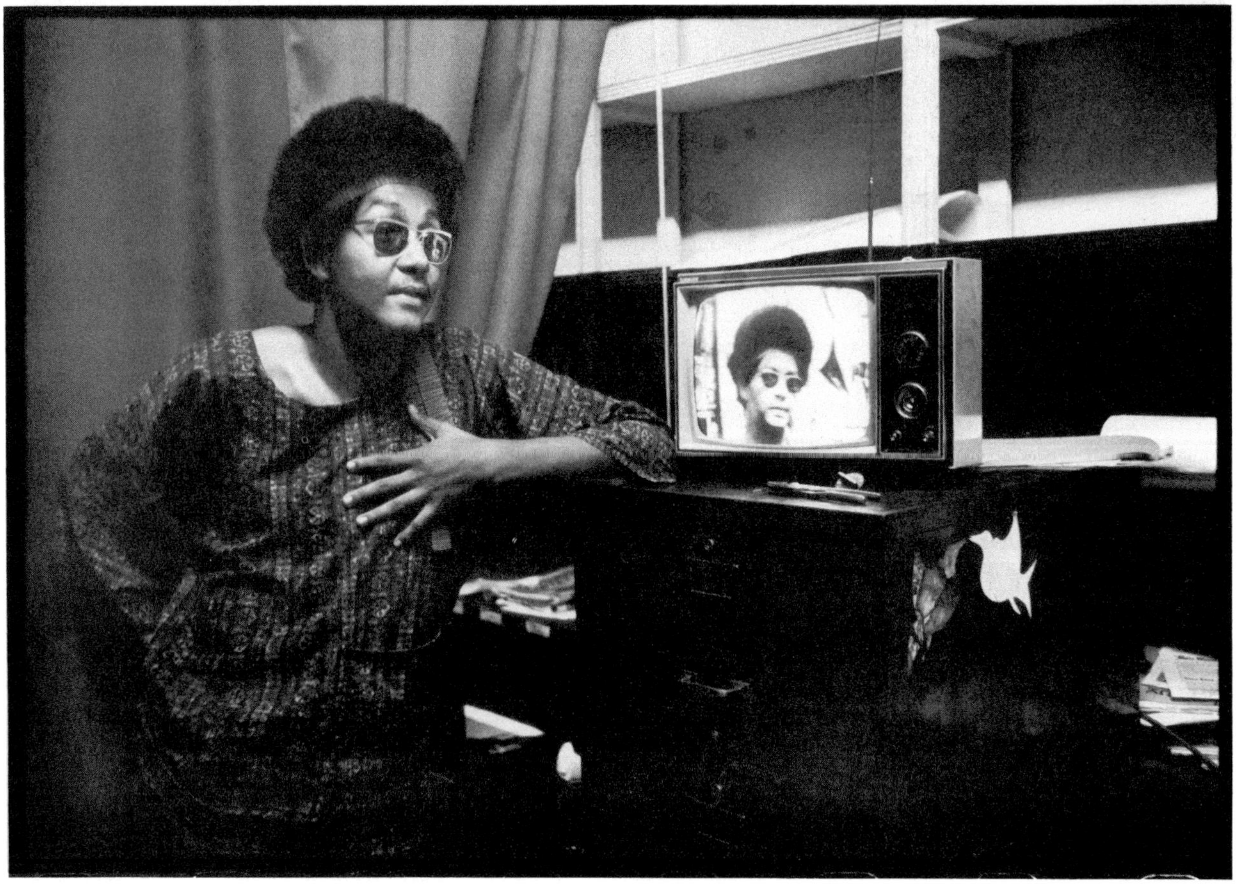

YORUBA, MINISTER OF INFORMATION, SIX O'CLOCK NEWS, BRONX OFFICE, JUNE, 1970

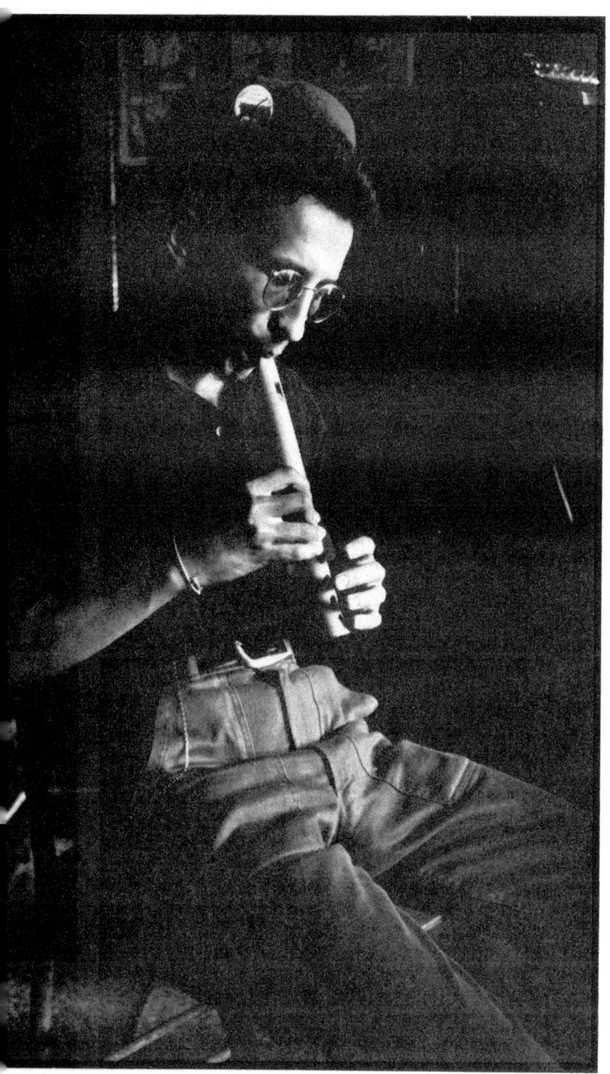

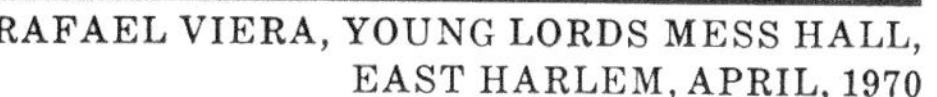

RAFAEL VIERA, YOUNG LORDS MESS HALL,
EAST HARLEM, APRIL, 1970

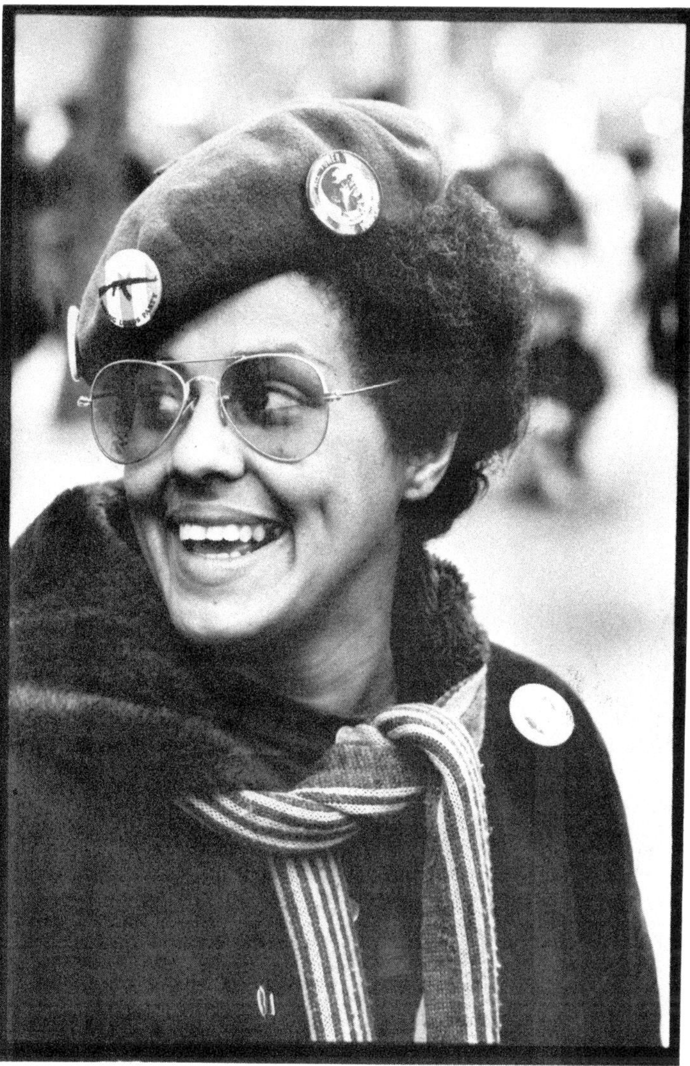

AIDA CUASCUT, UNITED NATIONS
DEMONSTRATION, OCTOBER 30, 1970

"The people dig an underdog;
that was the great appeal
of the Mets at one time,
and you have to understand
that that's exactly
what we are, underdogs.
Once the people can start
digging us for that,
we can tell them,
'Dig yourself for that.'"

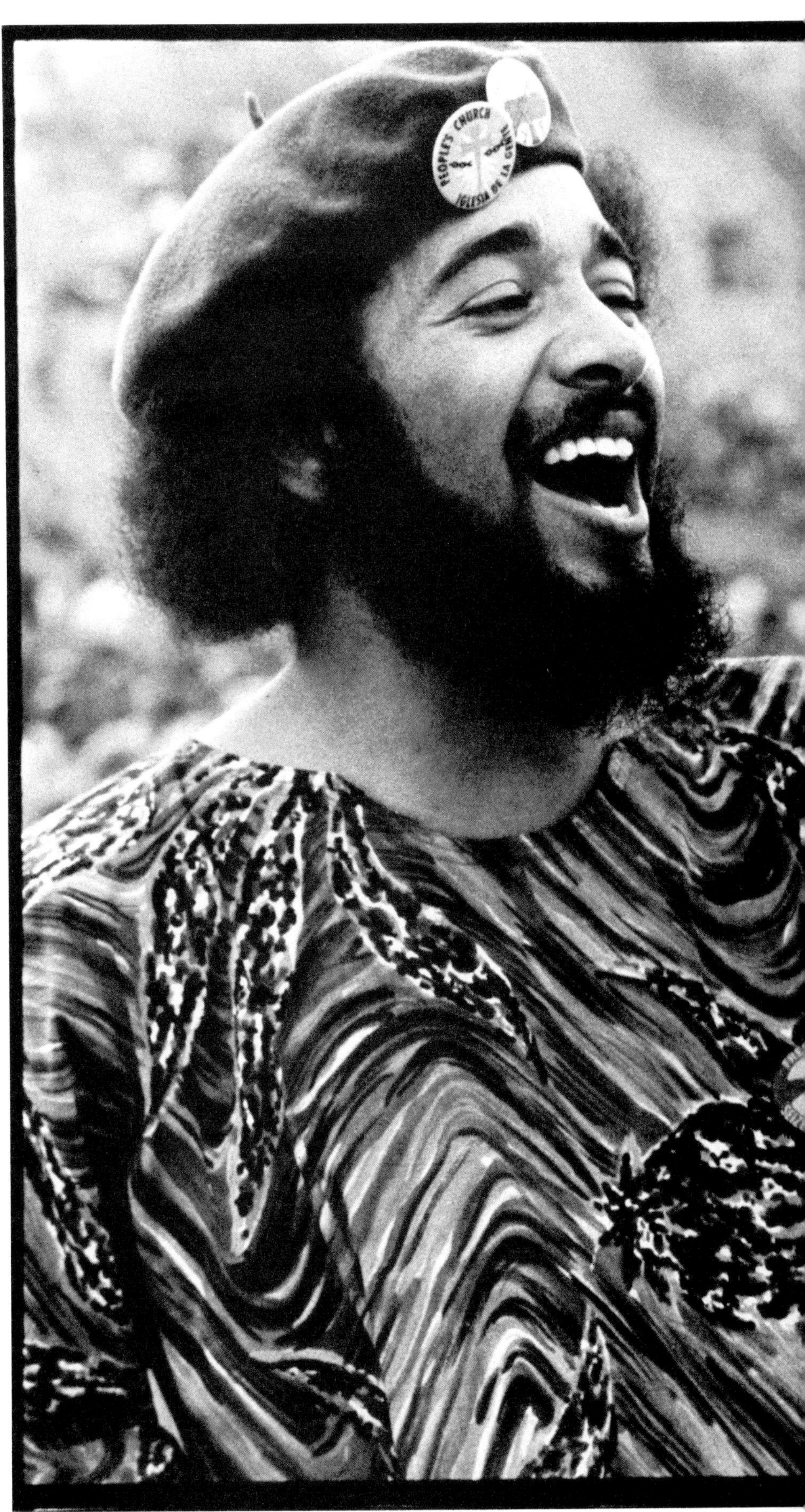

"Revolution is not something we want to do. It is bloody and cruel. But it is something we have to do to live decently and free."

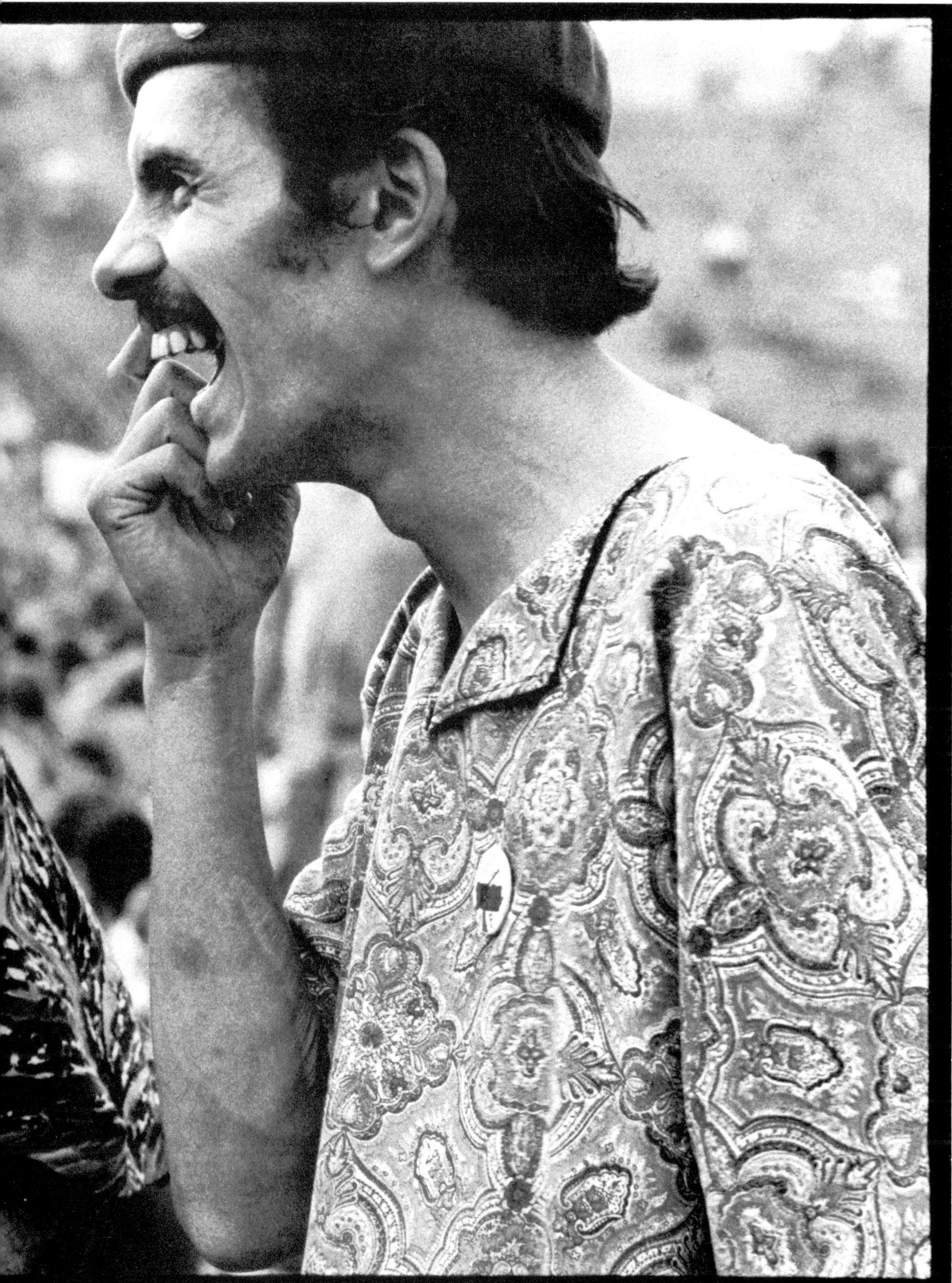

TENGO PUERTO RICO EN MI CORAZON

In January 1971, we announced that we were going to open a branch in Puerto Rico. This came after fighting for a year and a half in the united states of amerikkka, in the belly of the monster.

You see, one-third of the Puerto Rican Nation is in the united states, and two-thirds of our people are in Puerto Rico. We always knew in our minds and hearts that the Party would be expanding to Puerto Rico. That's what our button is saying: "Tengo Puerto Rico En Mi Corazón." Those ain't just words to us. We saw right from the beginning that one of the first steps in our struggle for National Liberation would be the uniting of our nation.

And now it's done. The one-third and the two-thirds are together. We've opened two branches in Puerto Rico—one in Aquadilla, the home of Julio Roldan, and the other in El Caño. The response of our people was beautiful.

On March 21, we joined the Nationalist Party and marched in a demonstration to commemorate the Ponce Massacre. (In 1937, colonial police, acting under the orders of amerikkkan governor blanton winship, killed twenty Nationalists and wounded 200 others who were holding a peaceful demonstration.) When we started marching, everyone was quiet, checking us out to see if all those things that the mass media in Puerto Rico had said were true—were we really "terrorists," "fanatics," "lunatics," "murderers"? We lined up in three columns and half-stepped in cadence.

The people related to our discipline—it told them we were serious, for real. A new member of the Party was in the crowd taking pictures, and he heard people saying that we weren't lunatics after all, like, the papers had lied. Some people felt that the war of liberation was going to take off right there.

The march was long and hot, but we were all very proud and kept the pace up. People joined us, marching with us, relating to the discipline of the Party. Finally, there were about 700 people marching—there had never been that many people before on March 21.

It was one of the proudest days of our lives. We had been sort of worried that the government scare campaign would frighten our people, but the people voted for us again—in the streets. The Lords who marched were feeling chills and at points we felt like crying when we thought about all the people who had fought and died so that our struggle could move forward. And how strong we will have to be to win.

But we will win. Because our *compañeras* and *compañeros* everywhere are together. They are strong, dedicated, and filled with love.

Que Viva Puerto Rico Libre!

The Young Lords Party
March 21, 1971

ABOUT THE AUTHORS

Palante is the first book about the Young Lords. Through photographs, essays, and interviews with members, the book captures the spirit and actions of the sixties movements. The Young Lords fought for the rights of Puerto Ricans in the United States and for the independence of Puerto Rico.

Puerto Rican and Latino activists founded the Young Lords Organization in Chicago in 1968 taking inspiration from the Black Panther Party and other national liberation movements across the world. In July 1969, a Young Lords chapter was formed in New York, and it became the Young Lords Party. They expressed their political beliefs in a 13-point program, published and distributed a newspaper called *PALANTE* and produced a weekly radio show on WBAI also called *PALANTE*.

The YLP focused on community issues—from the lack of affordable housing to police brutality—and organized street garbage cleanups, "serve the people" programs, and door-to-door health testing for tuberculosis and lead poisoning. Through dramatic takeovers of institutions—such as The People's Church and Lincoln Hospital—and mass mobilizations, the YLP brought media and public attention to the socioeconomic and political situation of people of color in the United States and to the colonial status of Puerto Rico.

Iris Morales is an activist, educator, media producer, author, and attorney. Her lifelong commitment to social justice is inspired by the Puerto Rican peoples' struggles for equality and self-determination as well as by the community's vibrant contributions in arts and politics. A member of the Young Lords for five years, she rose through the ranks to become Deputy Minister of Education and leader of the Women's Union. *!Palante, Siempre Palante!*, her award-winning documentary about the Young Lords, was broadcast on national public television and continues to be screened in schools, universities, and community venues across the United States.

Michael Abramson is a graduate of Kenyon College and the University of Chicago, and—since 2009—a bona fide inventor. In his more than 25-year career as a photojournalist for Time-Life and others, he has photographed a wide range of subjects—from deaf street gangs to American presidents—and has traveled the world. His book credits include *Our Portion of Hell*, *Inside Las Vegas* (text by Mario Puzo), *Amy: The Story of a Deaf Child*, and *Roy Lichtenstein: The Artist at Work*. He recently finished his first novel, a future-set political thriller entitled *Rebecca Tree*.